For Eliza

Once, I was telling some children in Warsaw about Africa. A small boy stood up and asked, 'And did you see many cannibals?' He did not know that when an African returns to Kariakoo from Europe and describes London, Paris, and other cities inhabited by *mzungu*, his African contemporary might also get up and ask: 'And did you see many cannibals there?'

Ryszard Kapuściński, *The Shadow of the Sun*

Contents

Contents

ACKNOWLEDGEMENTS

A big thank you to James Fry, Amar Grover, Raph Bonnaud, Ted Morgan, John Nichol, Mungo Park and his grandson, Tom Sutherland, Sophie Ransom, Rossini, Deepa and Letay Silveira in Port Harcourt, Ali Baba in Timbuktu, Sophie Mew in Djenné and all at Hope and Homes for Children.

I am further beholden to Tom Finchett and all the team at Swanbourne, especially David Edmondson, Stuart Greenwood, Pete Willie and Phil Timmins. Carol O'Brien, Sylvia and Bruce Corrie, Barbara Levy, Bob Crow, David and Jo Fox-Pitt, Katie Lawson, Aldo Zanetti, Roger Jefcoate, all at the Ark in Milton Keynes, Patrick and Sarah Westropp, Julian and Alice Kennard, Matt Todd, Tony Baldwin, Lucia Pinto, my cousin Peter Berry and the one and only Gina Rodriguez have all been stars too. Not forgetting my long-suffering family – Mum, Dad, the Duncan Smiths, the Stanleys and the Roches – there for me as always.

Most of all I would like to thank the people of West Africa, whose generosity and friendship were an inspiration through-out my journey. Many of you appear in these pages. I only hope my story does you justice.

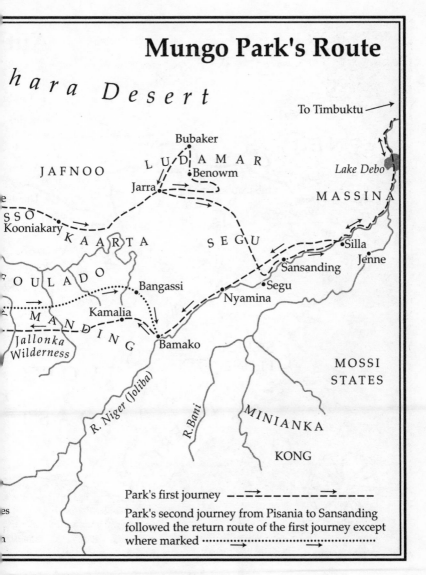

Mungo Park's Route

hara Desert

To Timbuktu →

Bubaker

L U D A M A R

JAFNOO

Benowm

Jarra

Lake Debo

MASSINA

SSO

Kooniakary

K A A R T A

S E G U

Silla

Jenne

OULADO

Bangassi

Sansanding

M A N D I N G

Kamalia

Nyamina

Segu

Bamako

Jallonka
Wilderness

MOSSI
STATES

R. Niger (Joliba)

R. Bani

M I N I A N K A

KONG

Park's first journey ----→------→----

Park's second journey from Pisania to Sansanding
followed the return route of the first journey except
where marked ·········→·············→·······

es

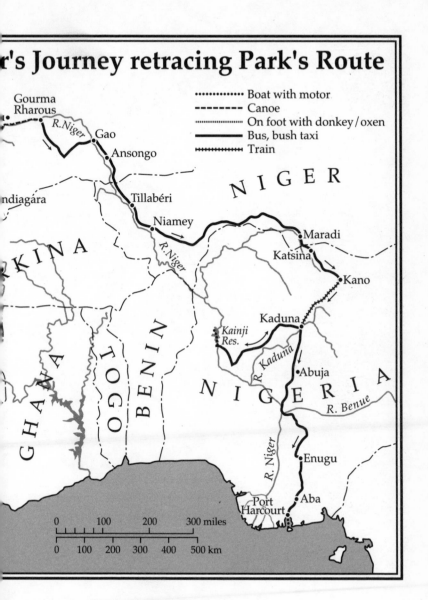

r's Journey retracing Park's Route

••••••••••• Boat with motor
--------- Canoe
On foot with donkey/oxen
Bus, bush taxi
+++++++++ Train

Gourma
Rharous
R.Niger
Gao
Ansongo

ndiagára

Tillabéri

Niamey

R.Niger

N I G E R

Maradi
Katsina
Kano

Kaduna

*Kainji
Res.*

R. Kaduna

Abuja

N I G E R I A

R. Benue

B U R K I N A

G H A N A

T O G O

B E N I N

R. Niger

Enugu

Aba

Port
Harcourt

| 0 | 100 | 200 | | 300 miles |
| 0 | 100 | 200 | 300 | 400 | 500 km |

PROLOGUE

Three cups of tea in the wilderness

THIS MORNING is the coldest yet. I exhale a plume of wispy, gas-like breath. Writhing in my sleeping bag, I grope for the tent's toggle, yank it, and unzip a fresh world.

All around me is a washed-out sea, a canvas devoid of colour and life, as if yet untouched by the gods. Just for an instant I'm in its thrall, lost in its emptiness, suspended somewhere between light and darkness; so much so I don't quite know who I am, or what I am doing here.

A white camel trots across the pale, tussocky skyline and breaks the spell. I watch it for a while. The camel is being ridden by a Tuareg swathed in indigo. The desert is his home, his orbit, and he moves like a dark star through the neutral haze of dawn. On his hip is a dagger, winking silver.

The Tuareg reins in his camel near the tent and looks at me. A soft breeze teases his headdress, so that it shimmers imperceptibly, like lake water stunned by a pebble. I notice the hilt of his dagger is peppered with green jewels. The wasteland beyond him is as bleak as anything I have ever seen, but there is beauty in the desolation, and fear. Always fear.

We move in the direction of our fear, so the sages tell us.

But surely we do not really wish to do this. No, we move to-wards what stirs us, thrills us, punishes us and, if lucky enough, heals us. Right now, in this wilderness, I have found a world so utterly out of sync with my own, I cannot help but be sucked in. There is nothing of home here. No familiar tree, bird, creature, cloud, star, number, name or face. No thrum of engine, no whir of computer and no bogus light: not one recognizable sound or stink. Nothing. I love my home but I also love being a stranger, a wanderer, a jumblie in a sieve: and this is the place for it.

Perched high on his mount, the Tuareg clears his throat, spits and begins to laugh, a high-pitched and contagious sound. He clearly finds my little one-man tent, with its fancy zips and mosquito gauze, a grand joke. The fact I am cocooned in ther-mal underwear, tight as a wetsuit, only exacerbates his mirth. I look at him, he looks at me and together we laugh.

Of course, this has all happened many times before. When the Arctic explorer William Parry docked near Baffin Island in 1821 a group of Polar Inuit, believing they were the only people on earth, asked him: 'Are you from the sun or the moon?' I realize with my space capsule tent and incongruous long johns, I may as well have dropped out of the sky too. This Tuareg has surely seen white men before – aid workers in Land Cruisers, chancers on motorbikes – but perhaps never in quite such an absurd and solitary context as this.

Soon the Tuareg's laughter is sated and he moves on. Using his bare feet he stabs the camel on its neck, his splayed toes acting as a steering device. The spectral beast lollops off towards the sun, which slouches on the horizon, cold and wan, like stabbed egg yolk.

Once dressed, I eat some bananas and dates, pack up my gear and write for a while. Then I stride off to explore my surroundings. The sun is up now and already the sand and sky are welded together in a fume of heat. A hoopoe flies by in a flash of pink, chirruping wildly.

Although no village is in view there are still some faint tracks in the sand. I can see bicycle tyres, dog spoor, donkey hooves. In time the sand thickens and bird prints, neat and regular, like midget hieroglyphics, dominate the path. Soon even these dissolve and just the camel pads and thorn bushes remain.

I do not want to stray too far from the main track so I think about turning back. Then, up ahead, I see the Tuareg's white camel. Another mangy, dun-coloured camel is slumped next to it. Both animals are dozing in the shade of a tree with yellow blossom. The blossom looks almost celestial in its isolation. Hunkered down with the Tuareg is a darker-skinned man in a white turban. The pair of them beckon me over.

They have made a twig fire. The Tuareg places a small, delicate-looking teapot into the flames and together we sit down and wait for it to boil. The Tuareg speaks no French, but his friend in the white turban knows a little.

'*Trois fois! Trois fois!*' explains the friend, his half-mast eyes popping open in excitement. 'Three times we drink this tea. Ah, yes, three times.'

From a goat-skin bag, the Tuareg tips out three tiny glasses; the sort of glasses that would be used for schnapps or tequila in another hemisphere: fast drinks for fast lives. Not here. To fill these glasses in the West African bush takes time, time for the tea to be lovingly mixed, brewed and poured. Time for those who drink it to sit back in the meagre desert shadows and tell a story or two.

Along with the precious glasses, a bag of sugar falls from the Tuareg's goat-skin, and two silver crosses engraved with desert symbols: stars, moons and camel humps. There are *ju-ju* items too, a scorpion amulet, a cobra skin and a locket containing verses from the Koran.

The Tuareg gestures for me to buy something but I refuse. He smiles and puts the items back in his bag. He rubs his face, now stained deep blue from his headdress, and finally lifts the teapot from the flames. Concentrating hard, he pours the tea into the glasses from over a foot high. The cascade of brown liquid froths and settles.

'This first glass of tea is strong, so strong,' says the white-turbaned man. We each take a glass and sip in silence. The tea tastes bitter, but very smooth, leaving an afterglow in the pit of the belly. 'This tea is for death,' he adds solemnly, but there is still humour in his eyes.

He continues his commentary throughout the protracted brewing ceremony. After ten minutes the second pot of tea is ready. It is sweeter than the first but still with some bite. 'This tea is for life,' he whispers, straightening his turban. 'Do not waste any.'

The Tuareg assists with the third brew and measures out a pile of sugar in the palm of his hand. He then spills the sugar into the little teapot with quiet finesse. Once completed, he passes the pot over to his white-turbaned friend, the real tea connoisseur, who puts the finishing touches to the third glass, the final one, the sweetest of all.

'This last one is pure sugar,' says the connoisseur, pouring fresh tea into my now sticky glass. I take a slug of the liquid sweetness.

'This last one,' his narrow eyes pop open again, 'is for love!'

The two men gulp down their glasses in unison and start to laugh. I laugh too. We are all just glad to be here on this sunny day, drinking tea in the sand, raising toasts to love.

'Death, life and love!' shouts the turbaned tea maker, as if high from all his brews. 'Death, life and love!' He leans over and whispers very slowly in my ear. 'Today, *toubaboo*, you drank Africa.'

CHAPTER 1

NAYA'S DANCE

JUST FOUR hours after take off from Gatwick I was soaring over the Sahara gazing down from my window seat. Far below stretched a blur of unfamiliar colours: greys and whites, sickly reds and dirty golds. Apart from the odd dark fissure, or rash of hardy vegetation, there was nothing. No break in the monotony: no movement at all.

'That's pure magic,' said Dave, my neighbour, a Maths teacher from Birmingham, as he leaned over to catch a glimpse of the desolate strangeness beneath us. 'Magic!' he repeated, awed by this great desert the size of America, but with a population less than his hometown. He shook his head as if it was all a bit much, then returned to watching Jamie Lee Curtis on the in-flight movie.

Later that afternoon we landed in The Gambia.* Considering this was one of Africa's smallest countries, I thought its

*After independence from the British in 1965 Gambia's name was changed to The Gambia. For the sake of simplicity I have at times used the old name.

1

airport runway looked comically over-sized. I mentioned this to Dave, as he put on his Raybans.

'NASA funded the runway here, mate,' he told me. 'That's why it's so long, in case America needs to land a space shuttle on it.'

The Gambia is known as 'Africa for Beginners', but that all depends on which way you turn out of the airport gates. Due north are the luxury Atlantic beach resorts, while further east is the tiny capital city, Banjul.

Just for a moment I was tempted to tag along with Dave and my fellow passengers. We all stood on the airport concourse, whey-faced and sweaty, smarting at the brightness of our new world. London, with its apocalyptic winter skies and fuggy coffee shops was long gone. Everywhere here was bathed in light.

A jolly, perma-tanned brunette, clearly a tour rep, began calling out names. It was time for me to peel away. There was no mini-bus waiting to whisk me off to some air-conditioned pleasure den. I have come here to see Africa, I told myself pompously. I shook hands with Dave and a few others I had met on the flight, stuck on my hat, and walked out into the sunshine. Nobody else was heading to Banjul.

'Welcome to the Smiling Coast,' said my cab driver, who looked a bit like Huggy Bear from the *Starsky and Hutch* TV show. He wore a cowrie shell necklace and was picking at his teeth with a long twig.

His taxi's windscreen was cracked and the boot did not shut properly, springing up and down, like argumentative jaws, as we bounced over random potholes. We drove through a barren, scrubby landscape, swerving now and then to avoid stray goats. The radio blasted out some upbeat reggae.

After nearly an hour we reached Banjul's harbour. Amid the cargo boats and fishing skiffs were the gunnels of a wreck prodding out from the surf. I was dropped off on the bustling seafront opposite the Ferry Guesthouse.

'Why you stay here?' asked the driver. 'It's a dump, full of Senegalese. Let me take you somewhere cool.'

I thanked him but still decanted myself. I walked past a mango-seller in a fez, then a girl in a purple shawl frying omelettes on a brazier. Complicated smells of diesel, dried fish, salt, smoke and donkey dung permeated the rubbish-strewn streets.

Shouldering my rucksack, I slogged up the Ferry Guesthouse stairs into a sun-dappled reception area. Half a dozen spectators were watching a football game on a portable TV. A blizzard of white fuzz made the ball's position hard to trace.

'Hey, brother, you want a room?' said one of the crowd sleepily. He was spread-eagled on a prayer mat, wearing only a pair of shorts. When I nodded, he dragged himself up like a boxer trying to beat the count.

'Here, let me show you. My name is Mohammed. You want some tea?'

Mohammed, a thick-set youth with brilliantine hair, led me to a room with creaky floorboards and a broken ceiling fan. There was no lock on the door and mosquito blood stained the walls. Outside was a poster of the Spice Girls in their heyday.

'Black Spice very sexy,' said Mohammed, pointing at Mel B. 'Beckham Spice too.'

I dumped my stuff and took a shower. When I stepped back onto the veranda, wrapped in my towel, an elderly, bare-breasted woman was putting some washing on a line. She smiled warmly. I waved and bolted for my room.

Back in reception the football match was heating up. It was the beginning of the Cup of Nations, a tournament that clearly had the whole of Africa hooked. We were watching the opening match. Tunisia, the host nation, was taking on Rwanda. I asked when the Gambian team was playing its first game.

'Gambia is too small,' said a sulky, dreadlocked girl in the corner. 'We no play. Not big enough, not good enough.'

After a while Rwanda scored a goal. Mohammed and his friends whooped and high-fived each other.

'Do you support Rwanda?' I asked him.

'Yes, yes,' he replied, slapping my palm. 'Rwanda are in the tournament for the first time. They are a little country like us. They have terrible civil war ten years ago, one million dead. Terrible. We wish them better luck now.'

Mohammed returned his attention to the game. Before long Tunisia equalized with a cracking penalty and the group around the TV were just as delighted. One man jumped up and danced a jig.

'Do you want Tunisia to win now?' I asked Mohammed, confused. 'You're cheering them too.'

'Yes, yes, I like Tunisia,' he replied above the noise. 'They are also a small country. It would be good for them to win.'

'So who do you like best?' I pressed him.

'I like Rwanda and I like Tunisia too,' shouted Mohammed gleefully. 'But most of all, brother, I just like goals. In Africa more than anything we like goals, goals. GOALS!'

* * *

Later that evening, after witnessing Tunisia defeat Rwanda 2–1 and drinking some bottles of Julbrew, the local beer, I trudged upstairs to set up my mosquito net. The net was more like a miniature tent: a dome supported by two flexible poles. I had bought it on a whim the day before, thinking it would be useful on the River Niger.

Soon I realized, either I was being very stupid, or there was a serious design fault. No matter how hard I tried, I just couldn't get the poles to fit into their sockets. I began hurrumphing and cursing, my hands were sweating so badly I couldn't get a grip on anything.

'*Bonsoir, monsieur.*'

A fleshy, very dark girl with a rook's nest hairdo appeared at my door. She had obviously heard the rumpus I was making from downstairs. She quickly surveyed the scene and walked over to help me. She had an air of absolute confidence.

'*Merci,*' I said, as she took hold of a corner of the mosquito gauze.

'*De rien.*'

The two of us wrestled with the intractable netting for a good five minutes, ping-ponging ourselves back and forth across the room, before finally wrenching the poles into place.

'*Voilà,*' said the girl, laughing, 'but that tent, no good!'

We both sat down on my bed. I noticed the girl's cotton dress, brocaded with gold lace, still looked immaculate. In contrast my blue T-shirt was sodden, great saddlebags of sweat under my arms.

She told me her name was Naya, from Senegal. She had been earning a pittance, odd-jobbing in Dakar and had come to Banjul to make a clean break. She said she knew Madame M, the owner of the Ferry Guesthouse, who had given her a job.

'Banjul is small, very boring,' she mused. 'Dakar is big, very crazy. But, ooooh, too expensive. My brother owes much money, my father is sick. I need money. In Banjul I save many dollars.'

My French was as bad as her English and we shifted between the two languages, speaking in the only tense we both knew: an endless present. This seemed right. Just now, the past and the future had ceased to exist for me. Fuelled by too much beer, the suffocating heat and the heady smell of Naya's perfume, I was inextricably locked in the moment.

'What is your work?' I asked her.

'Oh, my work is cooking, washing and, you know, other thing . . .'

Mid-conversation Naya grabbed my hands and pulled me up to my feet. She was taller than me and physically strong. She unhitched the straps of her dress with her thumbs and pushed herself against me.

'You like me, England man,' she whispered, pecking my check. 'I know you like me.'

'Yes, of course, but not . . .' I protested, stunned at the immediacy of it all, yet still clinging on to her. We tottered around the room, in a comic last dance at the disco routine.

At times I half-heartedly tried to push Naya away but somehow I couldn't. I was overcome by her smell, an intoxicating blend of musk and earth and sweetness. I was high on it, as if I hadn't smelt anything properly for years. Her cantilevered cleavage was now squeezed tight against my chest: it felt like she had about ten heartbeats. As we danced I looked up to Naya's face, her smooth, dark skin was beaded with droplets of sweat. I kissed her cheek and slowly pulled away.

'You like me, England man, you like me.' Naya held on to my waist, flashing a lovely smile.

'Yes, I do, but . . .' Her hands moved down to my navel. 'Oh no. Naya! No, no, *no* . . .' Gradually I extricated myself from her pungent embrace.

'*Je suis désolé,*' I said. 'I'm sorry if I led you on. You're lovely, but no. I can't.'

'No problem, England man.' She gracefully hitched up her dress straps and began to laugh.

'You are shy boy,' she teased, using her words as a good-natured insult. What she really meant was: 'We could have some fun, rich foreigner, then you pay a little and what's the harm in that.' I sat back on the bed, my head reeling. Naya was

6

tough and savvy, and clearly didn't see herself as a victim; but I still felt I'd let her down.

'Naya, wait,' I said, as she made for the door. I wanted to give her something. Her circumstances were tricky. She had told me this, utterly matter-of-factly, without fishing for pity or dollars. In fact she had asked for nothing at all. I fumbled around in my money belt and handed over a fiver's worth of Gambian dollars.

'That's for the dance.'

'The dance?'

'The dance around the room,' I explained. 'I won't forget it.'

'Ah,' she shrieked, 'you are too funny, England man.'

She took the money, laughing uproariously, and swung the door shut. I collapsed inside my mosquito-resistant cocoon. It was airless inside, heavy with heat, but I was exhausted and soon fell asleep. I woke up early, a head full of wild and vivid dreams. In Africa I was to dream almost every night.

*   *   *

As I supped coffee the following morning while overlooking Banjul's chaotic harbour, I pondered what had lured me here. My West African adventure had been sparked, not only by a blatant urge to hit the road, but by Mungo Park, the explorer in whose footsteps I soon hoped to tread. I had been captivated by the ambitious Scot the moment I first read about his ground breaking travels to the River Niger.

Park, a mustard keen, 24-year-old surgeon, had struck out for West Africa in the summer of 1795, docking on the Gambia River and making his way eastwards towards the then mystical Niger. Throughout the two and a half year expedition, funded by the African Association (a philanthropic group of London movers and shakers), Park was treated with both immense kindness and startling cruelty.

Some tribes believed the tall, freckly explorer to be a cat-eyed devil who had been dipped in milk while others welcomed him like a long lost friend. One moment Park was being tortured by the Moors of Ludamar, the next taken in and fed by a good-hearted slave. The presence of this lone, pale-skinned Christian terrified and fascinated the local people in equal measures.

Near the end of his travels, after being shunned by a succession of village chiefs and nearly attacked by a lion, Park, half-starved and riddled with disease, latched onto a coffle of slaves and staggered back to the Gambia coast. It was a near miracle he made it home alive.

On his return to London in 1797, the humble explorer became an instant celebrity. Although he never made it to Timbuktu, Park had still earned his spurs by confirming (near the river port of Ségou*) that the Niger flowed eastwards: a crusading discovery. Once settled back in the Scottish borders, Park completed a book about his journey. The eagerly awaited *Travels into the Interior of Africa* was full of high adventure and tribal lore. It became a quick-fire bestseller.

I had recently discovered Park's diary and, as I read it, realized it was coming up to the two hundreth anniversary of his death. (The explorer had drowned at Bussa Falls in northern Nigeria in late 1805 or early 1806 during an ill-fated return trip to West Africa.)

As I flipped the pages of his diary, ideas flickered in my mind like lightning strikes. The River Niger appealed immensely as a theme for a journey. Not only was it Africa's third longest river – after the Nile and Congo – but it was also a geo-

*The contemporary spelling.

graphical freak. Unlike most rivers, which run to the sea, the 2,600-mile Niger flows from its source in the highlands of Sierra Leone towards the Sahara: straight to the desert. It then curls like a question mark around Timbuktu before purling on south to its mouth on the Nigerian coast.

By the time I had devoured Park's diary the lightning in my head had frazzled away all hope of restraint. Oh yes, I thought, this was the sign, the burning bush moment all journeys require. The moment you know there will be no turning back.

So how would I trace Mungo Park, this man every bit as intriguing as the river he had so doggedly pursued? Park had sometimes travelled by wooden canoes and yes, I would do the same. I might use donkey or ox carts at times too. As I only had three months, I would have to rely on hitchhiking or public transport for certain stretches, but this did not curb my enthusiasm. In fact, it all posed an irresistible challenge.

And so here I was in Banjul, all set, as Park dramatically wrote in his diary, to travel 'to the world's end'. It had all sounded so easy over a boozy Christmas lunch with the family a month before, but now, as I imagined the dark, mangrove-infested waters that lay ahead, I was gripped with fear.

* * *

Banjul, or Bathurst – as it was known before Gambia gained independence – did not exist in Mungo Park's day. Instead, after his 30-day voyage from Portsmouth in the summer of 1795, the callow explorer docked at Jillifree, a remote trading station near the mouth of the Gambia River. I would soon be hot on Park's heels but first wanted a few days to find my feet in Banjul.

I fast discovered it was a capital with a difference. In fact, with only 50,000 people – less than Taunton or Aylesbury –

Banjul felt more like a market town than a metropolis. Apart from one or two colonial façades it was a hodgepodge of tatty warehouses, street stalls and cheap hotels.

There were no civic show-stoppers at all: no grand memorials to Empire, no skyscrapers (three storeys was about the limit) and, praise the Lord, no Starbucks. The one landmark I came across was Arch 22, a hideous white structure, which only Yahya Jammeh, the Gambian president, is allowed to drive under. The arch celebrated 22 July 1994, the day 29-year-old Jammeh staged a successful coup in the capital, becoming one of the youngest leaders in the world.

I liked Banjul. The people waved and smiled at one another, the soldiers outside the gates of the presidential palace said, 'Welcome to our country, Holland man', and the women at Albert Market wore the most colourful clothes I had ever seen. Hummingbirds flitted through the neem trees while children rolled hoops and wrestled in the dust.

At the Ferry Guesthouse I ate my meals with Mohammed, Naya and the rest of the staff. We all sat cross-legged around huge tureens of rice, fish and vegetables. We ate with our hands and drank lots of sweet tea. Naya joked that she wanted to marry me, but only so she could see where Princess Diana had lived. Mohammed told me he would do anything to get out of Banjul.

'My life is so quiet here,' he said. 'Banjul is getting smaller every day. Most capitals grow, but we shrink. What hope is there here? All the tourists are up the coast. I put my faith in Allah. He is all I have.' His eyes lit up. 'Unless I meet an English girl. Or maybe a German girl, a French girl!' He stopped and lifted his hands to the air. 'Or, Allah be generous, a Spice Girl!'

CHAPTER 2

GODS AND GURUS

ON SUNDAY I heard some Gospel music in the town centre. It was coming from St Mary's, a sturdy Anglican church, with white walls and stained-glass windows. More through curiosity than religious yearning, I decided to join the congregation.

The church was beautiful inside. Sunlight lanced through the windows, spotlighting the stone memorials, some to Gambians who had fought for the Allies in the war. A reassuring smell of wood polish, damp stone and freshly laundered clothes enveloped the nave.

I sat at the back, the only white face. The choir, all in purple robes, sang a selection of rousing but unrecognizable hymns. At one stage we all gave each other the sign of peace. Hugs were exchanged as opposed to the usual crisp handshakes I was used to. The Gambia was only five per cent Christian but being a minority clearly gave St Mary's congregation an intense and joyous solidarity.

At the end of the service the preacher – a dead ringer for James Brown – asked in his zealous, boom-boom voice, for new members of the congregation to stand up and introduce themselves. I wimped out: this was a one-off attendance for me. Most newcomers to the flock were local, but one, Robert, had recently arrived from Freetown, the capital of Sierra Leone. He rose up, a tall, rangy man with tightly cropped hair.

Robert had fled Freetown, he announced to us, to start afresh in The Gambia. He was a trained tailor, but work was hard to find in his country in the aftermath of the civil war, a war in which his brother had been killed. Robert confessed he had little money now, having walked and hitched his way north. His hopes were pinned on a cousin in Banjul, another tailor, with whom he planned to join forces.

After Robert finished his story, the preacher spread his arms out towards him. 'Our doors are always open to you, young brother!' he said, his voice unsteady with emotion.

The congregation dispersed and mingled outside in the churchyard, the air thick with tropical blossom. I approached Robert and asked him if Sierra Leone was a Christian country.

'About half the population,' he replied, undoing his tie in the heat. 'More than here, but Sierra Leone is not as safe. Gambia is better.'

He explained that although his country's civil war was over, he still felt violence could erupt again. Many of his family had already left home; one brother now lived in Burkina Faso and a sister in Guinea. Then there was Omar, his brother killed in the war.

'He was only 16, just a child,' said Robert bitterly. 'He was always the wild one. But there were boys younger than Omar fighting, some not even teenagers. It makes me so angry.'

Robert told me in the past children rarely fought in wars because the old-style rifles, like Kalashnikovs, were too heavy for them. But now, with light, easy to handle firearms, more youngsters were press-ganged, and if no guns were available, knives and clubs were handed out. Robert said children often made good soldiers, fuelled with the invincibility of youth.

'My brother, Omar, he was a good boy.' Robert clenched his fists as he spoke. 'Now he is gone. Sierra Leone is so beautiful. God gave us so much and look what we have done.'

He stopped talking and perched on the edge of a bench, resting his hands on his lap like a child about to say grace. A swallow swooped overhead and landed on the church roof.

'It was worse next door in Liberia,' Robert said suddenly. 'One terrible leader after another. Samuel Doe, the old dictator, had his ears cut off. The crazy people who did it made a video. You can still buy it in the markets. Think of it! I'm sick of this cruelty!'

Robert plucked some moss from a nearby grave. 'I had many foreign friends in Freetown,' he said, his voice softer now. 'One girl, Sally, gave me English lessons. She told me about Robin Hood, the man who robs from the rich and gives to the poor. She joked that in West Africa it's the other way round, the rich take from the poor and hang on to it. Sally told me about your country,' he paused, smiling at the memory. 'About the freedom you have. How you can travel all over Europe. Study until you are 25. That's amazing to me. Sally still complained about the rain, the greyness. But that made me laugh! Who cares if it rains with all that freedom.

'Understand something, Tom.' He wagged a calloused finger at me. 'I will only ever know Africa, but I don't mind. I love Africa, you see. I love Africa and I love Jesus. But you and Sally live in such a different world to me.' He stopped and shut his eyes. 'I cannot believe the same God watches over us.'

* * *

That evening I invited Robert to the Ferry Guesthouse to join in with the usual communal meal. Naya had prepared chicken in a spicy peanut sauce and we all plunged our hands into the pot.

Mohammed was holding court, telling us he had a close friend who, if he summoned up sufficient magic, or used the relevant *gris gris* (charm), could make himself immortal.

'Even if a knife is stuck in him,' boasted Mohammed, rolling a ball of rice up in his hand, 'no blood comes out.' When I asked him if I could meet this miracle man, Mohammed told me it was impossible because he lived in a village far from Banjul. Mohammed sensed my scepticism and offered to introduce me to a magician instead: a fortune-teller, who was 120 years old.

'A hundred and twenty years old!' I said. 'Come on, Mohammed, that's too much.'

'Okay, clever white man,' he chided. 'If you doubt me, you must meet this old man tonight.'

I shot a glance at Robert. I sensed he was also unconvinced, although he was careful not to offend his new friends. He simply stated that anyone reaching 120 years old was highly irregular; in most West African countries the average lifespan was well below 50.

Whatever the validity, I could not refuse such an offer. After the meal Mohammed, Naya, Robert and I walked out into the night. The dusty streets were bathed in moonlight. Other than the odd moped or prowling cat, the city was asleep.

After ten minutes we came to some mud buildings near the Albert Market. Opposite us was a large poster proclaiming: VOTE YAHYA, YOU KNOW HE IS OUR MAN, with a picture of the youthful leader in a green scarf and an orange conical hat. An election was due to be held in a few months, The Gambia being one of the few recognized democracies in Africa.

When I asked Mohammed and Naya about Yahya, they both approved of him. He was young and strong, they agreed, a good man. Robert, who was more politically-minded, told me Yahya's record was far from untainted. During his rule there had been rigged elections and a student rally fired on by soldiers, but in comparison to Sierra Leone, he accepted, Yahya was probably on the side of the angels.

'Is youth respected here?' I asked.

'Both youth and age are respected,' replied Mohammed, as we entered a courtyard engulfed with jungly plants. 'The young for their strength, the old for their wisdom. This 120-year-old man is the wisest man in Gambia, but he is too old to be president.'

'Not in China,' quipped Robert. 'I've heard they have leaders who are too old to even stand up!'

'Shhh,' said Mohammed, 'we are at the fortune-teller's hut.'

Mohammed stooped down and pulled back a grubby curtain. One by one we crept into a Spartan room, lit up by dozens of candles. The old man sat on a heap of cushions in a corner. Mohammed shook his hand and they chatted quietly for a while. He then gestured for me to come over. I gave the old man a handful of kola nuts, the recommended gift. Some of the nuts were red, others white, they were supposed to possess hallucinogenic qualities, and he enjoyed chewing them.

The fortune-teller looked little over 70, with immaculate bristly hair, animated eyes and only mildly weathered features. I soon discovered he also had three wives, one who was my age. If he was 120, I thought, I'd better start chewing kola nuts too.

The old man pulled at the hem of my shirt. I crouched down and he reached out with his arms, sinewy as hawsers, clasping my forehead between his palms. I fell down on my knees and all the others followed suit. The old man started to groan and wail. He released my head and shook his fists wildly, as if he had dice in them.

The others began to groan in unison. I found the whole scene almost unbearably funny, but managed to keep my composure.

The old man spoke in Wolof, one of the local dialects, and Mohammed translated in between the groans. 'He says you are going on a long journey, Tom.' Not exactly a piece of Holmesian detective work, that one. 'He says it will be difficult sometimes.' Bravo, Nostradamus, such lucid foresight. 'He says you will see a great river, and you will follow it a long way.' I realized this was all heavily staged but I didn't mind, I was enjoying myself.

A gust of wind rattled the corrugated roof above us. I snuck a quick look round at the others, thinking they would be larking about, but they were all completely absorbed. Mohammed seemed to be hallucinating, his eyes shut tight and Naya was quiet and serene as a Buddha. Only Robert looked a little ill at ease.

'He says you have left your family,' said Mohammed in a possessed, robotic voice. I suddenly felt less comfortable. The old man was groaning horribly now, as if he had something malign trying to eat its way out of him. 'You are without a home.' The old man began shaking and making terrible, preternatural noises. He abruptly stopped and slumped his head, like a toy run out of batteries. The room was silent, but for the whine of mosquitoes.

It was an age before the fortune-teller, now recovered from his funk, looked up again. He was exhausted, utterly spent, the boyish glint in his eyes long gone. He seemed much older, nowhere near 120, but still an old, old man. He mumbled a few more words and then told us to leave.

'He says you have a child, a daughter,' related Mohammed, as we walked from the hut. 'He says you must be careful on your journey, you must return to her.'

'How does he know I have a daughter?' I asked Mohammed anxiously. 'How can he know that?'

'He is, how do you say, a guru,' said Mohammed, pleased by my response. 'I told you he knows everything.'

Then I clicked. I remembered I had told Naya I was a father, who had probably told Mohammed, who in turn had told the old man. I kept quiet but reassured myself this was the explanation.

'Don't worry,' whispered Robert, before he branched away towards his home. He could see I was still a little rattled. 'It's all just guesswork and nonsense.'

I could tell Robert hadn't been won over by the evening's *ju-ju,* or by the elderly sage. More than anything, though, he was enraged about my lapsed Christianity, leaving a daughter at home.

'You have a daughter, Tom,' he said, as a parting shot. 'How can you leave her for so long? What are you doing here, all alone?' He grabbed my shoulder tightly. 'You must be a good Christian, my friend.'

And before I could provide a litany of feeble excuses he had vanished like a djinn into the darkness. It was the last I saw of him.

* * *

Later that night, sweating in my bed at the Ferry Guesthouse, my mind echoed with the fortune-teller's groans. In my restless, dream-like state I thought back to my last meeting with Eliza, my daughter, before I left for Africa.

I had travelled up to her London home from Oxford. When I arrived I already smelt of the road, my jumper steaming with rain, bus pongs and other people's cigarettes.

Eliza, her hair a rick of blonde curls, bounded up and swung on my legs like a monkey. She buried her head in my jumper and shouted, 'Daddy!' with such sweet affection, that I almost collapsed. She then ran back to Amanda, her mother, and held her the same way, shouting 'Mummy!' Back and forth she went, delighted at having, however briefly, the right number of parents.

Mummy! Daddy! Mummy! Daddy!

Amanda had always been Eliza's centre of gravity, her home star. I was simply a meteor with visitation rights, whizzing into her life and out again, a whirl of irresponsible love. Amanda was now happily remarried and bringing up Eliza in a grounded and loving environment. This gave me immeasurable comfort. But, even so, I was about to leave her. I was not the NUMBER ONE DADDY on my Father's Day card. I was RUNAWAY DADDY.

At the end of my visit, I held Eliza very tight, for a long time.

'Can you put me down now, Daddy?'

'Okay, Eliza Lou, I'll be home very soon,' I lied. Three bloody months! 'I'll think about you everyday.' Oh, the horror of departure, how I hated the sound of my clichés and forced, singsong voice.

'Where are you going, Daddy?' Eliza asked for the umpteenth time.

'Gambia in Africa.'

'Da-addy, what's Gambyafrica? Sounds funny.'

'A place, Eliza Lou, just a place. I'll be back soon.' I bundled her up in my arms one more time. 'Oh, how I'll miss you.' As I put her down I bumped my head on the stairwell.

'Bugger it.'

'Da-addy, you swore,' Eliza whispered, utterly over the moon. 'You said bugrit! Bugrit, bugrit!' I wonder if in the entire history of goodbyes a father has ever managed to say anything remotely less poignant to his four-year-old daughter.

'Shh, shh, don't tell Mum,' I joked, putting her down. 'You be a good girl, Eliza Lou.'

'It's okay, Daddy, I'll be fine,' she said, in a strangely adult voice belying her tender years and FINDING NEMO pyjamas. 'I'll be fine, fine, fine, fine.' I eventually let her go and she ran towards the kitchen. 'Biyee, Daddy.'

I walked down the corridor, stepping over Bonny, the family Labrador, and out into the open. The wind ripped into my face, as if to say: 'You are free now, off you go.' And there was a relief, a letting go, coupled with an aching emptiness.

As I walked off I heard Eliza banging on the window. She was bashing and waving madly, like Dustin Hoffman at the end of *The Graduate*.

I ran over to the window. She stood on tiptoes. 'Listen, Daddy, listen,' she shouted through the glass and the wind. She took a deep breath and sang a couple of lines of 'Twinkle Twinkle Little Star'. I clapped, knowing exactly what would come next: it was an ongoing joke between us. Eliza smiled wickedly, morphing from angelic choir girl to cheeky ingénue.

'Twinkle twinkle chocolate bar,' she sang, 'my Dad's got a rusty car.'

When Eliza finished she burst into laughter. I watched her, sick with love and pride. Then I played out my part of the game, turned my hands into bear claws, growled and pretended to grab at her through the rain-spattered window. She shrieked in ecstatic mock terror and charged back into the kitchen.

Alone again, I strode off against the wind.

CHAPTER 3

A DIFFERENT SLAVE

NEXT MORNING I felt punch drunk. What with Robert's sad stories, Naya's dancing and centenarian fortune-tellers I was undergoing a sharp, 1,000 volt culture shock. In fact, so swept away was I by my new surroundings, I had lost track of why I had come here: to follow Mungo Park.

Before heading off in his wake I wanted to remind myself what potent Sirens had drawn the young explorer to West Africa. I opened my copy of *Travels into the Interior of Africa* and a couple of other Park-related books in my rucksack.

In many ways it is not surprising Mungo Park became an explorer. In the late eighteenth century, Scotland, with its savage climate and volatile economy, was the perfect breeding ground for young men thirsting for adventure overseas. Fellow Scot, Alexander Mackenzie, became the first man to cross the Rocky Mountains in 1795 – the same year Park struck out in search of the Niger – while some 17 years earlier James Bruce, known as 'Abyssinian Bruce', was credited with discovering the source of the Blue Nile. The following century, of course, there was Dr David Livingstone, the doughty Lanarkshire missionary, who, inspired by the Bible and Park's journal, mapped out Lake Victoria and the Zambezi River.

Mungo Park was born in 1771 just north of the English border near the town of Selkirk. His father, also Mungo (probably named after the patron saint of Glasgow), was a hardworking tenant farmer who was determined to give his children a leg up in the world. Although the Parks were upwardly mobile, life was not easy. The large family was crammed into a squat, cold cottage* in the village of Foulshiels. Mungo was the seventh of 13 children, five of whom were to die before adulthood.

For all the ill-health and cramped conditions, the farm was in an idyllic setting, amid rolling, sheep-dotted hills fringed by the River Yarrow. This was a romantic landscape, filled with the ballads and folklore that Park came to love, as did his future friend, the local writer, Sir Walter Scott. Nearby were the ruins of Newark Castle, a reminder of Scottish-English conflict; fierce times which had shaped proud, hardy Border folk such as the Parks.

Young Mungo attended the local grammar school and at the age of 15 became apprentice to a doctor, Thomas Anderson, whose daughter, Ailie, he would later wed. Mungo Senior was disappointed; he believed his quiet, serious son would be better suited to a career in the church. Yet, beneath his bookish façade, teenage Mungo was increasingly driven and plumped to study medicine at Edinburgh University. It proved a good choice; he worked hard and blossomed socially, joining debating societies and writing poetry in his spare time.

---

*The Parks' family cottage still exists, albeit roofless and smothered in tall weeds. It lies four miles west of Selkirk on the Moffat road. Modern Foulshiels Farm, next door to the cottage, is still lived in by a sheep farming family. They told me they had fielded less than a dozen inquiries about Park over the last 20 years.

When he left Edinburgh in 1791 Park landed on his feet, thanks to his brother-in-law, James Dickson, a seedsman and nursery keeper. Dickson invited the 21-year-old graduate on a botany expedition in the Highlands. It proved a triumph and prompted Dickson to introduce his young relative to a well-connected friend, Sir Joseph Banks; a meeting that was to seal Park's destiny.

Banks, both extrovert and scholarly, had made his name as a botanist on Captain Cook's first expedition, collecting plants from Australia, New Zealand, Tahiti and Brazil. By the time Park met him in London, Sir Joseph had become one of the capital's most prominent figures and President of the Royal Society. Lord Hobart, the Foreign Secretary, put it beautifully when he said of Banks in 1793: 'Wide as the world is, traces of you are to be found in every corner of it.'

With Banks as his patron the world was as good as Park's oyster too, and within six months the ambitious Scot had secured a job as a surgeon's mate on the *Worcester*, an East India Company ship bound for Sumatra in Indonesia.

Before departure, Park wrote some revealing letters to his friend and future brother-in-law, Alexander Anderson. In these, the quiet man of exploration exposes his rabid ambition. 'Macbeth's start when he beheld the dagger was a mere jest compared to mine . . .' wrote Park, admittedly in one of his more overblown moments.

The Sumatran journey was uneventful but Park made full use of his time. While the *Worcester* was being loaded with pepper and arak (an aniseed spirit), the trainee surgeon eagerly collected plant specimens and painted watercolours of the local fish. It was a pivotal time for Park. His passion for exploration and natural history burgeoned; already medicine had begun to play second fiddle.

On his return from the Far East three months later, Park learnt of his father's sudden death. He spent time in Scotland with the family, then travelled down to London with his Indonesian plant samples and fish sketches. Sir Joseph Banks was impressed by Park's work, and very excited. The grand old statesman realized his protégé was ripe with potential.

Without knowing it, Mungo Park had secured his passport to West Africa.

* * *

Mohammed lent against the railings of the jam-packed ferry, chewing on a mango. The wind buffeted his unruly hair. Rather than heading up the Gambia River as Mungo Park had done, we were sailing across its mouth to the port of Barra, directly opposite Banjul. After the half hour voyage the plan was to hail a bush taxi to Juffureh near to where Park had first landed.

Between mango bites, Mohammed explained that the Gambia River was much the same as in Park's time. There were still no bridges or tunnels, so, unless you owned a boat, the ferry was the only way across.

On arrival at Barra, we were swept up in the brightly coloured scrum forging towards the ferry exit. An elderly woman in front of us balanced a bucket of potatoes on her head, while a Trotsky-bearded huckster tried to tempt us with a tray of coconut slices.

Present-day Barra was a mass of wheezy vehicles and tin shacks. The area had clearly gone downhill since 200 years ago when, according to Mungo Park, its king was the most formidable on the river. Indeed, he was able to charge a whopping £20 on every vessel entering his territory. Barra had been famed for its salt which was paddled up river in canoes in exchange for an incongruous mix of cotton, elephants' teeth and gold dust.

'What's this area known for now?' I asked Mohammed as we walked along the harbour front.

'Peanuts,' he replied, wiping his brow with his MIAMI base-ball cap.

'Peanuts!' I said, interpreting his remark as negative. 'I can't believe there's nothing here.'

'I told you, peanuts!' Mohammed looked at me strangely. 'They have peanuts. Groundnuts. Whatever you call them. Millet too.'

Mohammed tracked down a bush taxi, a rust heap of a Peugeot 504, which we shared with five other adults and three children. We juddered off east along a bitumen road that soon turned to dirt. It was a beautiful day, the sky a clear pale blue, the sun not too hot. Parrots squawked in the lush vegetation and at one point a troop of small grey monkeys paraded across the road, forcing our jalopy into an emergency stop. Purple blossom fringed the roadside and sweet, exotic smells wafted through the windows.

* * *

We were dropped off at Juffureh, opposite a large white building. EXHIBITION OF THE SLAVE TRADE, read the sign above the entrance. A mural depicting a gang of slaves, glum-faced and shackled together, had been painted on the outside wall. Inside the museum it was as cool and dank as a cave. It turned out to be an inspired exhibition; the displays simple, direct and moving.

I read that the Portuguese had been the first Europeans to discover the West African coast. They quickly realized its potential and by the mid-fifteenth century had set up a string of trading stations. Before long, the British, French, Dutch and Germans began jockeying for position, too. At first ivory, beeswax, peppers and gold were exchanged, but then the focus switched to a more urgent commodity: slaves, needed to work in the mines and plantations of the freshly colonized Americas.

Of course, the principle of slavery, of one man owning another, had already existed for centuries in Africa. Slaves had been traded not only between the people of black Africa, but across the Sahara as far north as the Middle East. But only when the European powers muscled in did this profitable human cargo start to burgeon. In West Africa alone it is estimated up to 15 million slaves were dragged away from their homeland across the Atlantic. Throughout the course of these sea journeys – some lasting up to three months – nearly half the slaves died of thirst, hunger, disease or asphyxiation. Sometimes whole cargoes perished.

While a few European traders made half-hearted forays into the interior of Africa, most stuck like limpets to the coasts, islands or river mouths. Their idea was to carry away as much as possible from the Dark Continent* with the minimum effort and cost. Indeed, over the course of 400 years in Luanda, in present-day Angola, the Portuguese did not dig a single well for drinkable water or light up one street with lanterns.

Although Park writes movingly about individual slaves he meets on his journey, he remains strangely ambivalent on the issue as a whole. That said, by the time of his 1795 visit, only 400 slaves a year (it had been more like 3,000 a century before) were exported overseas from the Senegambia region. Other areas further south, especially around the Gulf of Guinea, were proving richer pickings for the slavers towards the end of the eighteenth century.

---

*While the term Dark Continent later took on racial connotations, it was initially because cartographers shaded the unknown regions of Africa black – which, in the eighteenth century, meant almost everywhere between Cairo and Cape Town.

Slavery was abolished in all the British colonies in 1807, a year after Park's death. By then, with the Napoleonic Wars in full swing, no more colony in America, and steady advances in industry, Britain had little need for slaves. But slavery in one form or another was to continue across Africa for over a century: in certain isolated pockets it has yet to be fully stamped out today.

On leaving the exhibition I spotted one particularly grim quotation, which perhaps spoke more than all the statistics. The words were attributed to 'An Anonymous Source'. 'The negroes are wilful and so hate to leave their own country that they often leap out of the canoes, boats and ships and keep under water till they are drowned to avoid being taken.'

When I read this out to Mohammed he laughed, a sad, awkward laugh, not really a laugh at all.

'The white man thinks Africa is a wild place,' he said. 'But the black man thinks the *toubabs'* world is wild too. Of course, a slave wants to die at home, not in a place he is an animal, a place he cannot be free.'

* * *

From the museum Mohammed and I walked down to the neighbouring settlement of Albreda. On the riverside was a derelict French trading house and near to it a large iron cannon pointing across the water. We sat by the cannon, something Park may have even done, watching dragonflies and throwing stones into the jade-tinted water.

'Okay, let's do the *Roots* thing,' Mohammed said, stifling a yawn. 'The Alex Hailey thing. You know, the man who wrote *Roots*. Juffureh is supposed to be where his book starts.'

I'd never read the book but *Roots* had been one of my first and fondest TV memories. As a child the struggles and adventures of Chicken George and Kunte Kinte (the ancestor Hailey based his novel on) had kept me spellbound. I vividly remembered the scene where Kunte Kinte and his brother were seized by slavers while collecting firewood near the river. Mohammed told me some descendants of Kunte Kinte's brother still lived in the village.

As we walked towards Kinte's hut I got cold feet. A clutch of tourists had just arrived and the souvenir touts were circling. The scene was far from relaxed, the tourists and touts both becoming edgy with one another. The hut, from what I could see, was made of millet stalks and reeds, so unlikely to be the original. I decided to hang back; cling on to the positive memories I had of *Roots*.

'This village is messed up,' Mohammed whispered, pulling at my arm. 'We are right to stay away. The *Roots* thing is bullshit. Everyone says they are Kunte Kinte's relative. It's a joke. The slave museum is better, more true.'

We branched off towards the bush taxi stand, followed by a tawny, doe-eyed dog with a limp. It whined in pain each time its front paws touched the ground.

'What did Mungo Park say about slaves?' Mohammed asked.

'The slaves Park met treated him kindly,' I replied. 'By the end of his journey he was starving, dressed in rags. Slaves took pity on him, thought he was worse off than them.'

I paused, picking my words carefully. A naked child ran past and kicked at the dog. It yelped in surprise, before lolloping off towards the river.

'That's the odd thing about Park,' I continued, 'he was a sensitive man who saw the cruel way the slaves were treated, the beating, the ropes. He wrote well about it, but still stayed neutral. Never properly spoke out against slavery.'

'Like many *toubabs*,' said Mohammed, his eyes hard, indignant. 'Slavery was so bad for this country. Poisoned it. Whites paid blacks to catch slaves too, you know. Blacks catching blacks. Their own people!' He kicked hard at the dust. 'Slavery made the black man feel weak, not human. No wonder some African leaders are bad now. It is what the white man taught us. It made Africa sick. Gambia is my home. I love my people but I am a smart man, I want to do so many things. See so many things. But I am trapped, no chances, working in a boring guest house. I am a different slave.'

'Come on, Mohammed. Is it really that bad?'

'What do you know, Tom!' he shouted, furious now, his forehead creased and sweat-soaked. 'You are here following this Mungo Park. You are just a tourist. You are here less than one week. Tell me, what do you know about my country? What do you know about my life?'

CHAPTER 4

LOST IN THE FLOW

BY THE time we were back in Banjul, Mohammed had calmed down and returned to his usual genial self. I enjoyed his company. He was proud and opinionated, prickly at times but not without humour. I felt I was learning lots by spending time with him.

Mohammed knew I was keen to travel far up the Gambia River and had offered to help me out. That afternoon we bussed five miles along the coast to Denton Bridge, near a tributary of the river. Mohammed knew a man there called Captain Jim who owned several small boats.

All along the river bank were groups of men tinkering with engines and fishing tackle. We passed a dead cow. It lay on its back, its eyes glazed and peaceful. The rotting beast's legs had stiffened to such an extent it reminded me of an upturned table.

Captain Jim soon appeared in blue overalls and a panama-style sun hat. He looked me up and down, while primping his greying goatee. Mohammed explained my predicament and the two of them chatted for a while in Mandingo, Captain Jim's dialect.

Mohammed explained Captain Jim knew of a ferry plying up the Gambia River. It docked nearly 200 miles upstream in Janjanbureh. This was encouraging news. Janjanbureh (or Georgetown, as it was known in colonial times) was near to where Park had anchored and rested up before striking out inland to look for the Niger.

'The bad news,' said Mohammed, smirking, 'is the ferry sunk over 20 years ago.'

He told me the only way now was to hire a motorized skiff. My request was apparently most unusual. Standard boat trips for bird-watchers or fishing expeditions were no more than a few hours, whereas to reach Janjanbureh, would take three days at least. The fuel costs would be high, in the region of 3,000 Gambian dollars (£50) a day.

This was much more than I bargained for, but it was early in the trip, and my wad of 2,000 Euros (for the full three months on the road) still obscenely fat. I was also desperate to get going, to follow Park's trail. Besides, I trusted Mohammed; and Captain Jim, despite often being incomprehensible, seemed a good sort too. I haggled the price down a bit and struck a deal. The boat would leave at midday tomorrow.

Mohammed took a mini-bus back to Banjul, while I decided to walk. I made my way along the river until it segued into the Atlantic. I knew some of the coast farther west had suffered severe erosion, but the beach here looked unharmed and, even better, deserted. I stripped and crashed into the refreshing surf. To dry off I walked along the seafront, the sand still lukewarm from the heat of the falling sun.

An elderly couple sitting on deck-chairs waved at me. They were both very pale, shaded by a beach umbrella, which sprouted over them like a fairytale toadstool.

It was a beautiful, balmy evening and I sat down to watch the waves. I was high on anticipation. Tomorrow I would be heading east, the first stretch of my journey towards the River Niger, a journey many had taken before me.

* * *

For all Sir Joseph Banks' global influence, the enigmatic River Niger still seemed beyond his grasp. This was a source of escalating irritation to the proud statesman. It was not just the River Niger, but almost the entire interior of Africa that eluded him. Damn it, Banks must have thought, we have maps of frozen Siberian wastelands, of Pacific atolls, even charts of the surface of the moon, but we know nothing of this vast continent almost on our doorstep.

And what of the rivers: the Spaniards have already sailed down the Amazon, the Mississippi is extensively mapped out, and the great rivers of Europe are almost household names now. And yet, what little we know of the Nile, the Congo and, as for the Niger, we are completely in the dark.

It is easy to understand Banks' frustration. When the geographer James Rennell prepared his famous map of the interior of Africa in 1790, he was still forced to rely on information from Herodotus. A great scholar, Herodotus, no question, but he had died in 425 BC. The gap of over two millennia did not mean he was unreliable over the Niger though. In fact, Herodotus admirably managed to work out the then nameless river's unusual flow. He rightly assessed that it broke all the rules, running eastwards away from the sea and directly towards the desert.

In the first century AD Pliny the Elder concurred with Herodotus about the eastward flow, and by now this mythical river in the sand had a name, the Niger, derived from the phrase *gher n-gheren*, meaning 'river among rivers' in Tamashek, the language of the desert nomads.

Over the next two centuries information on the river became increasingly muddled. The Alexandrian geographer, Ptolemy, and the cartographer, Al-Idrissi, confused the issue by claiming categorically that the Niger flowed west. The balance was redressed in the fourteenth century when the great, and usually reliable, Moroccan traveller Ibn Battutah accurately described the Niger as flowing east. This might have settled things, but Ibn Battutah's books were not available in Europe in the late eighteenth century. He was a spot on, but invisible source.

The wealthy, Granada-born Moor, Leo Africanus, travelled to Africa almost a century after Ibn Battutah. He was a fearless adventurer and by the age of 20 had visited not only Tabriz in Persia but the fabled city of Timbuktu. His lavish descriptions of this mysterious place on the fringe of the Sahara, whose king owned sceptres of gold weighing more than ten men, sparked furious interest. The fact Timbuktu was near the Niger made it only more seductive.

But Leo's picaresque accounts were flawed over the direction of the Niger. Despite never being adamant, he still plumped in favour of the great river flowing to the west. Two more centuries were to pass with no more conclusive evidence coming forward. There was rumour and gossip about the Niger and Timbuktu, but it was always conflicting, trivial or simply outrageous.

By this time Sir Joseph Banks, having seen so much of the world himself, was champing at the bit. Not only was he frustrated over the dearth of knowledge about Africa, he was embarrassed, disgusted. Several other prominent Londoners felt the same way and on 9 June 1788 a group of 12 gentlemen, with Banks at the helm, founded a new society at a tavern in Pall Mall. It was called the African Association. Its stated purpose: 'For Promoting the Discovery of the Inland Parts of that Quarter of the World'.

They were a motley but distinguished group, with very mixed motives. Among them was an Irish aristocrat, a retired general, a bishop, a lawyer, a doctor and several wealthy landowners and dilettantes. Some, like the silver-tongued MP Henry Beaufoy, were committed to stifling the slave trade (William Wilberforce also joined the African Association in 1789), while others sized up Africa with a more commercial eye. Banks himself was something of an imperialist, seeing slavery as a necessary evil.

These wildly diverse individuals, however, were united in one goal. They desperately wanted to learn more of the interior of Africa, to succeed where governments had failed. Scientific inquiry and exploration were the nascent Association's top priorities. All they needed now was some brave, capable men who were up to the challenge.

* * *

John Ledyard seemed a perfect candidate. The impulsive, trailblazing American was a born adventurer. Even as a boy in Connecticut, Ledyard had run away from school and spent time living among the Indians. As a young man he bushwhacked around America for a while, living in the woods and paddling self-made canoes down remote rivers. At the age of 24, Ledyard sailed over to England and joined the crew of Captain Cook's ship, the *Resolution*. The ship set sail in the summer of 1776 in search of the North-West Passage, Cook's third voyage to the Pacific. Four years later the *Resolution* returned. In that time Ledyard had made ground breaking deals with Russian fur traders, floundered in ice while attempting to cross the Bering Sea and seen Captain Cook stabbed to death in Tahiti.

The American was soon thirsty for more adventure. But for all his hearty masculinity, Ledyard's journal at this time shows a more romantic side. He wrote that he saw himself as 'a traveller and a friend of mankind' who wanted to 'strew roses' on his sisters' laps and 'branches of palms beneath their feet'. After writing a book, *A Journal of Captain Cook's Last Voyage*, he prepared for his next grand scheme, to sail south around the Americas to the west coast.

Ledyard looked for backers in America and Spain, but struck it lucky in Paris, where he met up with the American consul, Thomas Jefferson. Perhaps inspired by Jefferson, Ledyard changed his plans. He now wanted to be the first person to circumnavigate the world by land, if possible travelling through Russia, Siberia and then over to the American north-west. With the patronage of Jefferson, and a small grant from Banks (who had heard of Ledyard's plans), he set off from Paris in the autumn of 1786.

Roughly a year later, having travelled on foot and horseback via Stockholm and St Petersburg, Ledyard ran into difficulty in Siberia. He had hoped to cross the Okhotsk Sea, but it was frozen solid. He decided to sit it out in the nearby region of Yakutsk and wait for a thaw. In the spring of 1788 his luck ran out. He was arrested as a French spy by Russian soldiers. Catherine the Great had got wind of his journey and was worried, correctly, he might have designs on the Russian fur trade.

Just 600 miles from his goal, Ledyard was marshalled back to Poland, and told he would be shot if he attempted to regain entry into Russia. A few weeks later he appeared, ragged and penniless, at Soho Square in London, the home of Sir Joseph Banks.

Banks wasted no time. He quickly introduced the indefatigable Ledyard to Henry Beaufoy, the secretary of the African Association. They hit it off. 'I was struck by the manliness of his person,' Beaufoy was to remark, 'the breadth of his chest, the openness of his countenance, and the inquietude of his eye.'

Ledyard was set a Sisyphean challenge. He was to make his way from Cairo to Mecca, then cross the Red Sea and 'traverse the Continent of Africa as nearly as possible in the direction of the Niger'. Beaufoy asked Ledyard when he could get going.

'Tomorrow morning,' replied the optimistic American.

It took a little longer than that but, even so, within two months of his Siberian ordeal, Ledyard was back on the road. He told Beaufoy he was accustomed to hardship and had known 'the utmost extremity of human suffering . . . If I live, I will faithfully perform . . . my engagement to the society; and if I perish in the attempt, my honour will still be safe, for death cancels all bonds.'

The African Association members were delighted with their new recruit. They had formed the society only three months ago and were already making progress. It was to be short-lived, though.

Ledyard landed in Alexandria that summer. He was not impressed with the once opulent Egyptian port, describing it as a place of 'poverty, rapine, murder, blind bigotry, cruel persecution, pestilence!' He visited some of the sights and moved on to Cairo.

Things did not improve here. The westbound caravan he was due to join was harried by delays. Ledyard was like an animal in a cage, desperate to stride off and seal his place in the history books. Then, like so many travellers to Egypt, he became sick; a bilious complaint. Ledyard took a dose of vitriolic acid, the recommended medicine of the day. In his haste to be cured, he drank too much. He died, his innards irreparably burnt, spewing blood. John Ledyard, the most travelled American of his time, was never to throw roses on his sisters' laps.

* * *

Back at the Ferry Guesthouse a power cut had put paid to the football on TV. Mohammed, Naya and the others sat slumped around the set in varying states of torpor. A bald man knelt on a prayer mat in the corner of reception, whispering devotions and fingering a string of beads.

I chatted for a while with Naya and retreated to my room. The following morning a friend of mine was due to arrive. Amar, a solicitor turned photojournalist, had been commissioned to write a piece on the Senegalese port of St Louis. Now he had finished this he was heading south to join me up the Gambia River and a small section of the Malian bush. I was used to travelling solo, but it would be good to have a friend on board for a while.

Amar's presence would also be something of a comfort. Before leaving for West Africa I had been bombarded with chilling news flashes. What about the Christian massacres in Nigeria? Tuareg banditry in Niger? Riots in Mali over the Paris-Dakar rally? Was the internecine fighting in the Casamance really over? Even on arrival in sleepy Banjul, the local paper blazed: 'Hyenas on the Rampage – threat to people in broad daylight is a new phenomenon'. Apparently sheep and goats were not enough to satisfy the hyenas of Upper Nuimi.

Most of this stuff I acknowledged, but tried not to stew over. In truth, I had been partly seduced by West Africa because of the risk it entailed. I sometimes wondered if, subconsciously, I had a Conrad-like calling to plunge into a dark, potentially hostile, place and not come out again; a subliminal urge to do myself in.

But, deep down, I knew this wasn't the case. In my experience, most travel, however daunting and uncomfortable, is rarely life-threatening. It was the same the world over. A regime might stink but the people on the street look out for you; and I always like to trust. I was no Beowulf in search of a glorious death. No, I was more like Bilbo Baggins, a timid soul who is surprised by his taste for adventure, just about summons up enough courage to see it through and then returns, delighted, to his hobbit hole.

This was to be the last of my big journeys. Over the past six years I had pedalled a bicycle 12,500 miles from England to Australia and walked across America with a mule. I needed to rein myself in from these long-winded jaunts. I knew there was a possibility I never would ('Once a bum, always a bum,' wrote Steinbeck near his sixtieth birthday) but I hoped this was not my destiny. In West Africa I was confident I had found a place that would stretch me, beat me up a bit, make me howl at the moon, and maybe, God willing, clip my wings.

But one recent story had dented my confidence. I had a couple of articles about it with me and skimmed over them that evening. The first was from *The Sunday Times*.

The story centred on a 28-year-old Englishman called Christian Velten. Velten had struck out on the trail of Mungo Park the previous year, beginning his journey in Banjul and heading east. Using a camcorder, he had been filming his journey for a documentary. The adventurer had last been heard of roughly ten months ago, from Kita, a small town in west Mali. At the time Velten had been travelling with a donkey and cart along one of Park's remoter routes. He had also employed a Gambian interpreter, but sacked him after an argument. Later he had hoped to canoe down the Niger. Velten's parents, with the help of the Foreign Office and Interpol, had arranged a search party. So far it had drawn a blank.

Before my departure I had clicked on to Velten's website and downloaded his exact route in case something came to light. Velten sounded like a practical, hardy man who had planned his trip carefully.

In a separate article in *The Evening Standard*, Velten's mother, Pauline, had written of her family's anxiety:

He [Christian] told me not to worry before he left, saying he knew what he was up against. Of course I did worry, but my husband and I have brought our children up to be adventurous . . . he liked travelling on his own, so took the risk, and I think he gets a buzz surviving hardship.

I have to believe my son is alive. The not knowing is tortuous – is he sick with malaria or typhus but alive in a village somewhere being looked after? Has he drowned, or has he been kidnapped? There are crocodiles and hyenas; as he was on his own in a tent in the wilderness, anything could have happened.

We have to find him, even if what we find is what we are dreading the most.

* * *

After John Ledyard the African Association already had another explorer waiting in the wings. This was Arabic-speaking civil servant, Simon Lucas, who had sailed out to Tripoli and was poised to head south towards the River Niger through the deserts of Libya.

Lucas boasted almost as colourful a past as Ledyard. As a youth he had been captured by pirates on a voyage from Cadiz to London and sold as a slave in Morocco. He was released three years later and, in a strange twist of fate, was offered a job as British vice-consul in the Moroccan court. He jumped at it. Returning to London 16 years later, he was appointed oriental interpreter to King George III. The African Association soon heard about his credentials and recruited him as their next explorer.

On his arrival in Tripoli Lucas blended in well with his flawless Arabic. In a letter back to his sponsors he described himself as growing his hair so long that 'he looked like a London Jew in deep mourning'. He began his journey by travelling east along the Libyan coast to the city of Mesurata. Here, he was warned not to turn inland across the desert because of warring tribes. Lucas was far less gung-ho than Ledyard and lost heart. He apologized to the Association, returning to England with only a selection of native seeds and some scant geographical titbits. It did his career no harm, though, and he soon became British consul to Tripoli.

And so the River Niger remained a mystery. Some believed it flowed into the Atlantic or perhaps linked up with the Nile, or maybe even a large lake in the desert. Others thought it plunged south and segued into the Congo. Whatever its course, it was time for a fresh approach. Next time, the Association would send a man down the Gambia River.

CHAPTER 5

FIRE BOATS AND
RIVER HORSES

AMAR was one of the first off the ferry from Barra the following morning. Of all my friends Amar is perhaps the easiest to spot in a crowd. Being of mixed ancestry, his father Sikh, his mother Irish, he had a most distinctive look: part Bob Geldof, part Punjabi nobleman. The fact he was sporting a purple shirt and hefting a rucksack the size of a hay bale made him all the more identifiable.

We ate breakfast at a popular street stall near the ferry terminus: bread and omelettes washed down with sweet coffee made with condensed milk. The man serving us had shrivelled fingers on both hands, but still poured the drinks with the panache of a Manhattan barman, the milk cascading into our plastic cups, settling in a jaundiced slick above the coffee. Fat, drowsy flies circled us.

After our sugary kick-start, I said farewell to my friends at the Ferry Guesthouse. As a thank you I gave Naya my deodorant ('Ah yes, England man, now I smell like Lady Diana!')

and Mohammed a phial of Deet mosquito-repellent. Amar and I then flagged down a taxi, chicaned past Arch 22 and out to Captain Jim's boat.

Captain Jim had evidently taken his rank to heart that morning and, along with his baggy track suit bottoms, sported a jacket with yellow epaulettes. He nodded his approval when Amar and I handed over our wads of Gambian dollars, then introduced us to Salif, our teenage guide, who would pilot the skiff up river. Salif looked hard-faced, with tiny tribal scars either side of his nose, but he turned out to be very shy, speaking with a stammer. He flashed us a brief, eager to please grin and busied himself priming the boat's engine.

Amar and I sat on the river bank. Other than the odd dive-bombing gull or fisherman threading a dugout through the mangroves the dark river was still.

All this was shattered when a middle-aged couple, both blonde and grilled to an unhealthy shade of butterscotch, revved by in a motor launch. Once level with the harbour the boat decelerated and sploshed to a halt, a spume of transient white in its wake. The chargrilled man stayed sitting at the wheel, while his partner, in a flesh-hugging mauve bikini, stretched over the deck to hand a fish to Captain Jim.

Standing on tiptoe Captain Jim grabbed the fish by the gills; it was about a foot long with barbells dangling from its mouth like hydra's hair. He stuck it in a bucket, then jumped on board and pulled another much larger fish along the gang plank. This great silver creature, the size of a pike, slopped down in front of us, its gaping maws displaying Dracula-like teeth.

'This fish is a capitaine!' said Captain Jim, watching Amar and me inspect the flaccid monster's dentistry. 'Very famous.'

'The capitaine fish, it bite even a hippo. Or bite a man when he swim. Bite here!' He gestured with his eyes towards his crotch, and let out a high-pitched laugh. 'Ouch, yes, very dangerous.'

I had read somewhere that the capitaine could reach four feet long. I looked at the dead fish's sharp, snaggled teeth and felt my testes flinch up, briefly reaching places I imagine only usually achieved by the very finest martial artists.

'No skinny dipping then,' said Amar decisively.

* * *

Soon we were gunning up river in our skiff, which was freighted down with backpacks and fuel jerries. Once out in the open, away from the narrow mangrove-hemmed creeks, we had the water to ourselves. It stretched like a wide sheet of steel in the midday sun, pockmarked by occasional clumps of migrating vegetation.

The Gambia River meanders like a 350-mile lifeline through the country that bears its name. Indeed, the British even drew up Gambia's frontier by steering a gun boat along the river and firing cannon balls at intervals to mark out the size of the territory. As long as the border was in cannon shot, that would suffice. For this reason, The Gambia today is like a small, spindly finger poking into the ample flank of her more progressive, French-speaking neighbour, Senegal.

Despite her suffocating, poorly thought out borders, The Gambia remains fiercely proud. The idea of a united Senegambia region has often been mooted, but always comes unstuck, partly because the smaller of the two countries clings resiliently to its own strong cultural identity.

After three hours Salif, now wrapped in a green anorak despite the withering heat, pointed ahead. What looked like a colossal raft unleashed from its moorings, shimmered in the distance. This was James Island, opposite the bank from Juffureh, where I had visited the slave museum the day before.

Salif docked on the island's south bank and threw the anchor, a tractor tow bar, into the shallows. It made a tremendous splash, turning the surrounding water the colour of cocoa. We all jumped on land and wandered up through a grove of stout, pale-trunked baobabs dripping with green fruit.

Apart from several DANGER − NO CLIMBING signs and a clutch of rusty cannons, all we found left was a ruined fortress with a single surviving room, perhaps once used for holding slaves.

The island certainly boasted a turbulent history. Baltic agents first laid claim to it in the mid-1600s; then the British, the French and, for one unlikely spell, a gang of Welsh pirates. By the time Park sailed past in the summer of 1795, the island had been long abandoned, the fort already in ruins.

It was such a hauntingly lovely spot we toyed with camping the night, but decided to push on. Park surged ahead at this stage too. Despite brief pit stops − one at the trading centre of Vintain, just beyond James Island on the south bank − the fledgling explorer travelled as fast as he could. He was keen to reach Pisania, some 180 miles upriver, from where he would strike out inland in search of the Niger.

During his brief hiatus at Vintain, Park noted the customs of the local Feloops. He calls them 'a wild and unsociable race of people', who liked to trade in beeswax and rice and intoxicate themselves with mead, a mind-pickling honey homebrew. He dismisses their language as 'peculiar', using their numbers from one to ten as an example. (For those interested, seven in Feloop is *footuck-cookaba,* and that's one of the shorter ones.) Park is more complimentary about the nearby Jaloff people who he calls 'active, powerful and war-like'.

At the outset of his journey Park not only provides thumbnail sketches of the people, but the wildlife. He spots sharks swimming near the mouth of the river, crocodiles and river horses (hippos) further upstream and elephants, panthers and hyenas on land. None of these potential killers concerns him much and he talks almost tenderly of the hippos' 'timid and inoffensive disposition'.

Though Park's *sang-froid* is commendable, animals would have been the least of his worries. It was malaria that was the chief killer. In 1795 the mysterious fever was still thought to stem, not from mosquitoes, but stagnant or putrid air (from the Italian, *mal-aria*, meaning bad air). Until quinine was first used as a preventative medicine in the mid-nineteenth century almost all Europeans visiting West Africa were struck down with the disease, many fatally. As the English sailors used to sing:

> Beware and take care of the Bight of Benin,
> For one that comes out there are forty goes in.

The Gambia River was especially unforgiving. Not long before Park's visit 200 British convicts had been posted upstream as part of an experimental penal colony. Within less than six months all but 50 were dead.

But Park was not one to dwell on such grim possibilities. If he came a cropper, so be it; that was his philosophy. Until then he would make the most of this exciting new world, which, for all its beasts, also boasted unrivalled beauty.

* * *

That first evening on the river, apart from the dull burr of our engine, I liked to think we were witnessing scenes very similar to Park. The sun was sinking slowly, turning the underbellies of the clouds a brilliant red. It was as if the hem of the sky had been doused in blood, before diluting to dove-grey and then the palest of blacks.

By now alternative sunsets had eclipsed the real one. In the surrounding mangroves, bonfires were being lit. They flickered in the crepuscular haze, intense and solitary, like distant glow worms. The smell of wood smoke occasionally wafted on the breeze.

The water surrounding us was bathed in moonshine. At one point a dolphin, mussel-shell blue with flapping fins, sprang up in front of the boat in a dazzling parabola. It lifted its beak as if to say, 'come on, play with me', and plunged down, pursued by a contrail of phosphorescent green.

Tiny silver fish began to leap into the skiff, at first one or two, then great shoals. They slapped against our legs and faces, danced on our laps, jittered across our luggage, or else vaulted clean over the bows. Amar and I tossed back dozens into the spectral water, except when Salif shouted for us to hang on to the bigger ones: any over a hand's length. Salif laughed as we grappled with the hapless sprats, and Amar and I laughed too. You could not help but be high on a night like this.

At one stage Salif killed the engine. Bar the flapping of the fish: silence. A fisherman drifted up to us. We had seen him from some distance away, a small fire had been burning in the centre of his dugout. At first I thought it must have some religious significance, so powerful was the image of the flames licking up from the little boat, but it turned out he was simply brewing a billy can. A tangled net was draped over his stern, the moisture droplets on it glistening like pearls.

Salif and he exchanged greetings. The fisherman was dark, hard to see, his voice sounded elderly, but rich and musical, as if used to telling stories. After speaking to the fisherman, Salif told us we would have to travel until midnight to reach Tendaba Camp, the village where we would sleep.

Amar said he didn't care if it took all night. Neither did I. Looking around, it was as if this was a half-finished land, an enchanted canvas where imagination could run free. The night sky was limpid, the stars like spilled milk. There were still fires blazing in the mangroves, rashes of phosphorescence in the water, occasional drum beats. It was a scene of unalloyed splendour.

The fisherman stood up and looked at us. He had been hard to see in the darkness but now his face glowed in the firelight. He was an old man, with mole-pelt sideburns specked with grey. He looked far too old to be out on his own fishing; 70, maybe more. Then a woman, invisible until then, stood up and looked at us too. She was his age, with withered cheeks and wide eyes. The couple stood together and when they smiled at us, the pair of them looked, just for a second, like children.

* * *

Mungo Park was not the first explorer the African Association sent up the Gambia River. That honour (or poisoned chalice, a cynic might have said) was bestowed on a 50-year-old Irishman, Daniel Houghton. Houghton was a tough, upbeat ex-army major, who seemed an even safer bet than Ledyard or Lucas.

The old soldier not only boasted Ledyard's hardy optimism but, having been based four years with the army on the island of Gorée off the coast of Senegal, he also had Lucas's insider knowledge of Africa. It was hoped Houghton's senior years would lend him a patience that Ledyard had lacked and a confidence that had evaded Lucas.

But Houghton had a problem. By the summer of 1790, when the African Association interviewed him, he had drummed up some heavy debts. He urgently needed to bolster his haemorrhaging finances, not least because he had a wife and three children to support. He was desperate for work and offered his services in West Africa for a paltry sum of around £260. Records show that another man, Captain Mason, had also applied for the job but demanded an extravagant budget of some £1,200. Ever keen for a bargain, Banks and Beaufoy plumped for Houghton.

Houghton's mission was to boat up the Gambia River, then travel eastwards overland in search of the Niger and, if possible, Timbuktu. Unlike Ledyard and Lucas who had set off into the unknown, the course of the Gambia River had already been well documented by previous British traders.

Houghton was not only to be a geographical crusader, but a political envoy, attempting to win local hearts and minds en route. Such was the Association's confidence in their new explorer, Banks arranged for him to meet William Pitt, the prime minister, shortly before departure.

Houghton's voyage started auspiciously. He reached the Gambia River in the autumn of 1790, the start of the dry season, an ideal time to travel. Like Park would do some five years later, Houghton stopped off at the trading post of Pisania. He secured a horse and five donkeys before moving on to Jonkakonda, some 16 miles east. Here, acting on rumours that his life was in danger, he crossed the river to escape ambush.

The southern bank was far harder going than the more travelled northern route but by March 1791 Houghton had still made it to the town of Medina, in the kingdom of Wuli, almost halfway up the river.

Houghton, whose life had been one of poverty and hard graft up until then, had to pinch himself to believe his good luck. In a letter to his wife the humble Irishman wrote of Medina as some kind of Elysium: 'You can live here almost for nothing: ten pounds a year would support a whole family with plenty of fowls, sheep, milk, eggs, butter, honey, bullocks, fish, and all sorts of game.'

The King of Wuli was initially welcoming to Houghton, even offering to supply guides to help him reach Timbuktu. It seemed all too good to be true, and, sure enough, just before Houghton set off again, disaster struck. One afternoon Medina, a town of some thousand thatched huts, was razed by fire. Houghton was to lose most of his belongings.

Probably due to this catastrophe the King of Wuli rescinded his offer to assist Houghton. The explorer was now in dire straits, his provisions meagre, his donkeys lost, his chances slim. To add to his woes, a replacement gun he bought blew up in his hands, badly wounding his face and arms.

But Houghton was lion-hearted and even the onset of the rainy season, with its muddy tracks and rampant disease, failed to stall him. He set off north but soon found himself caught in the thick of a war between the neighbouring kingdoms of Bambuk and Bondo. To keep the rival kings sweet, Houghton was forced to pay gifts, including the crimson waistcoat he had hoped to wear on arrival in Timbuktu.

Once the fighting had calmed, Houghton exchanged his paltry supplies for a horse and secured a guide. He headed off once more, having gained the King of Bambuk's blessing. It was the summer of 1791 and Timbuktu perhaps no more than a month away. Houghton was back on track, writing to his sponsors that he was in fine spirits and, thanks to his dark complexion and local dress, looked almost exactly like a Moor.

After this only one more note was received from Houghton. He reported that he was in a village called Simbing (some 160 miles north of Bamako, the capital of present-day Mali) and, despite having been robbed, was still in good health.

And then: silence. Rumours soon filtered back that Houghton was dead, but the African Association waited a full year before announcing he was missing. His long-suffering wife was not only distraught but broke, and thrown in a debtors' prison. The Association eventually bailed her out, supplied her with a pension and paid for her children's education.

Only over five years later, when Mungo Park followed in Houghton's wake, was the Irishman's fate revealed. Park was even led to the spot near Simbing where the resilient ex-soldier died, abandoned by those who had robbed him.

West Africa had claimed yet another explorer, but not in vain. Houghton had provided the first proper information on the Niger for some 200 years. He rightly claimed the elusive river was not the same as the Gambia River, or the Senegal River, which ran further north. Despite never making it to the Niger, Houghton was confident it flowed eastwards. But these were all the claims of a dead man, unable to report back in person. Houghton was soon forgotten.

It would be up to the next African explorer, a young untested Scot, to reach the Niger, make it home again and cement his place in history.

* * *

Amar and I couldn't get enough of the Gambia River. There was always something at which to marvel. The current was almost a mile wide in parts and would then taper so dramatically we could hear Red Colobus monkeys screeching on its fertile banks. But it wasn't all jungle. At times the river's edge would be bleak, washed out, studded with rocks smooth enough to have been squeezed from a tube. While at the next bend there might be tall, lush grasses performing Mexican waves in the wind.

Amar shot off photos while I scribbled in my diary. We took it in turns to bale out the permanently waterlogged skiff. Salif stayed at the rudder, his face shielded by a floppy hat. Occasionally he would sing, at first softly, but with increasing confidence as the journey progressed. His voice was frail and mournful, sounding as if the words strained hard to work their way out of him.

The three of us lived off baguettes filled with a combination of macaroni, oysters, raw onions and ground up stock cubes. Oranges, bananas and nuts were also in plentiful supply.

Our first night at Tendaba Camp had been surprisingly comfortable. As predicted by the old fisherman, we had turned up about midnight expecting to bivouac in the bush. Instead we were led to a jungle café and served icy sodas before crashing out in thatched huts equipped with fans and cold showers. As we drank coffee the following morning an osprey wheeled on the thermals overhead.

The next evening was spent in a fishing village. Amar and I slept top to toe in a mud hut, cocooned in a mosquito net with more holes than a Gruyère. The next morning we were woken by the most exquisite music; somewhere outside a *kora,* a multi-stringed African lute, was being strummed softly. As we packed up, old men watched us in silence from beneath the acacias.

By the third day – with some 150 miles clocked up – the river finally shrugged off the influence of the Atlantic. The water was now no longer salty or tidal, but entirely fresh. We passed the Baboon Islands, dense with palm trees and lianas. As the river narrowed Salif suddenly howled out: 'Heepo! Heepo!' I scanned the glassy water, unable to see a thing. Salif steered the skiff full circle, and slowed down to a gentle chug.

'Heepo!' And there it was in front of us: a lone hippopotamus, its head prodding out of the water. We all held our breath; it was only 20 yards away. The hippo looked at us, snorted, flicked its pinkish ears, then slipped below, dainty as a mermaid.

We all stayed silent hoping it would surface again, but the spell was broken by a park ranger jetting our way in a rusty tub. The engine took us by surprise. So far we had seen less than a dozen boats on the river and they had all been dugouts. This was the first loudly revving vessel since the bronzed couple in their motor launch.

The ranger cruised alongside us. He was neatly dressed in one of those green army jumpers with patched elbows. He looked well primped, his hair pomaded, sunglasses on forehead. He began firing questions. Who were we? Did we have a certificate? This was the Gambia River National Park, did we realize? As he interrogated us, a chimpanzee appeared out of the foliage. It stood on a branch, beating its chest furiously, as if castigating us for daring to come so close to its world. Having made its point, the chimp stopped its beating, screeched and fell backwards, swallowed by the rampant vegetation. We heard a brief crash of branches, a few more high-pitched 'arrr, arrr' noises and then it was gone.

The ranger explained the chimp was one of 50 or so that had been rescued and reintroduced into the wild. The project had proved a success and the relocated chimps were now breeding together.

'Why do they need rescuing?' asked Amar.

'Some jungle is being cut down for farming,' said the ranger, dragging on a cigarette. 'But chimps are also killed by poachers. They sell the chimp heads and fingers in the markets, as charms.'

'What about the hippos? Are they still hunted?'

'No, no,' replied the ranger, upset by the idea. 'They are protected. Less than 50 hippos live here on the river. But fishermen put down nets. These nets make the hippos angry, upset their homes.'

51

'Do they ever attack?'*

'Not often, they are vegetarians remember, but they will sometimes. A few years ago a family in a canoe were on the river. They saw a hippo and threw oranges at it. For fun! The hippo attacked them and their canoe went over. They could not swim. Some of them died.'

The ranger shrugged his shoulders and flicked his cigarette into the water. 'There used to be hippo poachers,' he continued. 'Hippos' teeth are valuable, like ivory. And if people are very hungry, hippos have lots of meat. But here, it is very bad to hunt hippo. There are so few. They should be left alone. Crocodiles too, not so many left.'

I remembered something from Mary Kingsley's book, *Travels in West Africa*. The canny and highly eccentric Kingsley, on finding a hippo standing near her canoe on the Congo in 1894, scratched him behind the ear with her umbrella and 'parted on good terms'. She liked crocodiles less and used her canoe paddle to bash one on the snout.

The ranger let us go without a fine. I had misjudged him; he was genuine and knowledgeable. He could have easily fleeced us but chose not to. We carried on upstream, the mangroves thinning out now. The river was so narrow that the air had become heavy and sour; the vegetation steamy.

Beautiful scarlet birds whooshed overhead in tight formations, and on the banks we could see yellow weavers,

---

*According to a recent AFP news report (July 2004) 11 fishermen have been killed by hippos on the Gambia River over the last ten months. Hippos cause more deaths in Africa than any other large animal, although many of the fatalities – boats capsizing, tents being trampled – are accidental. Hippos spend most of the daylight hours in water as their skin, although it looks robust, is very sensitive to sunburn.

sculpting away on their nests of grass and dirt. Some of the nests were works of art, hanging by threads from the palm fronds, fragile as Christmas baubles. A cormorant skittered up ahead, flapping wildly before soaring low over the dancing water.

Salif semaphored to some friends on the banks as we approached the town of Janjanbureh. They ran down to the river, waving and shouting, clearly delighted to see him. Salif told us Janjanbureh was his home; most of his family lived here. As we pulled up on the river bank, many others came to greet Salif. He wore a triumphant smile and when he spoke Mandingo now, his stammer vanished.

'Will you come back and live here?' Amar asked as we prepared to land. 'You are very popular!'

'No,' said Salif, tying the skiff to a hitching post. 'My father has a bike shop here but business is bad. Janjanbureh is no good to live. No work here.'

'So will you stay on the river?'

'No, no,' he said firmly. 'I want to be a welder. I can earn good money in Banjul.'

Amar and I both looked at him, incredulous. The idea of being cooped up in a welder's workshop seemed unthinkable if you could be cruising up and down the Gambia River. But we were looking at this through travellers' eyes, dreamers' eyes. Salif was clearly bright, ambitious and knew what he wanted.

'The river is not good money,' he said, shrugging, 'I have good time with you, but these long trips are few. Often I just stay around the harbour, fishing, fixing engines. The river is sometimes very boring.'

CHAPTER 6

VANISHING FOOTPRINTS

IN COLONIAL TIMES Janjanbureh, then known as George-town, was the most important trading hub on the Gambia River. Nowadays I expected the town, which sits on a long island fringed with coconut palms, to boast what my guide book called 'faded grandeur'. The 'faded' still applies, the 'grandeur' doesn't.

The first sight that met us as we walked down the main street was a ruined truck. It had no wheels, no windows, no roof. It was as if it had wheezed to a halt and been left, like a stricken beast, to be picked at by scavengers. Several young men sat inside the disintegrating chassis, while others lay spread-eagled in the shade, so listless they might have been felled by sniper fire.

There were odd signs of vibrancy; children playing football with a mango stone, bare-breasted girls laughing as they filled buckets from a stand pipe, black jackdaw-like birds cawing in the neem trees. The town was also home to The Gambia's only boarding school, the alma mater of many tribal chiefs, but it was deserted today. Little could disguise the pervading malaise.

Even Janjanbureh's once bustling warehouses were now verging on collapse, the masonry strangled by zealous roots. One derelict building was confusingly known as the 'slave house', but slavery had been abolished by the British long before it had even been built. All it contained now was a family of skeletal cats.

Janjanbureh's dramatic reversal in fortune was all down to one thing – a new highway. Now that traders preferred to use this road rather than the river, the town's life blood was ebbing away. A bridge connecting Janjanbureh Island to the mainland would have helped, but there was none. Ambitious young men like Salif were forced to seek a life elsewhere. As for the few tourists, most cast a cursory eye over the woebegone streets and made a beeline back to their eco-camps or Atlantic beaches.

The one ray of hope amid all the languor was a tree near the river bank. This arboreal runt was nothing much to look at, but the sign beside it was rather inspiring. THE FREEDOM TREE, it blazed. The Freedom Tree had been planted, so it said, to celebrate things all Africans could appreciate regardless of wealth: sunshine, laughter and freedom. After seeing the lot of the inhabitants of Janjanbureh, catching sight of it was like glimpsing hope at the bottom of Pandora's box.

* * *

Amar and I spent the night at Janjanbureh Camp, having been ferried across to the opposite shore by a motorized raft. In stark contrast to the town, it was a lovely spot, with monkeys crashing through the bushes and the chatter of insects all around. The camp ground was studded with white adobe huts, their thatched roofs making them look, from a distance, like witches' hats.

There was no electricity but we were each given a lantern to lead the way. A clutch of frogs were sheltering in my shower. When I released them outside, three of them hopped straight back in, joined by a beautiful lizard with an orange head.

Once we had scrubbed up Amar and I ate some spaghetti at the camp site restaurant. That evening a tribal dance was performed. The male dancers wore severe-looking face masks and the women, raffia-syle skirts and necklaces threaded with dark beads.

A group of drummers sat around a log fire. They began by gently tapping the drum skins with the tips of their fingers, then pounding with great ferocity. The rhythm was hypnotic, the dancers pulsing and flailing as if possessed.

Next Amar and I were called on to perform. Both of us tried our best to imitate the frantic gyrations, but we were still little better than drunk uncles at a wedding disco.

The handsome, heavy-set woman I danced with writhed with such energy it looked like she was being controlled by a series of strings. At the end of her exertions I expected to see her drop down in the sand, but she remained animated, unable to shake off her fierce inner rhythms until long after the drumming was over. I could see what Mungo Park meant when he described some dancing women in the nearby province of Kajaaga as 'displaying the most voluptuous movements possible'.

Seeing the furious face masks and the palsied motions of the dancers, reminded me of something else Park had witnessed. During the Gambia leg of his journey the explorer came upon a ritual known as Mumbo Jumbo. (Because of Park's description the phrase later became part of the English language.)

Park is not complimentary about Mumbo Jumbo, calling it 'an indecent and unmanly revel'. It's easy to see why. Park explains that it was performed by Pagans – non-conformers to Islam – who were allowed as many wives as they liked. This often led to matrimonial squabbles between the wives, and the Mumbo Jumbo ceremony was invented to deal with them.

To begin with the husband disguised himself in a costume of tree bark and grabbed hold of a metal rod. He then let rip with a series of ear-piercing screams from the nearby woods before entering the village. After this revellers danced and sang, the women nervous because one of them knew she was the reason for the event, the root of the problem. This sinister pantomime would continue until midnight when the guilty wife would be revealed, stripped naked, tied to a post and viciously beaten by Mumbo Jumbo's rod. Park was astonished to note it was the women in the crowd who shouted the loudest abuse at the victim.

Although this particular dance Amar and I witnessed was not a Mumbo Jumbo imitation, Salif told me it did still go on in certain Gambian villages, although just as a performance. He assured me the women were no longer hurt, or 'inhumanely scourged' as Park put it.

* * *

The following morning Amar and I set off to find a memorial in honour of Mungo Park near the village of Karantaba Tenda, about 12 miles away. We decided to travel by a combination of bus and foot, beginning with a trudge across Janjanbureh Island to catch a ferry to the river's south bank.

Away from the dismal town centre, the island, with its luminous rice paddies and soughing palm trees, looked far less run down. One group of children were particularly eye-catching. They shouted at passers-by from the side of the road while rattling castanets filled with peanut shells.

One child ran after us. He was wrapped in hessian sacks and carrying two rusty machete blades. His face was covered by a white hood with two large eye slits, making him look un-nervingly like a clansman. The child danced around us, wailing and clashing his machetes together.

'Jesus,' said Amar, quickening his pace. 'What's all this about?'

As I was the slower walker the child concentrated on me, whirling about, hooting and yodelling like a tropical bird. His faceless hood made the spectacle all the more chilling.

'What do you want?' I asked him repeatedly.

The boy's noises were becoming increasingly high-pitched and other-worldly; the movements of the blades frenzied. Another child appeared, an older boy with a gentle, tubby face who spoke good English.

'Don't worry,' he told me, jogging to keep up. 'All those boys will soon be circumcised. It's a ceremony they do, singing at the roadside. This boy is collecting money.'

'What for?' I asked.

'Circumcision is very important,' replied the older boy. 'They need money to pay for the ceremony. Then they can become men.'

I handed out a couple of notes to the little dancer. He snatched them from me and ripped off his hood. The trans-formation was extraordinary. A few seconds ago he had been a crazed spectre, armed and dangerous, the next he was simply a youngster with a gap-toothed smile and bleeding feet. He now looked almost cherubic. He took hold of his friend's hand and the two of them drifted back down the road.

Amar and I soon arrived at the ferry. We joined the other passengers in a tug of war, pulling the chain which hauled the creaky boat across the water. A conductor presented us tickets from a hand-cranked machine. HAVE A NICE JOURNEY, they heralded, clearly a cast-off from a London double-decker.

At the south bank Amar and I caught a relay of buses and bush taxis, all of them fit to burst, as far as a village called

Kunting. From here we walked the remaining seven miles to Karantaba Tenda.

* * *

As soon as I was walking, I felt a great sense of release. Striding along the sand tracks, the sun on my face, kissed by the breeze, I sensed this was a good way to see Africa. I felt more alive to the earth's ancient pulses, to the footsteps of those gone before.

One thing that had astonished me so far in The Gambia was the lack of people. This was one of Africa's smallest countries, but for its size it was also supposedly one of its most densely populated. On the river I had spotted only a dozen dugouts over three days. Even on the open road vehicles drove by very infrequently, perhaps one every half an hour.

In the West I think we have become, even in rural areas, attuned to the continual thrum of the internal combustion engine, our lives subtly ruled by arteries of bitumen, paths of speed. It is all a far cry from when the early Australian aborigines sang their maps into existence. There was no need for any tarmac then, no need for drawings or contours; just a few well chosen lyrics.

'Take a left by the billabong, sharp right at the red rock shaped like a turtle, then follow the sun until you reach Big Eddy's, if you pass a gum tree full of white cockatoos, you've overshot.'

These days we still all tell each other the best routes, but now there is no picture to imagine, just a mass of numbers.

'Take the A34 to Newbury, then turn off down the M3, that leads you to the M27 and take the third turn off for Romsey.' With this sort of imageless instruction, all that springs to mind is a sea of bitumen.

It reminded me of an experiment performed on an ape in California I had once read about. The ape was given paints and brushes and encouraged to put its ideas down on paper. All it produced at first were random blobs. More stimulation was needed, the scientists agreed, and so pictures of bananas, female apes, jungle scenes, were supplied to act as spurs. After a year the ape finally scribbled down lots of wavy black lines. The poor creature was drawing the bars of its own cage. Put this ape in a car, I decided, and it would paint an endless swathe of grey.

In West Africa, where most of the roads are dirt or sand, vehicles are the exception, not the rule. This means every bus, every bush taxi, every moped, is chock-full. To an African this squashed camaraderie is not only enjoyable, it is luxurious. Without it, one has to walk, not just as a means of movement, but of survival. This has its riches too. If you walk you might see fruits dropping from baobab trees, children singing by the roadside, lizards skitting over your feet and a great deal more.

That morning Amar and I met many people: a young girl with a broken flip-flop, a limping man pushing a bicycle and an old woman with a stack of firewood on her head. Without exception, every one of them looked up, smiled and greeted us with delight. They had no water, no hat and often no shoes, while Amar and I were doused in sunblock, clad in stout boots with water bottles and maps at hand. Of course the two of us looked absurd, utter aliens, but at least felt to a small degree, at one with our surroundings.

In the West walking is no longer a biological urge; it has become a bind, an inconvenience, often just a device to lose a few pounds at the gym. During my trek across the United States, where the car is categorically king, I had been amazed by a survey revealing Americans only walk an average of 1.4 miles a week. This whittles down to a disturbingly meagre 350 yards a day.

This contrasts wildly with most Africans. Indeed some nomadic tribes, such as the Kalahari Bushmen in southern Africa, believe when their last footprints are blown away that is the end of them. To them it is their footsteps that define their life.

* * *

Karantaba Tenda was a mud village set back from the banks of the Gambia River. On arrival we saw a group of elders sitting in the shade of a gum tree, Koranic texts open in front of them. Witnessing these men, swathed in dark robes, reminded me of another scene from the early pages of Park's diary.

Park mentions that the head of a Muslim village is known as an *alkaid,* the chief magistrate. The *alkaid*, who still exists in many Gambian villages today, was responsible for such things as collecting taxes and presiding over local disputes. These disputes were judged by calling together the village sages and holding what was known as a palaver (from the Portuguese *palavra*), where each side of the case is heard and then judgement reached.

Park was impressed by the sophistication of the palavers he saw and goes as far as admitting they might well surpass their counterparts in Europe. For me, looking at these old men debating in hushed tones beneath the eucalyptus was like a flashback in time.

The peace was broken by some nearby cheers. Amar and I went to investigate and saw two teenage boys wrestling in the sand. The fight was over very quickly with one boy locking the other in an unshakable neck clench.

Once we had been spotted, a posse of children swarmed around us, like a jailbreak of Fagin's urchins. When we mentioned we wanted to see Mungo Park, one of the older boys shouted, 'Yes, yes, we go now' and grabbed Amar and me by the hand, steering us through the baobabs and thorn shrubs. Some of the other children followed for a while but then fell away.

'Do you like to wrestle?' I asked our new tracker, whose name sounded like Gilly. Wrestling was another sport Park had witnessed on his travels, and organized bouts still took place in The Gambia today.

'I wrestle a bit,' said Gilly, 'but I like football better.'

We reached Park's obelisk after a ten-minute hike along a series of disconnected goat tracks. The obelisk was all that was left of Pisania, where the explorer began the overland section of his journey. It was rather a sorry-looking structure, about 20 feet high, the stonework cracked and dirty. The metal plaque, burnished by the sun, was barely legible. From what I could make of the faded lettering it read:

> Near this spot
> MUNGO PARK
> set out
> on the 2nd December 1795
> and
> the 4th May 1805
> on his travels
> to explore the course of the Niger

Surrounding the obelisk was a barbed wire fence, which had collapsed long ago. The wire was trampled into the sand, coiled and jinked.

'Do you know about Mungo Park?' Amar asked Gilly, as we inspected the plaque.

'I learned about him at school,' said Gilly, squinching up his eyes in an effort to remember. Then with great confidence he announced: 'Mungo Park died here.'

Many of the Gambians I had spoken to – Mohammed, Salif, the staff at Janjanbureh Camp – knew of Park through school lessons, but their knowledge was sketchy. So far all of them had thought Park drowned at Pisania, rather than set off from here. It was hardly surprising: Park had been dead almost 200 years, and The Gambia had been independent for nearly 40. It was only natural the explorer's legacy was fading.

Gilly shook the limbs of a spindly-looking tree near to the obelisk. A shower of yellow berries rained onto the sand. He picked up a handful and gave some to me. 'Coogoo berry,' he said. 'Very good.' I nibbled a couple; they were juiceless, but still sweet, fleshy and very tasty.

Amar shot off pictures and furiously scribbled in a reporter's notebook. I was fascinated by his approach. Having swapped his law books for a camera and notepad, Amar still retained his lawyer's attention to detail. He translated his jottings into tight-knit, elegant prose that appeared in broadsheet newspapers or geographical magazines. He was forever note-taking.

Having cut my teeth as a cub reporter on the *Wilts and Gloucestershire Standard* and later turned my hand to travel books, my style was worlds apart. I would soak up the day's events and pen them down in loose excitable ramblings in the evening. Whereas Amar's writing read like a purring, finely tuned engine, not a rev wasted, my own prose roared, thrummed, whistled and would then need ruthlessly panel-beating into shape.

'This must be one of the remotest monuments in the world,' said Amar, as we stood beneath the shade of a baobab, looking at the mouldering stonework. 'There isn't even a path down to the river, it's overrun by nature. Poor Park, what a lonely spot.'

'Well from tomorrow,' I reminded him, 'we'll be hot on his tail.'

'Ah yes,' said Amar, humour in his eyes. 'The Park lark commences!'

* * *

After Mungo Park's return from Sumatra, it wasn't long before he was snapped up as the African Association's next 'Geographical Missionary', and by the spring of 1794 he had already warned his family he may soon be bound for West Africa. By then Park would have heard rumours of Major Houghton's demise, but far from denting the fledgling explorer's confidence, it fired him up all the more.

In many ways though, Park was lacking in experience. He was comparatively poorly travelled, knew nothing of Africa and spoke none of the local dialects. All he had going for him were youth, ambition and his solid Borders pragmatism. But despite other candidates being better qualified on paper, his sponsors found qualities in Park that won them over. Beaufoy even described him as 'a young man of no mean talents'.

The African Association decked out Park far better than Ledyard, Lucas or Houghton and the young Scot was the first explorer to be offered a salary. Once on the Gambia River he was to be paid 15 shillings a day for up to two years, with a smaller sum to cover expenses before then. Money would certainly have been an incentive to him but not the overriding one.

'I had a passionate desire to examine . . . a country so little known,' Park wrote, 'and to become experimentally acquainted with the modes of life and characters of the natives.'

Park was provided with some useful equipment – a pocket sextant, a magnetic compass and a thermometer – much of it superior to that used by his predecessors. Being a trainee surgeon, he packed up a small medicine chest, hoping to avoid a grisly fate such as Ledyard's. Less essential items included two fowling pieces, a silver-topped cane, an umbrella and a dapper blue frock-coat with yellow buttons.

Park was stymied by delays. He had been due to sail out to West Africa as part of an expedition led by James Willis, the newly appointed Consul General of Senegambia. Willis constantly overshot his budgets and failed to meet deadlines, so Park, by now crawling up the walls in frustration, was told to go it alone. Tight controls on London shipping due to the war with France held the frustrated explorer up still further and he finally sailed out of Portsmouth on 22 May in a small brig, the *Endeavour*, on its way to Africa to pick up a cargo of beeswax and ivory.

A month later Park reached the Gambia River and, after his brief stop-offs at Jillifree, Vintain and Jonkakonda (the place Houghton had been warned of a potential ambush), he arrived in Pisania, now the site of his lonely obelisk.

Here, Park was the guest of Dr Laidley, a British trader, who had also briefly hosted Major Houghton. Laidley traded in gold and ivory, but principally slaves. Despite being saddened by the 'horribly treated' slaves he witnesses, Park seems to have got on famously with Laidley, probably much to the chagrin of some of the African Association's abolitionist members.

Park did not waste time at Pisania. He learnt some Mandingo, one of the region's principal languages. He also complimented the Mandingo people finding them 'of mild, sociable, and obliging disposition', although he was critical that they did not tame their elephants and put them to work.

All was going well for Park until late July when he was laid out by fever, locally known as 'the seasoning'. Park believed he became sick while taking a longitude reading during a lunar eclipse. 'I impudently exposed myself to a night dew,' he wrote. This seems almost comical in the light of what he would have to endure later. It is much more likely he was struck down with malaria.

The treatment for most fevers at the time was a series of largely useless bleedings and purgings. Park went through a hellish spell but was bolstered by Dr Laidley who, he remembered:

> contributed greatly to alleviate my sufferings; his company and conversation beguiled the tedious hours during that gloomy season, when the rain falls in torrents; when suffocating heats oppress by day, and when night is spent by the terrified traveller in listening to the croaking of frogs (of which the numbers are beyond imagination), the shrill cry of the jackal, and the deep howling of the hyena.

Early in December, some five months after his arrival, a fully recovered Park left the secure haven of Pisania. Accompanied by Dr Laidley and the Ainsley brothers (two other expat traders) it proved a jolly start, the opening night spent around a camp fire, smoking and listening to Mandingo folk tales.

The following afternoon Laidley and the Ainsleys left him, thinking secretly, according to Park, that 'they should never see me afterwards'. Park was still accompanied by Johnson, his interpreter, who had spent seven years working in England, and Demba, a reliable Mandingo-speaking slave, who had been assured his freedom if he served Park well. The explorer's transport consisted of a horse – 'a small but very hardy and spirited beast' – and his employees' two asses.

'I had now before me,' wrote Park, displaying rare fear, 'a boundless forest, and a country, the inhabitants of which were strangers to civilised life . . . and I reflected that I had parted from the last European I might properly behold, and perhaps quitted for ever the comforts of Christian society.'

Two days later Park reached Medina, the capital of Wuli. Although he avoided shaking the king's hand – not de rigeur in Wuli culture – he was nevertheless warmly welcomed. King Jatta was used to foreigners and had been hospitable to Major Houghton. Park paid a small tax and on top of this promised the king he would later receive three gallons of rum, courtesy of Dr Laidley.

For his part King Jatta pleaded with Park not to proceed, convinced he would meet a similar fate to Houghton. When he could see Park was not for turning he provided the young explorer with a guide to at least steer him safely to the edge of his kingdom.

On 6 December Park left Medina and a few days later crossed the frontier of Bondo (near the town of Tambacounda in present-day Senegal). So far it had been plain sailing for the happy-go-lucky Scot but all that was about to change.

CHAPTER 7

HOTTING UP

TO STAY on Mungo Park's tail Amar and I caught a mini-bus down a zigzag of dirt roads to the Gambian border. Time was tight, as Amar needed to reach Mali by the end of January before his visa expired. That left us less than two days to flog through Senegal and over the border to Kayes, a pit stop for Park and supposedly the hottest town on earth.

At the Gambian customs, there was a Land Cruiser with a jazzy tri-colour flag suspended from its bonnet. This vehicle, tyre-less (but decidedly tired), looked as if it was afloat on the sand, marooned in no man's land. Bird pats corroded the roof of the nearby passport-stamping hut, where a haughty soldier fired questions at us in French, now the lingua franca until English-speaking Nigeria, over 2,000 miles away.

Once in Senegal we ate sweetcorn husks in a café strewn with dead flies. An old man in a white fez, crazed by a combination of faith and sunshine, spouted Koranic scriptures to the crowds.

Before long a vehicle, like a baker's van, pulled up. Amar and I shoe-horned ourselves onto the wooden benches in the boot. As the engine fired we became enveloped in a miasma of dust, then suddenly, as if teased by a magic wind, the air was clear: we were on the bitumen again.

Through the flapping tarpaulin encasing us I noticed The Gambia's monotonous lushness slowly fade to Senegalese browns and greys. On the side of buildings occasional slogans flashed: WHO WANTS TO BE A MILLIONAIRE? read one. EDUCATE A WOMAN, EDUCATE A NATION prophesied another.

But the thing I noticed most were sheep, especially once we slowed down in the dowdy suburbs of Tambacounda. Sheep everywhere, hundreds of them: some dangling from roof racks, some riding pillion on mopeds, others in small flocks marshalled by turbaned herders. One Arab-looking boy controlled six or seven ewes on individual leashes, like a Hyde Park dog-walker.

This ovine invasion was down to *Tabaski,* the most celebrated of all the Muslim festivals. *Tabaski* honours the time Allah called on Abraham to sacrifice his son but then, seeing the prophet's unstinting faith, allowed him to kill a ram instead. For this reason at the start of *Tabaski*, Muslim families sacrifice a sheep to feast on.

Amar and I holed up near the centre of Tambacounda in a cheap, attractive hotel festooned with grape vines. Before crashing out we strolled over to a coffee shack opposite, dominated by a poster of El Hadji Diouf, Senegal's premier footballer, and also a Liverpool striker.

'*El Hadji Diouf,*' said the coffee boy, as he filled our cups, '*il est le David Beckham du Senegal.*' We sat in silence on miniature wooden stools, looking up at the stars and listening to the impotent bleating of soon to be slain sheep. The coffee boy worked on a sewing machine, chig-chig-chigging away as we sipped our drinks. He wore a necklace shaped like a crescent moon.

Before we left I asked him about the upcoming festival.

'*Tabaski*! Always so expensive!' fumed the boy. 'Every family needs to kill a sheep. *Every* family! It is a matter of pride. The sheep prices go crazy now, three or four times as high. I celebrate *Tabaski*,' he stopped his sewing for a while to look up at us, 'but I will celebrate the Senegal-Mali football game far more!'

Next day, having changed money in a hardware store – a sort of Malian Homebase that doubled as a bank – we made our way to Kayes on a heavily rutted road. Our mini-bus was the first I had seen with no cracks on its windscreen; although it had other signs of wear and tear. Most noticeably its left flank had been strafed with gun fire. The bullet dimples looked dull and rusted, though. Old battle scars, I reassured myself, not fresh wounds.

The Malian frontier at Kideri, some 90 miles away, took us seven hours to breast. After this the road disintegrated, the driver stopping every 20 minutes to top up the radiator. But all this was more than compensated for by the lovely views.

Fat-trunked baobabs, their limbs like gnarled tentacles, studded the desertscape. Occasionally pale, scimitar-horned cattle drifted into view in search of grass or shadows. And as for the sunset that night, it was enough to make a dictator sigh. The sky was a gorgeous rash of turquoise, orange and blue. In the midst of this celestial blur was the sun sliding downwards, casting blood red shadows that gilded the ambient sand.

'I *have* to take a picture,' said Amar, unable to hold his camera straight what with the road's perpetual jinks and judders. The sooty contrail belching from our van's semi-house-trained exhaust did him no favours either.

'There'll be more skies like this,' I reassured him, 'many more.' Actually there weren't. That evening was the best sunset I saw in West Africa. From then on we were in quasi-desert and, although the night stars continued to dazzle, the sunsets were diluted by a penumbra of dust that lined the horizon; a hazy girdle between the sky and the earth.

We pulled up at Kayes late in the evening having averaged 15 miles an hour. All the passengers were coated with a frosting of russet grime. Amar was so stained he looked like he had been rubbed in cinnamon powder.

Mercifully the city was not living up to its mercury-busting reputation and was cooled by a light breeze. We found a room above a mechanic's garage. Outside were a cluster of Malians huddled around a TV screen. We peered over to see what they were watching. It was Benny Hill. The tubby comedian was wearing a rictus smile and a flat cap, chased by a throng of nurses in suspenders.

Home suddenly felt a million miles away.

* * *

In many ways Mungo Park picked the worst possible time to visit West Africa. The areas he travelled through in the late 1700s, especially in modern-day Mali, were savage and unsettled.

But this hadn't always been the case. In fact, in the thirteenth and fourteenth centuries, thanks to its domination of the gold trade, the Mali Empire had been fabulously wealthy, stretching all the way from the mouth of the Gambia River, up beyond Timbuktu and down as far the frontiers of Nigeria. Prior to this prosperous period had been the equally flushed Ghana Empire (nothing to do with present-day Ghana), described by the eighth-century Arab writer, Al-Fezari, as 'the land of gold'.

But it is the Mali Empire that history most remembers, partly because of lavish descriptions of the previously mentioned Moroccan traveller, Ibn Battutah, who visited in 1324.

He was greatly impressed by the strong, sophisticated govern-ments, the widespread lack of oppression and, largely down to the spread of Islam, the richness of the culture.

'There is complete security in this country,' noted the scholarly wanderer. 'Neither traveller nor inhabitant in it has anything to fear from robbers or men of violence.'

Yet for a man who clocked up 75,000 miles, dined with emperors, dodged the Black Death, passed judgements at royal courts and married countless wives, Ibn Battutah could also be surprisingly precious in his views of West Africa. The footloose Moroccan found it distasteful the way slave girls walked around 'with their privy parts uncovered' and was disgusted with the custom of eating donkeys and dogs. That said, the majority of his diary entries, were positive, often verging on awestruck.

Perhaps the most lasting testament to those glory days was the pilgrimage to Mecca of Mansa Musa, the greatest ruler of the Mali Empire. The king set off in 1324, clashing with Ibn Battutah's African travels. Mounted on his stallion, the flambo-yant and generous monarch was preceded by 500 slaves, each bearing a staff of gold. To add to the entourage, which was made up of some 8,000 people, were a caravan of camels, their saddlebags laden with treasure.

The Mali Empire finally overstretched itself and collapsed in the fifteenth century, replaced by a third great empire, the Songhai, its nerve centre at Gao in present-day eastern Mali. During Songhai domination, ambitious forays were made north and east into the desert, but this all fell apart when the Moroccans invaded in 1591.

The Moroccans wreaked instant havoc, plundering and looting, but soon spread themselves too thin to maintain effective control. Within a few years the once orderly, affluent swathe of ex-empires descended into chaos. Central government was usurped by small warring states some of which embraced Islam, others proving more resistant. Before long the burgeoning slave trade only added to the confusion.

By the time Mungo Park visited 200 years later the whole region was in a mess; ruptured, violent and anarchic.

* * *

While it took Amar and me one bumpy day of travel to reach Kayes from Tambacounda in our bullet-strafed jalopy, Mungo Park, using a combination of horse and foot, needed the best part of three weeks. Having lost the services of King Jatta's guide at the Bondo frontier, Park hired some local elephant-hunters to help lead the way. He naively paid them gold in advance, and the following morning one had run off.

This was an ongoing problem and the exploration party continued to fluctuate in size as the journey progressed. Park finally worked out that feeding his companions slap-up meals at the close of each day helped inspire loyalty and one night near the Faleme River as many as a dozen people joined him for a feast of mutton and corn.

Once across the river Park penetrated farther into the kingdom of Bondo. One of the first things that impressed him was the large number of schools teaching Arabic and excerpts from the Koran. In fact Bondo is thought to have boasted a higher level of literacy than England at the time – over 60 per cent. But not everything about this new region charmed Park. At one stage his party was molested by a clutch of wailing Bondo women, grabbing at his coat buttons. In a rare flash of temper Park berates them as a gang of harpies.

At the capital of Bondo, Park was put up in the hut of a friendly *slatee* or trader. The tired Scot was wary of meeting the local ruler, King Isata, having heard he had treated Major Houghton cavalierly. But the king proved more gracious with Park, although he was confused by the explorer's refusal to trade in slaves or gold. Park described the king's attitude to his journey in his diary: 'The notion of travelling for curiousity was quite new to him [King Isata]. He thought it impossible . . . that any man in his senses would undertake so dangerous a journey.' To be fair, the suspicious monarch was not alone in his opinion.

The situation was mollified after Park, wearing his blue frock-coat with the yellow buttons, handed over a range of gifts to the king. Despite being presented gunpowder, tobacco and amber, it was Park's umbrella that delighted the monarch most, and he furled and unfurled the 'wonderful machine' repeatedly. But still this was not enough, and before long Park was pressurized to hand over his smart blue coat too.

The following day, a much less dandified Park, set the tongues of the royal brides wagging when they inspected him. The women could not believe his vanilla complexion and the prominence of his nose. In fact they were so amazed, they concluded the explorer must have been dipped in milk as a child and his nose pinched every day until reaching its 'present unsightly and unnatural conformation'.

Ever the gentleman, Park took the insults with good grace. He then complimented the women on the 'glossy jet' of their skin and the loveliness of their noses. His flattery was not well received, however, and he was warned that 'honey mouth' was not the done thing in Bondo. This did not stop the women sending him some fish and a jar of honey later that night.

The next stage of Park's journey was through the kingdom of Kajaaga, inhabited by the Soninke people. Park describes them as a 'jet black trading people', who are 'indefatigable in their exertions to acquire wealth'.

They certainly got their pound of flesh from Park who, on Christmas Day in the town of Joag, found himself surrounded by 20 horsemen armed with muskets. He was accused of crossing into the King of Kajaaga's territory without paying. Park realized his mistake and handed over some gold he had been given by the King of Bondo. But this was not sufficient and the horsemen rifled through his baggage, grabbing half of it.

The next morning, not wishing to reveal any other belongings which might be robbed, Park and his group went without food. That evening the dejected and hungry explorer sat down and chewed on some straw. He was spotted by an old slave woman who insisted on treating him to a handful of ground nuts. This incident greatly touched Park and he wrote: 'I reflected with pleasure on the conduct of this poor untutored slave, who, without examining into my character or circumstances listened implicitly to the dictates of her own heart.'

Despite this cheering episode, Park was now in a vulnerable state and his guides nervous about the road ahead. Not for the last time, serendipity played its part. Demba Sego, the nephew of the king of the neighbouring district of Kasson, saved the day. He was in Kajaaga on a mission to improve relations between the two rival kingdoms. Hearing of Park's plight he offered to guide the explorer on the next stretch of his journey.

And so, with Demba Sego smoothing the way forward, it was only four days before Park and his companions had the Senegal River and the town of Kayes (then Kayee) in their sights, the very place where Amar and I now watched Benny Hill.

* * *

'I never shoot in the sun if I can help it,' said Woody Allen once, 'everything looks so much better without it. The sun is the bane of my life.'

Strangely the people of Kayes might agree with the angst-ridden New Yorker. But whereas the sun only interferes with Allen's camera angles, it positively dominates many Malians' lives. Kayes's hotter than hell reputation – at times nudging 50° Celsius – was nowhere in evidence that first morning. I had woken early stirred by the faraway yodel of a muezzin. As I left the guest house I realized this was, in fact, the coolest place I had visited in Africa so far, gusts of wind whipping up dust devils that scurried like genies along the deserted main street.

I had expected Kayes to be pulsing with life due to the start of the *Tabaski* festival. But other than the odd tethered sheep, bleating plaintively, there wasn't a soul around. A church bell stunned the quiet dawn. Despite the early morning breeze the town did have a parched look, the mud buildings evidently baked dry as biscuits by the usually record-breaking heat. Houses looked so fragile they might crumble at a touch. The local market was still empty, a labyrinth of mud and corrugated tin, stinking of urine, rotting vegetables and diesel. A hank of sinewy meat hung from an awning, flies buzzing around it like drones around their queen.

The one bustling place was the Senegal River, its banks splashed with colour. Magpies squawked in the papaya trees, men in bright turbans watered their vegetable plots, while tall, sinewy women thrashed their washing against riverside boulders, before stretching it out in the nascent sun. Calabashes, like mutant oranges, were stacked up near the river bridge, now alive with the toots of the first commuters.

* * *

Later in the day Amar and I visited Medine, a village some nine miles upstream from Kayes. The taxi that took us there cost

A portrait of Mungo Park while still in his mid-twenties

The ever-radiant Naya embracing a friend at
the Ferry Guesthouse in Banjul, The Gambia

Scene painted at
the Exhibition of
the Slave Trade in
Juffureh, The Gambia

Children on the Gambia River

A ruined vehicle near Janjanbureh, not far from the
spot Mungo Park struck out into the African interior

Amar and Salif on the Gambia River

An anxious sheep on a roof rack in Tambacounda,
Senegal, soon to meet its fate at the *Tabaski* festival

Malian football fans in Kayes, thought to be the hottest town on
earth, overjoyed when their team score against Senegal, the favourites

Bubakar steers Ramadan and Mango into the
wilderness south of Nioro du Sahel, Mali

An elegantly dressed
mother with her children
in the village of Bema, Mali

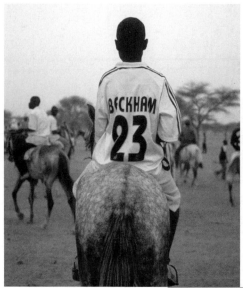

A teenage jockey (and David Beckham fan) at the horse race in Nara, Mali

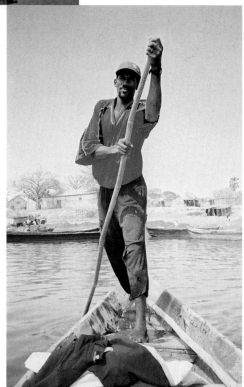

Karim piloting the pirogue down the River Niger

Boisterous crowds at the girls' football match in Massina, Mali

Paddling the pirogue
beyond Massina

The grand mosque at Djenné

Market day at Djenné

CFA 1,000 (roughly £1) and played 'Living Next Door to Alice' by Smokie on its hissing stereo. Medine was near to where Mungo Park crossed the Senegal River at the Chutes du Felou, a series of rocky rapids that still exist today.

Park describes these rapids, hamming it up slightly, as a 'considerable cataract'. It takes him and his team over two hours of robust chivvying to usher his cattle and mules across. Park's canoe then capsizes when his guide, Demba Sego, stretches over to peek in one of the explorer's tin boxes. After swimming across the river and wringing out his clothes the sodden Scot continues east towards Medine.

That morning at Medine the Senegal River was still as glass. Amar and I watched it from the ramparts of a ruined fort, built by the French as a defence post over 50 years after Park's visit. The site was now overrun by blossom, thorns and a couple of feral donkeys.

Walking back to Kayes in the heat of the day, we clambered over a rock escarpment, before returning to the main path fringing a railway track. On arrival, sun-baked and thirsty, we stopped for water at a street stall near Kayes railway station. The station, though grubby and run down, is integral to Kayes' history and is still a stop for the sluggish, infrequent trains between Dakar and Bamako, Mali's capital. As we meandered back through town, we passed a row of sturdy colonial warehouses, a nod to when Kayes had been a thriving administrative centre. Some of the buildings still served as departments of fishery or forestry, but many had fallen into disrepair, their pretty tile roofs riddled with holes.

On the closing stretch of our walk Amar and I we were ushered over by a gaggle of *Tabaski* revellers. The women in the group looked especially spruced up for the occasion, sporting blues and greens, oranges and yellows, purples and pinks. Malian women often dress vibrantly but today they were in a league of their own, able to steal the show on any Parisian catwalk. The colourful party sat gossiping on benches near a cinema billboard displaying two Chuck Norris movies and another called *Sylvia's Revenge!* depicting a flame-haired lady firing off a Gatling gun. DON'T MESS WITH HER! warned the poster.

I realized I was standing near a pool of blood, which left a dull stain in the dust. It was clearly the scene of an earlier sacrifice as everyone was chewing on hunks of mutton. A podgy man, with kohl eyes and tribal scars on his upper cheek, handed me a piece of the meat. He was the only enormously fat person I had seen on the journey to date, and his white T-shirt struggled to rein in his equatorial jet black paunch.

'For *Tabaski*!' he said happily, his breath sour with beer. The meat was greasy, fatty and basted in a mustard dip: it tasted wonderful. For a minute the incongruous flavour transported me home, perhaps to a Sunday lunch or a summer barbecue, but then I was offered a swig of sweet, minty tea – now a taste that could only mean Africa.

* * *

After Mungo Park had resurfaced from his capsized canoe on the River Senegal he forged on eastwards. It was now that his guide, Demba Sego, the nephew of the King of Kasson (in whose territory Park had now entered) showed his true colours and demanded payment. Keen to keep the peace, Park handed over some amber and tobacco but was then forced to stay ten more frustrating days in Kasson after Demba Sego made off with his horse. On finally receiving the animal back, Park was fleeced of yet more belongings before moving on. If this rattled Park, which it surely must have, he does not show it in his diary.

The remainder of Park's journey through Kasson enjoys better fortune. He meets a trader who owes Dr Laidley some slaves. Back in Pisania, Laidley had authorized Park to receive this payment in gold, providing the explorer's dwindling finances with a welcome boon.

Park pens one of his most moving diary excerpts at this stage too, when he witnesses a blacksmith, part of his travelling party, return to his home village. The explorer is humbled to see the singing, feasting and general euphoria that the blacksmith's return ignites, especially the reunion with his frail, hobbling mother.

> Every one made way for her and she stretched out her hand to bid her son welcome. Being totally blind, she stroked his hands, arms, and face with great care, and seemed highly delighted . . . From this interview I was fully convinced, that whatever difference there is between the Negro and European . . . there is none in the genuine sympathies and characteristic feelings of our common nature.

It is a powerful observation and about the closest Park comes to implicitly casting doubts on the thorny issue of slavery.

By 8 February Park had crossed the border into a new territory, Kaarta. The explorer is lucky to be welcomed whole-heartedly by the local ruler, King Daisy, who he finds sitting on a leopard-skin throne, his soldiers to the right of him, and his women and children to his left. A sheep is generously sent to the weary explorer's hut for his dinner.

Daisy later warned the resting explorer that a war was brewing between him and Mansong, the King of Ségou, whose territory fringed the River Niger. Rumour had it Mansong was fast advancing his army northwards, angered over a recent cattle dispute. King Daisy told Park that he must move on to avoid the incipient conflict.

Park also wanted to crack on at this stage to avoid difficult travelling conditions. Summer was not far off, and then the rains would come, causing the twin horrors of all West African journeys: delay and sickness. Simply heading straight for the Niger was no longer an option as he had to avoid Mansong's invading army. He chose instead to make a detour north into the lands of the Moors, the feared desert traders and bandits, and then head south by an alternative route.

Park's first experience in this new territory acts as a suitably dire omen. On 16 February, in a place called Funingkedy, the explorer is woken by screams. He climbs on to the roof of his hut, only to see five Moorish horsemen round up the best of the village's bullocks. Park is astonished by the lack of resistance and only one of the villagers, a young herder, tries to intercept. As the Moors gallop away with their bounty this brave youth is shot below the knee, causing severe bleeding.

Park tries to console the boy's mother, who repeatedly wails her son's praises with the words '*Ee maffo fonio*', or 'he never told a lie'. The explorer recommends amputating the boy's leg at the knee, but the villagers are appalled, believing Park to be some 'sort of cannibal for proposing so cruel and unheard of operation'. The young invalid is instead surrounded by praying *bushreens*, hoping to ease his pathway to paradise, and he dies later that evening.

Two days later Park reaches the tiny village of Simbing (only some 160 miles from the Niger) near to where Major Houghton met his fate. Park remains unsure whether Houghton 'perished of hunger, or was murdered outright by the savage Moham-medans'. Later that afternoon he moves on to the nearby town of Jarra.

Predictably, it is at this point Park's companions stall,

reluctant to press on into such blatantly hostile terrain. Park is sympathetic and gives Johnson his precious explorer's notes, with instructions to return them to Dr Laidley. However, he is pleased that his faithful slave boy, Demba (not to be confused with brattish Demba Sego), chooses to stay with him, despite the possibility of being recaptured and put in chains.

Thinking it prudent, Park sent a messenger to visit Ali, the ruler of Ludamar – a territory to the north – asking permission to travel through his realm. It does little good and after only a few days on the road he and Demba are harassed and spat on by a party of local Moors.

But a week later Park's luck returns when the chief of a remote village kills a sheep in the explorer's honour and offers to escort him for a while. A pleasant afternoon is spent with the genial headman, spinning yarns and quaffing corn beer. Park settles into a relaxed, almost complacent mood: 'In the midst of this harmless festivity I flattered myself that all danger from the Moors was over. Fancy had already placed me on the banks of the Niger, and presented to my imagination a thousand delightful scenes in my future progress . . .'

But Park's journey to the Niger was far from over and his happy reverie about to be irreparably shattered. In fact his troubles had only just begun.

CHAPTER 8

LUDAMAR BLUES

AMAR and I were due to catch a bus north from Kayes in two hours. But for now we were bunched up with the rest of the Malian football fans. It was the big game, Mali versus their arch rivals, Senegal. Of course, Mali was expected to be blitzed, kicked into touch by their sure-footed, CFA-flushed rivals. Senegal was top dog in the African Cup of Nations: a sleek, *über* greyhound taking on the lolloping St Bernard that was the Malian XI.

Still, nothing could dampen the frisson of excitement on the streets of Kayes that afternoon; last-minute prayers were winging their way east, *ju-jus* and talismans were being fondled in hope. The moustachioed man in the red beret sitting next to me nervously clacked a string of beads together.

The Kayes sun was back to its legendary ferocity. Amar and I sat under a tin shelter at the bus station, watching a clunky TV the size of a microwave oven. The volume knob was broken but many fans held shortwave radios to their ears, keen as children listening to sea shells. As soon as the game kicked off my neighbour with the red beret began a commentary. He was

82

clearly the leading pundit, Malian public transport's answer to Des Lynam.

'That El Hadji Diouf, he's so arrogant,' he shouted, playing to the crowd. 'He's like all the Senegalese. They think they are so much better than us. Look at him, like some proud bird.'

A growl of assent came from the crowd. Similar murmurings no doubt occur in Glasgow pubs every time David Beckham hoofs a free kick, but with a good deal fruitier language.

Shortly before the close of the first half, Mali scored. All hell broke loose. Beatific faces were raised heavenwards, even the more elderly fans bellowed, danced and shamelessly taunted Senegal's dismal defence. One man, with an explosive beard, immediately threw down his prayer mat, and sent a direct Allah-bound high five. Lizards on the fringing mud wall skittered off in all directions. Senegal equalized during the second half but the score line stayed at 1–1. A draw was seen as a major coup by the Malians and put everyone in a triumphant mood as we boarded our bus.

By now it was late in the afternoon and the worst of the heat was over. The bus was the spiffiest I had seen in Africa to date. None of the windows had the slightest splinter or nick, the radio worked, the engine purred, there were even one or two spare seats. It was very comfortable, and strangely dull.

We sped along a freshly built bitumen road. I had hoped we would stop off at the village of Koniakary,* a brief blip on

---

* English traveller Peter Hudson, stayed in Koniakary in the early 1990s while doggedly pursuing Mungo Park's route, village by village, on a moped. During his visit there he met a descendant of Park's rascally guide, Demba Sego, but the 90-year-old man had been too frail to say much. Despite Hudson's thorough retracing of Park's first journey, this old man was the only person in West Africa he found with a direct link to the explorer.

Park's timetable, but the new road veered off north before reaching it. As we edged towards the Sahara the bleaker the landscape became, although at one village a lake carpeted with blossoming white lilies dominated the view. The land surrounding it had been planted with maize. The lush shoots, tall as men, swished in the breeze, a sea of immodest green.

Amar and I were the only two to stop off at the oasis town of Yélimané that evening. Once the bus had trundled on into the night, the silence was deafening. No cattle were lowing, not even a cicada chirruped. A man in a black cowl appeared. He lifted his face, smiled warmly at us, and walked on. His hair was that of a black man but his face was moon white: an albino. Just for an instant I felt we had fallen off the map.

* * *

Amar and I were now deep into the Sahel, the vast, ancient savanna that stretches along the entire southern fringe of the Sahara from Senegal to Ethiopia. A dry, scrubby swathe of wilderness, prone to drought, it is becoming more fallow by the year. Indeed, over the past half century an area roughly the size of Egypt has been eroded as the Sahara's shifting sands surge gently southward.

The Sahel means 'shore' in Arabic, and in many ways it does act as the shore to the swelling ocean of the Sahara. But it is a shore pounded by many different waves; pale sands lap at its northern rim, while more tropical, jungly currents sweep its lower reaches at Guinea and the Ivory Coast. This huge area is sparsely populated, but the human diversity is rich. Here, some of the darkest people on earth mix with the fairer skinned descendants of the Moors. It is a land where wandering pastoralists live side by side with sedentary tribes who have been rooted for centuries. With its many conflicting cultures and beliefs the Sahel has proved a volatile place and continues to be so, whether through petty livestock wrangles or full scale wars.

While I was enjoying the Sahel's desolation I could tell Amar was struggling. I did not say anything, but I could tell after our magical few days on the Gambia River, this lackadaisical township we now stood in was not, as the Texans like to say, blowing the wind up his skirt.

To be fair, Yélimané was not an obvious place to stir the senses. The town square was nothing more than a line of lantern-lit street stalls selling their usual stuff: biscuits, soap, batteries, matches, dates, Bics, eggs, rice and peanuts. We slept in a grungy CFA 2,000 (£2) room near an airstrip, host to a weekly flight from Bamako. The following morning it was time to move on.

The road north from Yélimané was notoriously rough, the bitumen having petered out into heavy sand. I was desperate to shun public transport for a while and walk, as Park would have done. I tried hiring a donkey and a guide but nobody was willing. I was told the only place to do this would be Nioro du Sahel, another six hours on. This suited me fine as Nioro was in the heart of the old kingdom of Ludamar, where Park had spent several months.

The following afternoon, we blagged a lift in a northbound Land Cruiser called Lion du Forêt, with as many passengers on its roof as inside. Most of them now had light skin and colourful turbans – a look of the desert about them. The journey was trouble-free until the market town of Kirane, where Amar and I were ushered into the local army barracks.

The soldier in charge clearly wanted to intimidate us, and, I have to say, he didn't do a bad job. The interview room we were led to was suitably menacing. A haunch of on-the-turn mutton hung from the ceiling, while languorous youths

85

pottered by, holding their guns casually as tennis rackets. Our interrogator was wearing a combat jacket and a rather effette white silk scarf. He began shouting in French.

'*Tes papiers pas bons!*' he informed us. 'Your papers are bad. Why don't you have a special pass? This is not a place for tourists. It is a military area.' He pointed at his gun, knocking off some red peppers from his desk. 'You are near the Mauritanian border, there are problems here. The Iraq war means more terrorism. There are Tuareg bandits in some places. Tell me, what are you doing here?'

Amar, who spoke much better French than me, answered his flood of questions patiently and clearly. We are just tourists. We know nothing about the area. We just want to go to Nioro.

'Yes, yes, it's okay' said the soldier suddenly, his voice soft now. He had dazed, world-weary eyes, like car headlights dulled from being left on all night. The switch from his maniac shouting to this rather soothing whisper was unnerving. He was turning into a one-man version of good cop, bad cop.

All was quiet. The soldier stared at our passports, while slowly rubbing his teeth with a twig. Geological ages passed, ice caps melted. It was as if he was trying to decipher Sanskrit engravings. If I hadn't been quietly bricking it I would have laughed, the silence and the sheer silliness of it all were hugely infectious. Our visas were valid, our yellow fever certificates in place, surely there was nothing he could do. He was just fishing for a bribe.

'Why does one visa say "tourist",' he snarled, bad cop had suddenly been reborn. 'And the other one say "vacation". Why?' His voice was loud again. 'Why? Tell me. Why?'

'They both mean the same thing,' I replied. I wanted to add, 'Could you please stop this macho, swinging your balls around routine and let us go', but what I actually said was: 'We're terribly sorry, sir, but we've done nothing wrong. Vacation and tourism, there's really no difference.'

'No! You're wrong,' he harrumphed. 'I need to call my boss. I will call him at five o'clock. You will wait here.'

We had been held for 20 minutes. The driver of Lion du Forêt appeared, demanding how much longer we would take. He was ready to go. The soldier ushered him away.

I took a chance and pointed at the mutton, asking whether the soldier had enjoyed *Tabaski*. Good cop reinstated himself. Yes, it had been a great *Tabaski* with his family, thank you very much, and wonderful food. Amar followed this up with a question about the football. Yes, yes, a fine game, we whipped Senegal, the next match is against Guinea. We must watch it.

The soldier was onside now and, perhaps sensing Amar and I were unlikely to hand over a juicy bribe, casually threw our passports back. We shook hands and bolted for the vehicle.

* * *

An overheated Lion du Forêt pulled up at Nioro du Sahel later that evening, dropping us off at the local *campement*. It was getting cheaper the further north we travelled. This room cost us CFA 1,000 (£1): a concrete cell with a foam mattress in the corner.

Amar sat down in our glum surroundings and peeled an orange.

'You okay?' I asked.

'Fine,' he said. 'Just not sure I get West Africa. We seem to be travelling a hell of a long way for very small rewards.'

This was unlike Amar. I had travelled with him before, most memorably on a long trek in Tibet when, on the last night, we had stupidly stranded ourselves on a 4,000-metre pass, with no tent, no stove and only a couple of raw turnips left to eat. When it started bucketing rain we were in trouble; dancing and singing to stave off our shivers. We walked all the next day, finally reaching a monastery, full of burgundy robed monks and guttering candles. We dried off and feasted on yak stew and walnuts. It had been a close call, but unforgettable. The sort of traveller's tale de luxe we could bore each other with every time we met. At the time Amar had only just stopped working as a solicitor and was on his first trip as a fledgling photojournalist.

Amar was passionate about photography and travel. When he raved about a place, it made you want to drop everything and go, right away, pronto, get out of town. But on this journey, once we left the Gambia River he had been decidedly under-stimulated. He had tended to rhapsodize about previous trips instead: walks in Kashmir, castles in Syria, mosques in Iran.

'You've been talking a lot about past trips, but never Mali,' I told him, while unpacking my stuff. 'When you mentioned Stoke Newington today I really began to worry.'

'I suppose that's not a great sign,' he admitted. 'But if I mention Milton Keynes, then it's serious. Look, Tom,' Amar said, rubbing his hands over his face very slowly. 'To be honest, I don't really want to walk through this desert with a donkey. Mountains, jungles, historic forts, yes. But this!' He gestured to the encircling wasteland. 'Look, I can see you love all this, this desolation.' He paused. 'But, well, you've always been odd, very odd, and you've got an unhealthy obsession with mules, donkeys, livestock in general.'

'Don't knock it till you've tried . . .'

'You don't mind, do you?' Amar interrupted, suddenly serious. 'I said I'd go to Bamako with you. I don't want to let you down.'

'You're not letting me down at all, but I think you're a complete lightweight.' I was enjoying myself, knowing Amar was a considerably hardier traveller than I ever would be. 'A shameless wuss. A milksop.'

There was a brief silence as we watched a line of ants march across the mildewed wall.

'I loved the Gambia River, Tom. I really did, but the rest is so, just so . . . empty.'

'I can tell you're missing your better half,' I said. 'Much better half. It's understandable.'

'Yes, I am.' Amar spat out an orange pip. 'I mean, come on Fremantle, a stumpy mule-fancier like you is hardly a substitute for a green-eyed Belgian Amazon.'

The last time Amar and I had travelled together was seven years ago. Things had changed for us both since then: we talked of home far more now. We were fathers this time and Amar and his girlfriend Cath, were about to celebrate their fifteenth anniversary. Amar was now a jobbing journo, his travels short, focused, commissioned and always resulting in an article or two. He still liked to travel adventurously but with a degree of control, eagerly consulting maps and guide books.

As I wrote books, not articles, my trips were much less frequent, but longer. It gave me time to dive into a country headlong and ride whatever current swept me up. It was like a mild madness, the strangely appealing chance to prove the Prophet Mohammed's maxim that 'a journey is a fragment of hell', but with that, I always found, came a slither of heaven.

'I'll split tomorrow then,' Amar said, standing up. 'Come on, let's celebrate. The sweet tea's on me. Then you can go donkey rustling.'

* * *

Nioro du Sahel had all sorts of imperfections – it was dusty, fly-blown, susceptible to flesh-searing heat in the dry season, and street-destroying floods in the wet. My guide book called the town's mosque 'one of the most important in Mali', but neglected to mention that, to everyone except Muslims, all that could be seen were four impregnable mud walls.

But the isolated town had several redeeming features. It was peppered with mango trees, the locals were goofily helpful and most important of all it was a wonderful place to hire a donkey. In fact, I flagged down the very first donkey drover who trundled by the next morning. His name was Bubakar, a Fulani herdsman, and he agreed to travel with me as far as Diéma, roughly 70 miles south of Nioro.

Bubakar was very no-nonsense, a maker of quick decisions. He had an open, weathered face, his smile as flexible as a vaudeville clown. He told me he would harness up two donkeys to carry my luggage while I walked. Bubakar knew people in all the villages en route; he spoke decent French but little English.

I asked Bubakar if he had ever done anything like this before. He laughed good-naturedly, saying nothing, which either meant yes, he did it all the time (vastly improbable) or no, he'd never heard such a daft proposal (a safe bet). We shook hands and agreed to meet in three hours. He needed to tell his wife he would be gone for a week. And that was that.

I rushed around the market buying food for the journey. It was the most bounteously equipped shopping venue yet. I grabbed tomatoes, garlic, chilli peppers, carrots, tins of Moroccan sardines, bananas and dozens of tiny green oranges: sour, juicy and delicious. The colour of the market totally transformed Nioro, from a dun-coloured backwater into a swirl of chatter, laughter, music and haggling, full of primary hues and strange glamour.

A gypsy-looking man, bare-chested and gap-toothed, sharpened knives on a whetstone, Arab boys with grey eyes touted I LOVE AFRICA buckets and Saddam Hussein T-shirts, a row of Mauritanian women swathed in blue-black cloaks, hunkered down in front of great orbs of soap, hard and round as croquet balls. The women gossiped, their smiles flashing gold – a coven of beautiful, fairytale witches.

*   *   *

After an hour I dashed back to the *campement* with several heaving bags. Amar was chatting to Louis, a straw-haired car dealer from Munich, with a *laissez-faire* attitude to shampoo and the sound of his own voice. Louis had parked his Toyota van outside the *campement* late last night and today was moving on to Bamako. It looked like Amar had found himself a lift.

'I do this every year,' the garrulous German told us, re-clined on a cushion, chewing a melon slice. 'I drive down to Mali with an overland vehicle and sell it.'

'Who to?' I asked.

'It varies. Sometimes to big shots in a city like Bamako or Ségou, sometimes to hicks in the middle of nowhere.'

'What was the best price?'

'The best, huh?' Louis shut his eyes. 'Ah, yes, that's easy! It was in a remote village on the River Niger. The village chief hid all his money under his bed. Truly, he did! He distrusted towns, never visited them. I had to drive hundreds of extra kilometres to meet him. But it was worth it.' He paused and clapped his hands. 'He paid five times the price.'

Louis revealed he usually bought a 4WD vehicle, it didn't matter what type, for around 1,500 Euros and sold it on for 5,000 or more. He had never made a loss. His current Toyota vehicle was nothing special. In fact it looked of the most dubious pedigree, half removal van, half caravan with a few other cannibalized gizmos thrown in. Travelling with a pair of donkeys was certainly the more sensible choice.

'Yes,' said Louis, perhaps sensing my critical stare. 'I know it doesn't look much, but the engine is great. As long as somebody pays the price I paid for it I'm happy.' He bent under the chassis and grabbed a jerry can. 'Now you must excuse me, gentlemen, I need a shower.'

'So did you get a good deal?' asked Amar, as we headed back to the room for our backpacks. 'I hope your beast's got some stamina.'

'Yeah, not bad, but Park only paid two bars of amber per donkey. And guess what, sod's law, there was no amber in the market today.'

'Of course not.' Amar hefted up his immense rucksack. 'You need to go to Stoke Newington for things like that.'

'See you back in London then.' I shouldered my pack too. 'Next time we'll be travelling with our children.'

'Yes, stuff changes, doesn't it,' said Amar, as we shook hands. 'I'm ready for home this time.'

* * *

We last left Mungo Park in the territory of Ludamar, drinking corn wine with a jovial village chief. This brief spell of merriment was soon interrupted by a party of Moorish horsemen, who insisted that Park accompany them. Apparently Queen Fatima, the wife of their ruler, Ali, desired to see a white man. Within seconds Park had switched from imminent conqueror of the River Niger to hapless prisoner.

It was to be the start of a harrowing two and a half months for the young explorer. He was instantly escorted to Ali's camp at Benown, a collection of shabby tents north of Jarra, on the edge of the desert.

The first thing Ali, an old, white-bearded man of 'sullen and indignant aspect', ordered Park to do was kill a pig. As pork was considered unclean by the Moors, the explorer sensibly refused, telling Ali he never ate such food. Ali then ordered the pig to be unleashed, thinking it would attack the nervous Scotsman. Ironically, it scampered around madly before seeking refuge under Ali's own couch. That night Park was held in a hut with only the pig for company, describing it as a 'disagreeable inmate'.

The explorer's mettle was to be tested to the full. These were not the refined Moors of Fez and Marrakesh but a far wilder variety, used to the harsh, dog-eat-dog ways of the desert. They spat at Park and hurled abuse. He was repeatedly made to take off and put on his clothes, as they had not seen buttons before. Women studied his fingers and toes simply to check if he was human. Before long he had been reduced to little more than a circus freak.

Park soon convinced himself that being a stranger, a Christian and on top of this, an utterly defenceless one, was 'sufficient to drive every spark of humanity from a Moor'. There was even suspicion that he might be a spy.

On 18 March, a week and a half after he was first captured, four Moors arrived with a fresh captive: Johnson, Park's guide. When they failed to find any gold on Johnson, Ali ordered Park's belongings to be searched again, this time unearthing gold, amber and the explorer's precious compass.

Ali was especially intrigued by the compass, and why its needle always pointed towards the Great Desert. Park, thinking on his feet, told Ali it pointed to the direction of his mother, so he would always be able to find the way home. It was a clever explanation and Ali returned the compass in fear, believing it possessed magic qualities.

Scary rumours filtered back to Park that the Moors were keen to cut off his right hand, or gouge out his eyes, as they were thought to resemble those of a cat. These potential horrors were to be put on hold, however, until Queen Fatima, who was currently travelling in the Sahara, had inspected him.

To add to Park's woes it was the hottest time of year; so hot that the thirsty, half-starved explorer found the wind rifling through the crevices in his hut painful on his skin. One time Park was plagued by fever but forbidden to even lie down; on another occasion while seeking shade outside he was falsely accused of trying to escape. A gun was put to his head and fired twice, but the chambers were empty. This type of taunting was commonplace.

And yet, Park kept his sense of humour. The fact his spirit never broke was strongly illustrated when a group of women visited his tent. They told him they wished to find out if Christians were all circumcised. Park joked with them that this sort of public peeking did not happen back home, but suggested the youngest and prettiest girl do the honours, while the others retire. This tickled everyone and the chosen girl, although she never did perform the task, later sent him some food and milk.

Finally, Queen Fatima returned from her travels, and on 3 May, just shy of two months since his capture, Park was introduced to her. The meeting actually took place in Bubaker, a dismal settlement north of Benown, where Ali had retreated after reports that King Mansong's army was fast approaching.

At first Fatima was uneasy around Park and shocked by his appearance. But, after a translator deciphered the explorer's polite words, she relaxed. At the conclusion of the meeting she even offered Park a bowl of milk. Park noted that Fatima was enormously fat, but understood this was the ultimate form of feminine beauty to the Moors. Indeed, daughters were often force fed hearty portions of couscous and milk by their mothers to make them more alluring.

Park's time at Bubaker, a place even hotter and more water-starved than Benown, was miserable. At one stage he was so desperate to slake his thirst he thrust his head between two cows and greedily drank from their trough. But before Park's condition deteriorated further, there was a sudden spark of hope. King Mansong's army had now withdrawn, and Ali was eager to travel south again. Queen Fatima showed compassion to Park and pressed her husband to let the explorer accompany him. They set off on 26 May.

Two days later Park was shocked to learn that Ali had stolen his servant Demba, and was using him as his own personal slave. For the first time on his journey Park lost control, accusing Ali of the most appalling cruelty and injustice. Ali told the explorer to hold his tongue or he would be sent back north. Park was cruelly instructed he could keep 'the old fool' Johnson, but must split with Demba. On their parting Park and Demba held each other, both of them in tears. Park's diary reflects his anger: 'There is something in the frown of a tyrant [Ali] which rouses the most secret emotion of the heart . . . and for once [I] entertained an indignant wish to rid the world of such a monster.'

Having completed his business in Jarra by 8 June, Ali hot-tailed it back north, abandoning Park. The explorer was momentarily overjoyed, but this was still no time to relax. King Daisy had been far from finished off by Mansong's invasion and was now trying to restore his power. He soon set about attacking Jarra, where some of his rebellious subjects (who Ali had promised to help but then let down) had taken refuge. Park was caught in the cross-fire and fled the city with nothing but his horse, now a 'perfect Rosinante', his compass and a few clothes.

But Ali had sent a party of Moors to recapture the bedraggled explorer, and they soon caught him up 'whooping and brandishing their double-barrelled guns'. In a state of near meltdown Park accepts his lot with astonishing *sang-froid*, facing his rowdy captors with the 'gloomy relief' that this was the worst that could possibly happen to him. This was not to be the case. The Moors escorted Park for a few miles then decided to simply rob him rather than return him to Ali. They took the one valuable item Park still owned: his cloak – his only defence against inclement weather and mosquitoes – and swiftly rode off.

'It is impossible to describe the joy that arose in my mind,' wrote Park, 'when I looked around and concluded that I was out of danger. I felt like one recovered from sickness; I breathed freer; I found unusual lightness in my limbs; even the Desert looked pleasant.'

This was another short-lived moment of euphoria, as he was now dangerously dehydrated. There was not a drop of water for miles and his thirst became 'insufferable', his mouth parched and inflamed. 'Here then,' mused Park, 'after a short but ineffectual struggle, terminate all my hopes of being useful in my day and generation; here must the short span of my life come to an end.'

But serendipity struck just in time. A freak sandstorm whipped up, then 'vivid flashes of lightning, followed by a few heavy drops of rain'. The explorer spread out his clothes on the ground and sucked the moisture from them. He was saved once again. His only possessions the shirt on his back and a heart full of hope; his only goal the River Niger, luring him ever on, like a Ganges-bound sadhu on a quest for immortality.

CHAPTER 9

RAMADAN AND MANGO

'HAH, HAH, harrah,' bellowed Bubakar, while tapping his donkeys' rumps with a tamarisk branch. Not that the beasts needed much chivvying; they had been clipping along at a breakneck pace since we left Nioro that morning. I was forced to yomp just to keep them in eye shot.

The bigger of the two donkeys was called Ramadan. The other, a runty beast with a scabbed left ear and rakish expression, was unnamed. During our first rest stop I suggested that we christen him. How about Mungo, I told Bubakar, explaining why the name was relevant.

'*Oui, oui,*' said Bubakar, patting the donkey's punkish mane. 'I agree. We will call him Mango. MANGO! A very good name for a donkey.' I decided to let it stick. I'm sure the little beast didn't mind much either way: long dead Scottish explorer or succulent fruit, at least he had some sort of identity.

The road to Diéma was nothing more than a strip of graded sand, almost entirely free of trucks and pretty much everything else. At one stage a black-turbaned herdsman wandered up ahead of us surrounded by his cows. As we passed he stopped to look at us, perched on one leg like a flamingo. Other donkey carts occasionally shimmered into view.

Towards noon a man on a white horse drew level and reined to a halt. He looked magnificent in dark, billowing robes; his horse's fetlocks and tail dyed the colour of mulberries.

He fired off a question at Bubakar, who replied, and then fired another question back. This strangers' small talk I had heard many times already in West Africa. It seemed the more remote the setting, the more long-winded the exchange, often padding out for several minutes. From what Bubakar told me, the conversation went something like this:

'*Salaam aleikum*. Peace be unto you.'

'*Aleikum asalaam*. And peace by unto you too. Are you fine?'

'Yes, praise be to God, I am fine. And you?'

'Yes, fine. What about your wife?'

'She is well. And your family?

'Yes, they are fine, thank you. What about your cows/ sheep/camels?

'Not bad, but they need rain? So where are you going?'

'To Diéma. Is there plenty of water in the wells on the way?'

'Yes, all are working. Will you travel far today?'

'Until the sun falls, God willing, but now we must find some shadow and rest.'

One of the most touching questions I heard was: 'Is there anything I can do for you?' And if the answer was negative, the reply might be: 'Sorry for all the things I have never done for you.'

In my experience the latter comment is the sort of thing a husband might say to a wife, or a brother to a sister, probably after a blazing row or a substantial absence, but in the Malian desert complete strangers said it to one another and I liked that. It seemed both respectful and humbling.

As the heat intensified the donkeys' pace slackened, and I was able to decelerate from a yomp, to a walk to a comfortable

trudge. Apart from all the protracted conversations, something else had begun to slow us down. Bubakar was proving a
serial worshipper. Early in the afternoon he slipped off the
wagon and handed me his tamarisk whip. 'You keep the donkeys going,' he ordered, 'I need a quiet place to pray.'

I vaulted onto the wagon's rickety wooden platform and
grabbed the reins. It was a surprisingly easy job, the donkeys were
on auto-trot. I swayed about, occasionally shouting 'Har!' or
'Mango!' or 'Ramadan!' if we confronted a mild gradient or deep
sand. Then after 15 minutes Bubakar would appear again, gasping,
and resume command while I walked. From dawn to midnight
Bubakar told me he always prayed at least five times. In fact
Bubakar never really stopped praying. Even when jockeying his
little wagon, he fiddled with prayer beads and uttered mantras.
His prayers were remarkably unselfconscious. It didn't bother him
in the least that I heard him beseeching Allah with his impassioned
mumbles. He seemed in a state of permanent confession.

That said, in his brief devotional lulls, Bubakar was happy
to talk about our harsh surroundings. Many desert shrubs and
trees were armed with thorns, he warned, but I needed to be
especially aware of cram-cram seeds. Cram-cram were tiny
burrs with vicious spikes that stuck to everything: grass, skin,
socks, trousers and even donkey hair. They were notorious in
these parts, often drawing pinpricks of blood.

Of course, there were roses amid the thorns too. Bubakar
pointed out beautiful birds, their plumages bluer than the sky,
with long, black swishy tails that danced in the wind. The
reverential way he described these avian rarities did, however,
lose some of its poeticism when he told me they tasted great.
He pointed out green parrots, yellow dragonflies and a pink
barberry tree, its blossom making it look as if its branches
were on fire. More than anything, though, he talked of the
omnipresent, odd-shaped baobabs.

'The baobab is a special tree, Tom,' mused Bubakar, using his stick to point at one of the sylvan hulks. 'People have sat under them for hundreds of years. They have heard all our stories, all our history.'

Bubakar explained that baobabs looked the way they did due to evil giants planting them upside-down, but through time they had become both benign and useful. Baobab bark was made into ropes, its seed into fertilizer, its fruit into sauces and its flowers into a blood-stirring medicine. Baobabs could store gallons of water in their trunks and, as they were virtually fireproof, often lived for several centuries.

Before Bubakar's revelations I had always thought of baobabs as an arboreal ugly sister, a bit of a joke, with their fat, topsy-turvy trunks and spindly limbs. But once the moon was up that evening they took on a strong, reassuring quality, lit up like letters from an ancient alphabet, leading us on through the blue and starry twilight.

*　*　*

We finally pulled up in a village called Bema. Like any good stockman, Bubakar tended his donkeys first, unhitching them from the wagon and filling their water butts from a jerry can. The sun had long gone but a gibbous moon illuminated us so clearly there was no need for torches.

Bubakar led me through a gateway into a compound of mud huts. I was astonished to see a satellite dish sprouting from the hard earth, acting as a hitching post to half a dozen goats. A generator thrummed in the background.

A mass of villagers swarmed around a TV screen which was showing a Brazilian soap full of botoxed beauties sipping champagne. If only their dialogue sparkled like their teeth. Instead they were forced to say things like: 'Oh my God,

Bradley, I thought you were my brother, not my *sister!*' The Africans looked on in awe, oooing and ahhing, at these titillating snapshots of an unfamiliar world.

Bubakar introduced me to a man called Sylla. He was a bald, avuncular fellow in an orange robe whose whispery voice belied considerable power. When a group of noisy children swarmed around us, he lifted his hand and they scattered obediently, along with a posse of squawking chickens. It turned out Sylla was the chief. He had studied briefly in Paris and spoke good French and not bad English.

As we chatted, a pretty, lithesome girl in a green shawl brought over a cauldron of macaroni. Bubakar and I sat on the ground and ate greedily with our hands.

'This is my youngest wife,' Sylla said, gesturing to the smiling girl who had waited on us. 'I have three others. Muslim men are allowed four.'

'That's a lot,' I commented, mid-mouthful.

'Not really.' Sylla wiped some dust off his robe. 'The prophet Mohammed was allowed ten wives, Allah made an exception for him.'

'Isn't it hard for your wives?' I asked. 'Don't they get jealous?'

'No, no,' replied Sylla. 'They are all treated well and get on fine. I have children by all of them, eleven kids! Very different in age. I love them all and they love me.'

'What about you, Bubakar?' I asked.

'I am happy with one wife and one son,' he said, putting his hands in the air as if surrendering. 'More would be complicated. I am not a rich man. I am happy as I am.'

When I asked Sylla about his time in Europe he was not the least nostalgic. 'I did not really like France,' he told me. 'The food was horrible. Those greasy croissants! I made one or two friends but not real friends like here. I am a Fulani man, I like my home. I am not a tourist like you, no need to get away.'

'But I thought the Fulani were nomadic,' I interrupted.

Sylla explained that the Fulani – who were known as the Peulh by the French – had originally been nomadic.* These days the Fulani were still widespread, stretching from Senegal as far as Cameroon, but they were mostly settled farmers, living for generations in one place. I had read they were fervently religious and if Bubakar was anything to go by this was still the case.

I mentioned to Bubakar that Mungo Park had praised the Fulani (or Foulahs in his diary) for their cattle husbandry skills. I knew that back in Nioro, Bubakar owned a dozen cattle as well as tending a friend's herd.

'We sometimes look after our cattle better then we do ourselves,' he said, only half in jest. 'They are our life.'

It seemed this was not uncommon in Africa.† Sylla mentioned the Dinka tribe in Sudan who lived almost exclusively on their cows' milk, supplemented with blood occasionally drained from cows' veins. Dinka cattle were worshipped, loved and never killed. They were seen as mystical beasts and Dinka women were not allowed to touch them. Sylla stressed cattle were serious business in Africa and often led to tribal disputes, just as they had in Park's day.

'So did Mango Park travel with a cow?' Bubakar asked me, shovelling in another mouthful of macaroni.

---

* A small number of nomadic Fulani still roam remote areas of the southern Sahara in Niger. They are the only Fulani resistant to Islam and are some of the last true desert nomads.
† This bovine adoration is not unique to Africa and in Hindu culture the cow has long been a sacred beast. 'Hindus venerate oxen,' wrote the ubiquitous Ibn Battutah, while travelling in India prior to his African wanderings, 'and it is said that they actually drink the oxen's *urine* when they fall sick.'

'He mostly used horses and donkeys. But he does mention cattle briefly. I might try travelling with an ox at some stage.'

'Did he come through here?'

'No,' I admitted. 'But I'm only a bit off course. Many of the villages Park visited no longer exist. I'm really just trying to capture his spirit, see the sort of conditions he faced. I'll join up with him later near Bamako.'

We were flagging now and all of us holding back yawns. Sylla ushered over three neatly dressed children, two boys and a girl. One boy had a bad limp and a little goitre on his neck. Bubakar followed us. Before long the children pulled back a curtain and pointed at a bed for me to sleep on. Bubukar explained it was the children's bed but they could sleep on the floor. I insisted this wasn't necessary – I could sleep on the floor, or else set up my tent. Bubakar said I would cause offence if I didn't accept the bed.

As a thank you Bubukar handed the children an orange. The boy with the goitre peeled it and split it carefully in three, sharing it out equally. I noticed Malian children did this a lot; it wasn't just the eldest or the strongest who took everything.

I crashed onto the hard bedding and shut my eyes. Outside somewhere, a donkey was braying.

* * *

Ramadan and Mango let rip with a dawn chorus of sulky brays, accompanied by every other donkey in the village. The bally-hoo had a symphonic quality, the brays reaching a crescendo and then tailing off to make way for the odd solo artist, all of them equally ear-jarring.

I rolled out of bed, narrowly missing one of the children sleeping at my feet. The sun was peeking over the flat horizon, bright and shivery as a cigar tip. Bubakar was already up, feeding Ramadan and Mango on millet stalks. He picked up Mango's rear hoof and dislodged a stone, then set about the grooming. I noticed the donkeys' dung had not fallen in pats but pellets, shining like dark pearls in the early light.

I filled our jerries from the water pump and then worked on my diary. From his diary it is clear Mungo Park liked donkeys. He was particularly fascinated to witness one Fulani man put a forked stick in one of his beast's mouths to avoid it kicking. Ramadan and Mango seemed remarkably well behaved on the kicking front; nocturnal braying was their only vice.

But this also had a remedy, albeit a decidedly rum one. In 1872 Francis Galton wrote in *The Art of Travel* (one of the few books I carried with me) that the best way of silencing a donkey was the Chinese method of 'lashing a heavy stone to the beast's tail . . . as when an ass wants to bray he elevates his tail, and, if his tail be weighted down, he has not the heart to bray'. Galton neglects to add whether the ass kicked the living daylights out of him while attaching the stone.

Galton goes on to eulogize donkeys: 'Notwithstanding his inveterate obstinacy, the ass is an excellent and sober little beast . . . He is nearly equal to the camel in enduring thirst, and thrives on the poorest pasture, suffers from few diseases, and is unscathed by African distemper.'

Back at the compound, Sylla proudly introduced me to his other three wives, two of them pounding millet, another tending a fire. The youngest wife from the night before was nowhere to be seen. The three elder and considerably plumper spouses did seem genuinely happy in each others' company, laughing as they worked, no flickers of jealousy or upstaging one another.

While waiting for breakfast I played football with some of Sylla's children in the courtyard. After they had comprehensively trounced me they led me to a granary, a small mud building, suspended off the ground to keep the rodents out. On the outside wall a lizard had been carved into the mud, apparently as a warning to thieves – a sort of reptilian bouncer.

We headed back for breakfast. One of Sylla's wives, a stooped, jolly woman with a Marge Simpson hairdo, handed round a ladle of millet porridge. I took a swig, it was rather good, like scented Ready Brek. The next offering was considerably more unusual. I had offered to cook some of my food but Bubakar had got there first, brewing up a mess tin full of everything we possessed: tomato paste, sardines, sweetcorn, nuts, garlic cloves, peppers and coconut biscuits all in one large, indefinable stew.

We all tucked in and gave appreciative murmurs. That said, if I could have struck a Faustian pact to exchange my mess tin for a bowl of Crunchy Nut Cornflakes, I would have jumped at it.

* * *

Duly fortified, and having thanked Sylla and his wives, we headed south. It wasn't long before we were joined by a barefoot boy. He wore a filthy T-shirt advertising Camel cigarettes that read: NINE OUT OF TEN MEN WHO'VE TRIED CAMELS – PREFER WOMEN! He looked like he had been on the road for some time.

The boy, probably in his late teens, had appeared from nowhere. I had looked around and suddenly there he was, walking beside me. He understood no French or English. Bubakar spoke to him, beginning one of his long West African hellos, which soon fizzled out when he was met with silence. Bubakar said he thought the boy might be from Mauritania; he was very dark skinned and was probably heading to Bamako in search of work.

The boy seemed incredibly calm and unafraid. He offered us both a swig from his goat-skin *guerba*, or water-carrier. Bubakar took a swig and said I should drink too: it was polite. The *guerba* was not full of water but porridge, just like we had drunk for breakfast: except this time it was sour, the milk having curdled. It was clearly days old. I offered the boy some nuts and dates in return, the etiquette of the desert. The boy behaved as if he had been part of our team from the start. Without any prompting he helped Bubakar and me cut millet stalks and other foliage for the donkeys. He shook coogoo berries from the trees. He was always of sunny disposition, seemingly just delighted to have some company.

When we stopped at a well at one of the smaller villages he did something that astonished me. Staring intently at the ground he analysed a frog that had been squashed. The frog's steamrollered hide was in near perfect condition, dried out by the sun. The boy carefully unpeeled the frog, like masking tape, from the dust. Once it was free he walked to the well, peered over and threw it in. The frog took an age to land, a tiny barely perceptible plop. Bubakar laughed, sensing my amazement.

'Why did he do that?'

'He thinks the frog's spirit is still alive,' explained Bubakar. 'When he puts it in the water, he thinks it will swim again.'

That evening when we neared Dempa, the village where we wanted to sleep, Bubakar asked the boy for some identification papers. His usually open smiley face snapped shut like a fan. His mood changed instantly and irreparably. Bubakar raised his hands to make light of it, but the boy's pride had been punc-tured. He nodded his head in farewell, and began marching at a faster pace. Soon he was far beyond us.

'I didn't know if we could trust him,' said Bubakar, waving his tamarisk branch.

'He seemed harmless,' I suggested.

'*Evidemment*,' said Bubakar unhappily. 'But if he is a criminal, we might be in trouble too. We know nothing about him.'

A day later Bubakar and I reached the small chaotic transport hub of Diéma. The road east from here was not bitumen but still a superior dirt track to the one we had been on. After a celebratory omelette, Bubakar did an almost instant U-turn. We had been travelling for four days and, without my luggage, he hoped he could make the return journey in three. He fed and watered Ramadan and Mango and then packed up ready to retrace his tracks home.

'I will pray for you,' Bubakar told me as we shook hands. This was good news. Nobody prayed more than Bubakar, I would have an almost perpetual hotline to the heavens. He had been an exceptional guide, generous, honest and knowledgeable, I was sorry to see him go.

Not long after waving off Bubakar I jumped on the back of an eastbound lorry laden with oil drums. It chugged its way unhappily down the cattle grid of a road, the Malian passengers managing to sleep despite the judders and straining engine. After six hours I jumped off at the northbound turning for Mourdiah, a large village Mungo Park had visited shortly before his epiphany on the banks of the Niger.

CHAPTER 10

TWO ROADS, ONE RIVER

AFTER SHRUGGING off Ali's henchmen and sucking dry his rain-sodden clothes a refreshed Mungo Park plodded on south towards the Niger. Testing times still lay ahead for the destitute explorer. At the first village he was shunned by the chief, but an old woman took pity and fed him a bowl of leftovers. So overjoyed was Park by this simple gesture that he lifted his eyes to the heavens in thanks.

Next morning, having heard some Fulani were plotting to seize him and return him to Ali, Park surged on. He walked all day to the next village and that night, having only had two hours rest in two days, he was able to catch up on some much needed sleep. The following morning he exchanged his brass coat buttons with a shepherd who fed him a bowl of corn.

By 5 July Park fell upon a little town called Wawra. Ludamar and all its horrors were now behind him: he had entered the kingdom of Bambara. Things were to take a turn for the better. In the village of Moorja (modern-day Mourdiah), Park witnesses some of the locals getting drunk on corn spirit. He doesn't try the homebrew himself, but is touched when his hosts offer him as much corn and milk as he likes.

From here on south, whether the villages were Muslim or not, Park was able to find shelter for the night. One of his hosts even cut off several of Park's hairs, believing they had magical properties. The superstitious barber became so carried away that Park had to put his hat back on to avoid being fully cropped.

As he neared the Niger, Park tagged on with a group of fugitive Kaartans heading for the river port of Ségou. Some company was no bad thing as he was now in an area notorious for lions, where a lone traveller might make easy pickings. Park walked barefoot most of the time to preserve his boots; his emaciated horse being far too tired to carry him.

On 18 July the weary explorer encountered a slave coffle for the first time. There were seventy slaves 'tied together by their necks with thongs of a bullock's hide, twisted like a rope'. The sorry-looking party were heading for Ludamar, then across the Sahara and on to Morocco. With all the increase in human traffic Park realized the Niger would soon be in sight.

By the time he reached the village of Dooninkeaboo, Park was in such a mangy state that he felt even the local slaves looked down on him. The villagers refused to feed him. But Park knew he was near his goal and, despite being ravenously hungry and harried by mosquitoes, little could dampen his enthusiasm. On 20 July, along with his Kaartan companions, he made his way south. Soon he felt marshy ground beneath his feet and saw teeming crowds; it was market day at Ségou.

As Park craned forward to catch a glimpse of his prize, one of his party called out to him and pointed ahead: '*Geo affili*, see the water.'

'I saw with infinite pleasure the great object of my mission,' wrote Park, 'the long sought for majestic Niger, glittering to the morning sun, as broad as the Thames at Westminster, and flowing slowly *to the eastward*.'

Park then knelt down and drank from the Niger, or Joliba (great river) as it was known in Bambara. The secret of the mystical river, which had puzzled European geographers and explorers for centuries, had now been cracked. After all the adversity he had endured it must have been a sweet moment for Park. He did not lose his head though, and with characteristic humility, remembered to give 'fervent thanks . . . to the Great Ruler of all things' for allowing him to achieve his dream.

* * *

My own journey to the Niger, although a doddle compared to Mungo Park's, was proving almost as circuitous. Having reached Mourdiah, the town where Park had witnessed the locals getting drunk on corn spirit, I had a change of plan.

When I mentioned Mungo Park's name at a crowded coffee stall on Mourdiah's main street, everyone drew a blank. All except one, a mini-bus driver called Mamadou. Mamadou was a fierce-looking man with dreadlocks that drooped down to his hunched neck. He had a wart on his nose, like a glob of dried chewing gum, and seemed a little stoned.

'I've heard of Mungo Park,' Mamadou told me, as he munched on a hunk of bread. 'He was an explorer out here. But if you really want to learn about him, there's an American lady up in Nara, she'll know lots.'

'How far is Nara?' I asked, watching a couple of boys chase a rolling tyre across the street.

'Ah, *mon petit frère*,' said Mamadou, forceably grabbing my bicep, 'it's only another four hours. Around here that's nothing. There's nowhere to stay in Mourdiah, why not come to Nara, stay with my family. I am driving a mini-bus up there tonight.'

I pondered the idea. Mourdiah was quiet, attractive and like a host of other Malian mud settlements, but other than the bibulous and friendly behaviour of its inhabitants, Park had little to say about it. I checked my map. Nara was up near the Mauritanian border and looked even more seductively remote than Nioro, almost off the map. The fact I could stay with a local family clinched it for me.

The journey north was the worst to date. The mini-bus cabin was cooped in by prison-style bars and grubby panes of glass, the engine farcically throaty. All the passengers were so sardined together it was if we had each taken one of Alice in Wonderland's EAT ME pills.

Mamadou was a demon behind the wheel, thundering down the dirt road, veering over hummocks, ploughing through bushes, while at the same time singing along to Bob Marley, eating a banana and pointing out rock escarpments or passing camels. Nobody else said a word, we just sat, rooted to our narrow wooden benches, caulked in dust, praying for arrival.

We reached Nara after midnight. Since leaving Diéma that morning, over 15 hours had been spent on the road and less than 200 miles covered. Mamadou dumped off his 20-odd passengers at a litter-strewn depot and then drove on through deserted streets fringed by mud huts. Before long he pulled into a courtyard. In the moonshine I could make out a large cow, pale as a candle, sitting under a palm tree.

Mamadou led me to his room. He lit a hurricane lantern and gestured to a bed hemmed by a mozzie net. 'We will sleep here,' he said casually, then hunkered down and produced a brick of hash from his knapsack. He began chiselling away at the hash with his penknife, sticking equal sized portions into little envelopes. On the wall I noticed a poster which announced: WE ARE READY FOR WAR, with pictures of American soldiers juxtaposed with Taliban fighters. Next to it was a conflicting message: SAY NO TO WAR. I realized I knew next to nothing about Mamadou. I liked to trust people but I had never before shared a bed with a ganja-dealing bus driver with war propaganda splayed across his walls.

'Where are your family?' I asked Mamadou, anxiety evident in my voice. 'I thought they would be here too.'

'But they are here!' he protested, dragging on a freshly rolled spliff, the size of a small firework. 'All around here,' he gestured to the compound. 'This is my family. My parents, my sisters, my brothers. Only my wife and children live in Bamako. Hey, chill out, you want some dope?'

I turned down the proffered joint. Being an asthmatic, inhaling even a joss stick can make me wheezy. 'Are you selling this hash?' I asked.

'Yes, just a bit to friends and colleagues. I do it as a favour really. I can buy a chunk for CFA 5,000 in Bamako and sell it off bit by bit here. Life is hard. Driving doesn't pay a lot. I need any extra I can get.' He punched my arm playfully. 'Hey, *petit frère*, I'm a Rasta man, I love Bob Marley. I believe there is nothing wrong with dope.'

'What about the police. Isn't it serious to sell dope here?'

'The police! Ah, *petit frère*, I sell this to the police too! We are in the middle of nowhere. I am a Soninké, we trade with everyone.'

I pointed at the war poster and asked Mamadou where he got it. 'I can't remember,' he said, a little rattled by my questions. 'There's lots of them. I am a Rasta. I hate the war in Afghanistan and Iraq. I believe in peace.'

At this moment an elderly woman with pendulous blue earrings pulled back the door curtain and peered in. Her dark face lit up when she saw Mamadou. She walked up to him and touched his cheek. She turned to me and smiled, putting her hand on her heart. I did the same. She spoke to me. I understood nothing but could see that she exuded a quiet dignity. The old woman was Mamadou's mother and, seeing her, I relaxed completely. My pang of paranoia had been unfounded. Mamadou was not a drug-dealing Taliban extremist, but a family-minded peacenik, dealing out spliffs the same way Del Boy Trotter might dodgy toasters.

When the old lady left, I lay down on the bed, surrounded by a fug of aromatic smoke. Through a gap in the curtain I could see nocturnal clouds drifting through the darkness. Soon I was asleep.

* * *

The following morning I woke at first light. Mamadou was already up, chiselling at his hash. He gestured to a yellow water bucket by the door and told me I could shower with it. I walked across the compound to the mud-walled washroom. I poured the cold water over me and scrubbed off the grime from yesterday's journey.

By the time I finished the courtyard was a hive of activity. Two young girls were using long poles to pound millet into what looked like huge wooden egg cups. They threw the poles in the air and whammed them down repeatedly, occasionally clapping their hands between throws. An old woman with tribal scars on her forehead milked a goat, while two young boys scattered scraps of bread for the rest of the herd.

Three teenage girls appeared, each with a bucket on her head. Two poured some water for the cow, while the youngest of the group filled a trough for the chickens and doves. An old man sat in a deck-chair watching a young woman paint her feet with black dye. The sun was up but still shrouded in a pall of dust, looking more like a moon that refused to go down.

I drank some tea with Mamadou's parents and ate a hunk of warm, doughy bread. Malian bread was consistently delicious, no matter how remote the setting. As I watched the goings on in the courtyard it made me feel profoundly happy. So far the malaise of the bigger West African towns had been distressing, too many bored souls slouched around with nothing to do, no purpose in the world. Here in Nara there was stark poverty – some of the children had distended stomachs, some of the adults had hacking coughs – but everyone had a role, the whole place buzzed with a gentle urgency.

I took a few photos, trying to capture family life. I felt sure if Mungo Park had been able to carry a camera, he would have snapped similar scenes. The courtyard had a timeless quality. The goat milker, the silent elders, the three palm trees, the lone cow, the doves and chickens, the children balancing water buckets on their heads, the laughter, and all the time the pounding of the millet – *whump, whump, whump* – West Africa's steady and imperishable heartbeat.

* * *

Later on in the morning I went in search of Sandra, the American lady Mamadou had talked about.

Walking through the sandy streets, it was clear Nara was not a pretty place. There was a large, haunted-looking mosque but no hotel, no town square and no handsome civic buildings. All the fringing acacia bushes had plastic and other rubbish snagged on them. Although families kept their own courtyards shipshape, the place as a whole appeared run down.

Unsurprisingly, Sandra was the only Westerner living in Nara. Outside her gate sat a young soldier listening to the football on his radio. Mali had just beaten Guinea and he was clearly in a good mood. He smiled and handed me a cup of tea, which I sat drinking while he looked for Sandra.

When Sandra appeared I knew my presence would be an imposition. She was immediately tight-lipped and firmly on her guard. When I told her about Mungo Park and my journey, she told me she had no idea who he was: Mamadoo had got that one wrong. I felt rather embarrassed, as if I had tracked her down purely as a desert oddity, a lone *toubab* going troppo in this far corner of the world.

Sandra sat down between me and the soldier; we all looked into the distance, a plain of skeletal trees and scrub. I turned towards her. She was fortyish, heavy set, ghostly pale with a helmet of home-barbered hair.

'How did you get here?' she asked shyly. 'We don't get many visitors.'

'I took the bus from Mourdiah . . .'

'You took the bus! Oh my, I've lived here a long time and I've never done that. I always fly to the little airstrip. I've heard the bus is very dangerous.'

'No, not too bad,' I lied, making out that Mamadou's driving hadn't scared me witless. 'And the driver even puts you up for the night.'

This revelation seemed to soften Sandra and she began to relax. She told me she was from rural Iowa but had always been fascinated by Africa. After securing an agricultural degree in her hometown she had flown out to Bamako and worked for an NGO, advising on crop and vegetable growing.

'Six years in Bamako and I'd had enough of the city,' she said, still looking out into the bush. 'I've always been more at home in the boondocks. Nara is about as far out as you can go. I've been here eight years now.'

'Isn't it tough out here on your own?'

'I'm not on my own!' she countered. 'I have a whole town

surrounding me! And it's not tough for me. It's tough for the Africans. They are the ones who have to put up with the poverty. I can escape any time. I choose not to but I could if I wanted.'

It soon became clear Sandra was not some washed up eccentric or social outcast, but a person who hoped to make a difference. As we chatted several Africans stopped to chat to her – a cocky child, an elderly man supported by a stick and a young mother who had just been deserted by her philandering husband. Sandra knew them all by name and spoke perfect Bambara, good Fulani and a smidgen of Arabic. She asked them all about their families, their problems, their lives. The transformation in her among Africans was amazing. The closed, suspicious Sandra became a back-slapping, joke-cracking, problem-solving natural.

As we talked Sandra showed me around her vegetable patch. Onions, marrows, potatoes, carrots, tomatoes and a patch of broccoli, the latter a new experiment, all flourished. It seemed incredible all these plants were sprouting up from what was little more than watered sand. Sandra explained that this time, early February, was the most productive for vegetables. Millet was a winner out here too. It could be harvested within 80 days of planting and its deep roots meant it needed little rainfall, unlike the more demanding maize, which struggled in this semi desert.

When we slumped back down into deck-chairs, I talked a little about my walk with Bubakar and the wandering Mauritanian boy we had met.

Sandra said it was a typical time for young men in West Africa to be on the move. The harvest had been collected, money was in the bank and there was a lull before the planting season. It was a time for marriages, celebrations or else a chance for fortunes to be sought elsewhere, especially on the Ivory Coast. Mauritanians often headed south.

She said that Soninké men, like Mamadou, were also very go-getting and travelled far and wide to make a buck. The Bambara tended to be more laid back and sedentary, and the Fulani usually stayed at home to tend their livestock.

'How often do you head home?' I asked.

'Oh, once in a while,' Sandra said, sipping on a fresh cup of tea. 'I try to see my family every year. But my life is here now. I live very simply.'

She told me she had no air-con, no fan, and often slept outside. Her one luxury was a fridge run by a generator. She regularly travelled to remote villages, spending nights in the wild, checking on the local millet projects. She said projects in the villages were easier to run than in the towns, as you only dealt with one chief, not lots, making the politics more straightforward.

I asked Sandra who she turned to when times got tough. Was she at all religious?

'I have a quiet faith in God,' she admitted. 'Unlike the West, with all its wealth and distractions there are very few choices here. Life is hard, desert people need to believe in something more than just this,' she jutted her chin towards the horizon, 'whatever their religion.' She stopped as her pet collie nuzzled up to her leg. 'Oh, and if all fails I have Sheppy here. I don't miss home. I've made some good friends in Nara.'

'Do you think you'll end up back in America?'

'Oh my, oh my.' She laughed quietly. 'America's a different place from when I left it. I've been in the bush a long time! Some of my values have changed, I'm very self-reliant.' She paused for a while, and kicked at the sand with her sandals. 'When September 11 happened my thoughts turned to home. It was a horrible thing that shocked the world. Terrible. Quite terrible. Three thousand adults died in the Twin Towers, but people forget at least that number of children die every day of starvation across the world. Every day. I think my place is here. West Africa is so poor.* I can't do much, but I can do a little.'

We were both silent for a while, lost in thought, sipping our tea. Once I'd drained my cup, I thanked Sandra and made to leave. I felt very grateful to have met someone like her.

'Hey,' she said, abruptly, 'as you're here, you should go to the horse race tonight. I've got stuff to do, but my friend Sammy always goes. He'll take you. I'll get him to pick you up on his motorbike.'

* * *

Sammy, a wiry, hyperactive fellow with cowrie shells threaded in his hair, skidded to a halt outside Mamadou's courtyard on Dune Buster, his motorbike. Mamadou and I both scrunched onto the bike's ruptured saddle and off we revved. Initially Sammy struggled to keep control, before Dune Buster hit its stride and skimmed over the deep sand. I grabbed onto the back rail, my face jellied by the G force, my eyes smarting from all the sun and dust.

Within ten minutes we had reached the racecourse. Well, I say racecourse, but it was no more than an oval swathe of scrubland with random clusters of spectators. The atmosphere was electric. Horses were everywhere, some dowdy and quiet, others primped, prancing and raring to race. Women in bright

* Africa dominated the bottom leagues in the UN's 2004 National Human Development Report which draws on a complex web of statistics to measure the quality of life in different countries across the world. Trailing the list of 177 countries with the poorest quality of life was Sierra Leone (still recovering from its civil war) followed by Niger, Burkina Faso and Mali, all in West Africa. Norway topped the list as the best place to live, with America coming in sixth and the UK twelfth.

flowery dresses sang Gospel-sounding harmonies accompanied by a band of *tamba* drummers.

Most of the thousand-strong crowd stood. The only seats were for Nara's elite, the elders in black turbans, the younger set in polo shirts and sunglasses. Sammy and Mamadou were clearly well known in Nara and had a stake in one of the horses. They introduced me to some of their friends and we all pushed our way to the start line.

'Can I bet?' I asked Mamadou.

'You,' he said, smirking. 'Of course not.'

He explained that the only bets were made by the horse-owners. They each paid a lump sum to enter their horse in a race, and the winner won the grand total. When I told him about the role of bookies at European horse races Mamadou found the whole idea vulgar.

'Most people here cannot afford even the smallest bet,' he stressed. 'They come here for fun, to meet friends, to cheer the horses. During the dry season a race is held every other Sunday. It's a great event.'

Before the first race the 20 riders paraded their horses in a circle for the spectators to observe. All the jockeys were teenage boys, no more than 15 years old. Most rode barefoot, clad in bibs of canary yellow emblazoned with their number – a touch of pure Ascot.

By the time the jockeys were lined up, the crowd was in a state of incipient anarchy. Fists were being raised, synchronized cheers erupting, some of the more emphatic fans trying to burst through the cordoned area. All that prevented it bubbling into a full scale riot were the soldiers, each armed with an acacia branch and heartily thrashing anyone who broke through the lines. This proved most effective. Forget truncheons and tear gas, a well-aimed thorny stick was enough to quell even the most high-octane spectator.

The starter's white flag snapped down and the horses bolted towards the falling sun. Two of the jockeys careered off in the wrong direction. Several hyena-like dogs joined in, nipping at the stragglers' fetlocks. Then all was quiet as the sound of frantic hooves faded into the distance. After five minutes the pack thundered back into view. The acacia-wielding soldiers held the spectators at bay as the winning stallion breasted the finishing tape in a whorl of golden dust.

* * *

When the last race was over Sammy ferried Mamadou and me back home on Dune Buster. We bundled into the courtyard, high on adrenalin. Mamadou's mother had prepared us all a meal of mutton and couscous. We sat outside in the cool twilight, chewing the sinewy meat and drinking bottles of Castel beer.

'Cheers,' I said to Mamadou, raising my bottle. 'Thank you for bringing me to Nara.'

'Not cheers,' replied Mamadou, 'here we say Mali Mali. And when you say it you must look the other person in the eye.'

'Why?'

'Well, if you say Mali Mali and don't look the other person in the eye it means you cannot make love with a girl for seven years.'

'Seven years!'

'Oh yes,' Mamadou laughed and told me the story surrounding the strange toast. Apparently it stemmed back to the time when Mali's corrupt ex-president Moussa Traoré paid a state visit to China. Traoré had attended a banquet in Beijing with China's then president Deng Xiaoping. Deng had raised his glass to make a toast and said 'Chin Chin!' Traoré, thinking Deng had simply said China twice, allegedly replied: 'Mali, Mali'. Realizing his mistake, Traoré had then spilt his drink all over his suit.

'Traoré was a bad man, a dictator,' explained Mamadou. 'He squandered millions of our country's money. Malians like to joke that he used some of the money on his cleaning bill after spilling his drink in China.'

'He made such a fool of himself that night,' said Sammy, pulling up the collar of his combat jacket, 'that no woman wanted to be with him for seven years.'

It was a funny if highly improbable story of which I heard various differing versions during my time in Mali. I suspect it was simply a nice way of satirizing Traoré's corruption. It is a testament to the Malian people that rather than being strung up after a coup in 1991, Traoré served a prison term and now lives quietly in Bamako. Sammy and Mamadou both approved of Amadou Toumani Touré, the country's current president, regarding him as popular and benign.

Before long we had drunk several bottles of beer and put the world to rights. I had not touched alcohol since Gambia and it went straight to my head. Mamadou and Sammy made constant toasts. 'Mali Mali!' they repeated, chinking bottles. As I became ever hazier I forgot about the eye-contact rule.

'Do you have a girlfriend, Tom?' asked Mamadou at the end of the evening.

'No,' I slurred. 'My last girlfriend, ahh, she was so lovely. But she's with an Italian surgeon now.'

'That's just as well,' said Mamadou, holding back his laughter.

'Why?'

'Because, *mon petit frère*, now you cannot make love with any girl for the next 49 *years*!'

* * *

The following morning, I looked butter-faced and hollow-eyed with a mouth as fallow as my surroundings. Only after I drank some iodined water did I feel a little better. I vaguely remembered the previous night and Mamadou's prophesy. I tried to weigh up which was worse, a half-century of celibacy or the prospect of a ten-hour mini-bus journey to Bamako with Mamadou at the wheel.

After some millet porridge we drove to the bus depot. As was the case all over West Africa, Mamadou would have to wait until his mini-bus was full before heading off. Only that way could he justify the fuel costs.

Mamadou started touting customers at 8 a.m. but it was not until mid-afternoon that we were ready, the little bus groaning with luggage and excess passengers. This time I wimped out and paid for a front seat, sandwiched between Mamadou and a heavy, stolid-faced mother cradling a baby.

We gunned off down the long dusty road. Up above, scarves of cloud, brittle as smoke, hovered over the blue horizon. We passed donkey carts and solitary herdsmen, rallying their animals before sundown. I fell into a head-lolling doze and when I woke we had stopped.

'There is a machine working on the road,' said Mamadou, pointing up ahead. 'Look at all the dust. I can't see a thing, I must stop for a bit.' It surprised me Mamadou had demonstrated such caution, although just to show he hadn't completely relinquished his old ways, he pulled out a spliff from his top pocket.

While we waited many of the passengers took the chance to pray. It was a beautiful sight, all these colourfully dressed men and women prostrate on the sand. The dust stirred up by the bulldozers enveloped them in a sepia haze, making the whole landscape look ethereal and other-worldly.

Once the dust had settled Mamadou drove gingerly on. I dozed again and when I woke was glad to find we were back on bitumen, the first since the road out of Kayes. It was dark now and ahead of us a thin band of trees was ablaze. The flames looked far from the road but when we drove past, there was a brief whoosh of heat, like that from an open oven. It was nearly midnight and Mamadou was thrashing the mini-bus, which now sounded like a wounded beast. At least we were on the fringes of Bamako.

Oil drums blockaded the road ahead: a checkpoint. Mamadou shouted at a uniformed man standing sentinel, as if to say, hey, it's me, clear the way. Nothing was going to slow him down. The mini-bus chicaned past at some speed, bashing into one of the drums and sending it barrelling over an embankment.

We drove on through Bamako, which was as deathly quiet and meagrely lit as any West African village at this time of night. Only the odd concrete building gave any indication it was a capital city.

One of the African passengers began shouting at Mamadou, ridiculing him for running the road block. Mamadou shouted back. It all became very fraught and at the next checkpoint several soldiers ordered Mamadou out of the vehicle. They shouted at him and, as usual, he shouted back. Everyone began shouting at everyone else: passengers, soldiers, even the baby joined in. One of the soldiers asked for my identification. I handed over my passport. He said to me: 'England. David Beckham,' and handed it back, as if he now knew everything about me.

One of the soldiers pushed Mamadou. Mamadou handed him some money and then jumped back in the driver's seat cursing horribly. After five minutes we pulled up at a street full of food hawkers. Lots of passengers were still shouting at Mamadou. He looked exhausted from all the driving, close to snapping point.

I drank a coffee while I waited for my pack to be thrown from the roof. *Just a Minute* was playing on the World Service on the coffee-maker's short-wave radio. I grinned, Nicholas Parsons' voice sounded wonderfully incongruous. Finally my pack thwumped down. I grabbed it and hailed a taxi.

'See you, Mamadou,' I shouted, waving at him. 'Thanks for everything.'

'Hey, *petit frère*,' he replied from the mini-bus roof. Now that most of the passengers had gone he was relaxed again. 'Don't forget to send some pictures of my family. And remember, 49 years!'

Soon my taxi was gliding over a bridge. As there was no other traffic I asked the driver to pull over. I jumped out and hauled myself onto one the bridge's girders, my heart thumping. I looked down and there it was. A dull band of mercury flickering in the moonlight: the River Niger.

CHAPTER 11

BAMAKO

MUNGO PARK'S own road to Bamako was a far more troubled one than mine. After praising God for delivering him to the banks of the Niger, he found himself in yet another tricky spot. Mansong, the King of Ségou, believing Park might be a European spy, forbade him to cross the river he had just so triumphantly drunk from.

Indeed, the explorer's initial rapture was to be bitterly short-lived. He was left sitting under a tree as the light faded, alone and afraid, keeping half an eye out for lions and other wild beasts. Once again, a tribal woman proved his saviour. This Good Samaritan, on her way home from working in the fields, cooked him up a fish supper and provided him with a bed.

That evening, as Park tried to sleep, one of the other women in the family compound sang a sweet, melancholy song to capture the moment:

The winds roared, and the rains fell —
The poor white man, faint and weary, came and sat under
    our tree —

125

He has no mother to bring him milk; no wife to grind his
  corn.
Chorus – let us pity the white man; no mother has he.

Park was so grateful for the hospitality that the following
morning he cut off two buttons from his waistcoat and presented them as a gift.

Soon Park's future looked brighter. Although King Mansong
still refused to receive him, he agreed to provide the explorer
with 5,000 cowrie* shells and a guide as far as Sansanding,
some 30 miles downriver. Despite being personally cold-
shouldered by Mansong, Park is perked up by the offer of the
shells and the guide, and describes the king as a 'benevolent
prince'. It dawns on the explorer that Mansong may have forbidden him entry for his own good, knowing that a white man
would be vulnerable to attack in Ségou.

Before setting off again, Park told his new guide about his
adventures. His guide was clearly surprised by all Park had
endured to reach the Niger. Displaying perfect logic and unin-
tentional wit, he asked the explorer: 'Are there no rivers in
your own country?'

Walking on from Ségou, Park was impressed by the surrounding landscape thinking, almost certainly with a tweak of
nostalgia, that it bore a strong resemblance to rural England.
As he headed north though, the lushness diluted and he realized
he was once again nearing the land of the Moors. At Sansanding this was confirmed when a jostling mob squeezed around
him 'like spectators at an execution'.

The Moors insisted Park say prayers at the town mosque
but, being a devout Christian, he was reluctant. Instead, the

* Park mentions that 100 cowrie shells would be enough to support
himself and his horse for a day.

village chief let Park perch on a high seat in front of the mosque until sunset so that everyone could gawp at him. The bumptious crowd also wanted to witness him eat raw eggs, as they believed this was the staple diet for Europeans. Although not subjected to Ludamar levels of cruelty, Park was still treated as little more than an exotic plaything.

After this mild humiliation, Park moves on down the Niger. He almost stumbles upon a lethargic lion, and on another occasion is amazed to see a 'camelopard' or giraffe. But, despite these occasional thrills, Park is increasingly worn down by the mosquitoes and the intense heat. On 19 July, after being shunned from the village of Modiboo, Park's wretchedly tired horse collapses and he is forced to leave him to die:

'I surveyed the poor animal as he lay panting on the ground,' he wrote, 'with sympathetic emotion; for I could not suppress the sad apprehension that I should myself, in a short time, lie down and perish in the same manner, of fatigue and hunger.'

Six days after leaving Ségou, Park reached the busy town of Silla. It was here the derring-do explorer threw in the towel. He had heard Timbuktu was not far, perhaps only two weeks' journey, but his chances of making it were slim, especially now the tropical rains were making travelling conditions miserable. He had the sense to realize if he was to die now all his achievements to date would be worthless.

Park was exhausted, half-naked, demoralized and racked with fever. The further north he penetrated into Moorish territory the more his life was in jeopardy. Besides, he had no money to pay for guides and canoes. Park was not a quitter, but he knew the road ahead spelt suicide. Information about the rest of the Niger was also scant. The natives simply told him that the great river 'runs to the world's end'.

Park knew the return journey to Gambia would be an unspeakable slog, but his only chance of making it home, his only chance of glory. He turned around and stumbled back through the wilderness. On he plied, through dense forest and flooded savannah. At times villagers chased him with sticks or slammed their gates in his face, while others welcomed him and asked him to write them *saphies*, or charms.

At the port of Koulikoro, some 30 miles from Bamako, Park scribbled out the Lord's Prayer as a charm for his Bambaran host. The superstitious man then washed off Park's words with some water and drank them down, before licking clean the writing board, to make sure the white man's magic was wholly effective.

By 23 August Park trudged into Bamako but did not stay long, 'disappointed to find it only a middling town', despite its famous salt market. Two days later disaster struck. While walking west across some exposed rocky ground he spotted a posse of armed men. At first he thought they were elephant-hunters, but when they approached him one grabbed his hat and another drew a knife and cut at his waistcoat buttons.

Park was stripped naked and when he tried to retrieve his precious compass, one of the bandits cocked his musket. The thieves left him only his threadbare shirt and trousers but just as they were riding off threw back his hat. This hat was, in fact, Park's most precious item as it contained his travel notes in its crown. Fortunately the bandits had believed his notes might be magical and had discarded them in fear.

By now Park had reached the nadir of his journey. There he sat, naked, febrile, alone, near surrender. Fate had surely played its trump card. But then, as usual with Park, something put the fire back in his belly. It was a most unusual but effective *deus ex machina*: a small clump of moss. Seeing this delicate plant survive in such a hard place, inspired him to soldier on, 'assured that relief was at hand'. Tough, destiny-crazed men like Ledyard and Houghton had perished on their way to the

Niger, never to make it home. Could this young Scot, still only 25 years old, finally break the African Association's run of bad luck?

* * *

The Bamako I witnessed on my first morning was a very different place to the 'middling town' Park had passed through. Now with a population nudging a million,* it was in a state of upbeat flux. After the tranquillity of Mamadou's courtyard in Nara, the capital's boisterous streets rudely invaded my desert-calmed senses.

The Malian capital was certainly a city of smelly contrasts. One minute I would be walking amid blossomy gardens shaded by mango trees, the next zigzagging through a warren of corrugated shacks, their drains thick with scummy water. At times the whole city seemed enveloped in a fug of tainted air. Desperate hucksters would try to sell me phone cards or toothpaste or magic ointments that could treble my sperm count.

Although there were subtle indications Bamako was a capital city – Soviet-style high rises, traffic jams, billboards warning against AIDS – it came across as one sprawling and chaotic market. I opted to stay away from the central hubbub at a quiet Catholic mission on the south bank of the river. Crossing over the bridge each day I would ogle down at the Niger with its ever-shifting cargoes: a reflected cloud, part of a bamboo fence, a fishing boat, a drowned goat.

The word Bamako actually means 'crocodile river', but the capital's crocs had fled the city long ago, many towards the Niger's fast flowing source in the highlands of Sierra Leone.

---

* During Park's visit, Bamako's population was around 6,000.

When I looked down from the bridge though, it was always towards the east, where, some 2,000 miles away the river segued gently into the Gulf of Guinea.

This, the Niger's mouth, had been the principal goal of Mungo Park on his second expedition to West Africa. Much of this ill-fated follow-up journey had been undertaken in canoes, the first of which were launched from Bamako in the summer of 1805. I intended to track down a canoe too, or at least a pirogue, a sort of large West African dugout, and paddle off, if not to the 'world's end', then at least to Timbuktu.

* * *

Before pirogue shopping, I had a number of routine chores to deal with. I secured some detailed river maps, cashed travellers' cheques and applied for an extension to my one-month visa, saying a mute prayer as I saw my passport embedded in a land-slide of paperwork.

Finally I paid a visit to the British Embassy to find out if there had been any updates about Christian Velten. On arrival I was thoroughly frisked. My asthma inhaler (clearly suspected of containing toxic gas) and Swiss Army knife (equipped with toothpick and nail file) were apprehended before I could cross the heavily guarded lawn, where a Union Jack snapped in the breeze.

The embassy was manned by a cheery, barrel-chested Gambian called Benjamin, who liked to say 'God save the Queen' a lot, perhaps inspired by the portrait of Her Majesty above his desk. On the opposite wall was a photo of the well-groomed British ambassador, who resided in Senegal. Benjamin explained Mali was too remote and thinly populated to warrant an ambassador all to herself.

It turned out there was fresh information on Christian Velten. The young adventurer had last been seen, according to

Benjamin, not at the remote town of Kita, but actually in Bamako. After their argument, Velten had apparently split with his Gambian guide and walked on by himself. While in the capital he had been seen asking around for a boat to tackle the Niger.

'Christian's mother has called me a few times,' said Benjamin from behind his immaculate desk. 'I feel very sorry for her. I am a father. I can think of nothing worse than not knowing where your child is.'

Benjamin, gesturing to a wall map of West Africa, told me posters of Velten had been stuck up in key areas all along Mungo Park's route from The Gambia to Nigeria. There had been one possible sighting of the young Englishman in Gharum Rharous, a remote desert town near to Timbuktu, but this was now believed to have been somebody else.

'Mrs Velten told me Christian likes to live with the local people,' Benjamin told me, pouring us both a coffee. 'Apparently one time in Jamaica he ran low on money. He moved to a village and survived off sardines for several weeks. His mother thinks it's possible he's gone native, although he's usually reliable about staying in touch.'

When I asked about potential dangers on the road ahead, Benjamin rumpled his forehead. With the solemnity of an exam invigilator, he reached across his desk and handed me a fax.

GERMAN TOURISTS KIDNAPPED IN SOUTHERN SAHARA, read the headline.

The story concerned seven German tourists who had been kidnapped a fortnight before by gun-wielding Islamic extremists near Timbuktu. The hostages had been released within 24 hours, having been forced to promise they would convey some of the kidnappers' views to the people of Europe.

'This should not be a problem for you,' Benjamin reassured me, as I scanned the bleary message. 'Kidnappers always target groups in overland vehicles, four-wheel drives. Independent travellers like Christian and you should be safe from this sort of thing. If you are travelling by canoe, or bus or donkey, they aren't likely to be interested.'

'What about the Tuaregs?'

'They haven't kidnapped tourists for several years.' Benjamin paused and smiled weakly. 'The place you might need to be careful, my friend, is Nigeria. Ask about the situation when you get nearer the border.'

* * *

The good news was that for some of my journey, I would not be travelling alone. My oldest friend, James Fry, was turning up in Bamako any minute. I was delighted but amazed James had agreed to come. For the last 15 years he had been working as a manager at London Underground. The thought of James, a portly *bon viveur*, taking a month-long sabbatical to paddle down the Niger seemed most unlikely.

'Of course, I'll come!' James had announced, as we supped on pints at his East Finchley local shortly before my departure. 'This is just what I need.'

'You want to come to Africa,' I replied, choking on my Guinness. 'But I've only given you ten days notice.'

'Ten days,' mused James, rubbing his princely jowls. 'For you that's unexpectedly generous. Almost disappointingly free of spontaneity.'

'What about your work, James?'

'What about my work?' James crunched vigorously on a pork scratching. 'I need to change my life. I'm fed up with London, chained to the same job for years. Look at me. I'm plump as a bloody mole.' He rubbed his expansive girth, while reaching for another chunk of offal. 'My girlfriend's just dumped me. I've got no house, no children. Nothing. So, tell me, what have I got to lose?'

'What about pensions and bonuses and all that jazz?' I suggested. 'The greasy pole of promotion.'

'To hell with the greasy pole. It's time to uproot it, vandalize it, dance a lap dance around it. Damn it, Tom, I've been in a rut for years.' James was on a roll. 'Now I'm finally doing something about it and you're urging caution. You! Of all people, constantly buggering off with mules or bicycles.' He paused and fired up a roll-up cigarette. He now had the packet of scratchings in one hand and the rolly in the other, nicotine and cholesterol battling for his affection. His Guinness had already been drained.

'If I stay with the Underground,' James added. 'I'll be buried with the Underground. I've had some great years in London but now it's time to make a break for the light.'

'Even if that means following a Scotsman called Mungo to the world's end.'

'Especially,' James exhaled extravagantly, 'if it means following a Scotsman called Mungo to the world's end. I will settle for nothing less.'

'Bloody hell, you're serious.'

'Never more so. I just need to give work a month's notice.'

'Well, I'm heading out to Gambia next week. You could join me in Bamako in mid-February.'

'Excellent,' James tipped the remaining pork scratchings into his mouth. He paused mid-crunch: 'Where the hell is Bamako anyway?'

* * *

James had threatened to leave London before, but usually in a state of Friday night, Guinness-fuelled pique that had been allayed by the following Monday. That night in Finchley I sensed he meant it; and when I checked my emails at a Bamako internet café I knew he meant it. His flight was due in three days. James was taking a big risk to join me, sacrificing everything that was familiar to him. I was touched and grateful but I hoped he'd made the right decision.

While waiting for James I hung out at the Catholic mission in Badalabogou. It proved a relaxing spot, the rooms were Spartan but clean and cheap and the staff friendly. Every morning I was woken to choral music, the dawn filled with sweet protracted Alleluias and Amens from the nearby chapel.

I got to know the local hawkers, the waif-like girl who touted bananas near the rubbish tip, the workaholic baker who fired up his al fresco oven at all hours and the English-speaking Ghanaian family who I joined to watch Mali play Morocco on their TV one evening. Mali lost 4–1, the whole of Bamako letting out an agonized 'ahhh' at the referee's final whistle.

The other lodgers at the Catholic mission were residents in Bamako, rather than fellow travellers. There was Florence, a trainee nurse from Brussels, with the wholesome good looks of a Hogarth dairy maid. There was puckish Raph, a French engineer, who had taken time out to learn *djembe* (a type of Malian drum) and smart, intense Lilly, a Parisienne, who was completing a PhD on the effects of female circumcision in Mali. Then there was Julian, a mysterious Belgian, who chain-smoked Gauloise and never said a word.

We often shared evening meals together, prepared in the stygian gloom of the kitchen, where a resident rat slalomed around our flip-flops. One Friday night Lilly shepherded us all to a bar run by a Malian friend of hers. We sat on a mat eating sweet potatoes and dried fish.

The usually chipper nurse Florence was exhausted, her pupils suspended in nets of red wire. She had been dealing with stuff in Mali that she hadn't thought possible for a trainee nurse. That particular day she had acted as a midwife's assistant during a breach birth. The child, a baby girl, had died and the mother was still very sick.

'That's the worst thing about Mali,' Florence told us, running a hand through her dark hair. 'I'm used to seeing old people die in Brussels, but here it's the children. A quarter of all Malian babies are dead before their fifth birthday. A quarter! Fuck it,' she said, half crying, half laughing. 'I'm always bursting into tears here. The Malians cope with death, it's all around them, a child, a sister, a brother, a cousin. They've all lost someone way before their time. I'm just not used to it.'

'Why do so many children die here?' I asked.

'Malaria is a big killer,' replied Florence. 'Dysentery, TB, malnutrition. There's little medical back up in remote areas.'

'What about AIDS?' said Raph, nibbling at the remains of a capitaine fish carcass. 'I've heard it's not so bad here, compared to other parts of Africa.'

Florence explained only two per cent of Mali's population were HIV positive. This was in sharp contrast to somewhere like South Africa where one in five adults was infected, with over 1,500 new people becoming HIV positive every day. She stressed that in Mali it was the women who were most jeopardized. In a male dominant society, where husbands could take multiple wives, it was hard for young girls to say no to sex. Before their twentieth birthday at least half of all rural women in Mali were mothers. Another problem was seasonal migrations. Often young, job-seeking Malian men jaunted off to the Ivory Coast, the country with the highest HIV rates in West Africa, and then came home infected.

'Is it that hard for women here?' I asked. 'All the ones I've met seem so tough, so independent.'

'West African women are very proud,' said Lilly, who had been quiet until then. 'Considering how hard things are for them they are extraordinary. Many Malian girls never even get a chance to go to school.'

'Why?'

'Oh, you know. Tradition, poverty, staying home to tend the elderly or the animals.'

Lilly was sure things were changing, but slowly. She mentioned a high-profile story in the news about a woman who had just secured a major job organizing Mali's local elections, something that would have been unthinkable even a few years ago. A man would have got it every time.

But Lilly's main concern, and the focus of her PhD, was that over 90 per cent of Malian women were compulsorily circumcised. The operations varied hugely, Lilly told us, from a small cut on the clitoris to the dreadful-sounding infibulation, or the entire removal of the external genitalia. Female circumcision was widespread throughout West Africa. Even in countries like Senegal and Niger that had recently made the practice illegal, it often continued covertly.

'Some tribes think a woman who has not been circumcised is a disgrace, a dishonour to the family,' said Lilly, shaking her head. 'With this sort of view it's hard to stop it. It's the attitude towards women that really needs to change.'

'What age are girls circumcised?'

'Most used to be cut near to marriage,' Lilly said softly, 'but there were complaints it was too painful. Now over half the girls in Mali are circumcised as babies, soon after birth. The pain is milder but it's a far more delicate operation. Poorly done circumcisions can cause life-long pain. Things like infections, problems peeing, child birth complications. In villages with no scalpels, a razor or a piece of glass is used to operate. There was a move to have all the circumcisions done in hospitals. This has been banned now. I'm glad. Just because it takes place in a hospital doesn't make it okay. It needs to be outlawed completely.'

'Do you sympathize at all?' I asked. 'You're not worried you are poking your nose into a culture you don't understand?'

'Not at all.' Lilly flicked her wrist in dismissal. 'In my PhD I try to cover all sides of the story. Some men tell me female circumcision creates happy, loyal families; some of the local women say the same thing. But to me it all comes down to female subjugation. That's the bottom line. It's done to make sex less pleasurable for a woman, so she stays with her husband. I'm sorry, but it stinks.

'I wouldn't dream of trying to change most tribal rituals. But this genital mutilation is just barbaric, and so common. People think it's only a Muslim thing. But this is not the case. Female circumcision goes on in Ghana and Kenya, where there are large Christian populations. It's more a tribal ritual. I always try to show respect to other cultures, but regarding this, I just can't. It disgusts me.'

There was silence for a bit. Mopeds zipped by, somewhere in the distance a dog began barking.

'Oh, Jesus,' said Raph, breaking the mood. 'And I thought I'd had a tough day playing drums. Come on, we all need to unwind. I know just the place.'

*   *   *

We ended up in the far west of the city, in an open-air club called The Hogon. Florence, Lilly, Raph and I surrounded a wicker table close to the stage where a band were tuning up. In front of us sat six cross-legged drummers and to their rear a rank of *kora* players, all absorbed in strumming their intricate, lute-like instruments.

A singer swathed in a purple robe dominated the stage. He looked so slight in his billowy costume that when he danced he might have been floating. Lilly explained the man was a *griot*, a teller of stories, an itinerant singer. All over West Africa, a place where history is often preserved in stories rather than the written word, *griots* helped keep the folklore alive. I remembered Mungo Park had encountered several 'singing men' on his travels, many of them performing around village camp fires.

This *griot* turned out to be the warm-up act and his haunting stories were followed by a far more upbeat performer — a spitting image of a black Joe Cocker. He even sang with Cocker's same gravelly panache, as if he'd just swallowed a pumice stone washed down with Jack Daniels. Smartly dressed couples descended on the dance floor.

I danced for a while with Florence. Soon a Malian friend of hers, an anaesthetist from her hospital, joined us. I've always enjoyed dancing but have a disturbing lack of rhythm. Florence wasn't much better, gyrating about like a cheerleader on amphetamines. But Florence's friend had an internal pulse. He was a plump, vivacious man dressed in a sort of black poncho. He swayed and shimmered to the music with such elegance, I began to feel embarrassed by my own ungainly jerks and bounces.

I stepped down for a while and watched the dance floor from the bar. Rather than each dancer thrashing about to an individual rhythm, they all moved as one. This mass of swaying humanity looked like liquid, a silky sea of black, that ebbed and flowed, before draining away as each song ended, all the more splendid for its transience.

After a musical lull Florence and her friend grabbed me for

the last dance. We all joined hands and swung about in a woozy circle.

'This is Africa!' Florence's friend shouted. He was clearly boozed up. 'This is Africa!' he repeated delightedly, eyes a-google. Then once more, with increasing fervour: 'This is Africa!' as if the phrase was all his own, freshly minted. 'Yes, yes, Florence,' he said, swaying his arms in the air and breaking into laughter. 'Africa! Africa! Oh, Florence, you will never understand!'

* * *

The morning after, still groggy, I trawled Bamako for any trace of Mungo Park. I came up trumps in an obscure museum near the city centre where a stone mermaid with a vandalized tail reclined on the front lawn. Inside there were several topsy-turvy displays: cracked pots, a 1900 pirogue, an arsenal of fly swatters and, to my delight, a framed quote by Park.

The quote was nothing special, positively bland in fact, just a verbatim excerpt from his diary about Bamako's salt market. That said, it was my first contact with the explorer since leaving The Gambia: I was simply chuffed to see his name. When I asked the beige-uniformed museum guide about Park, he disappointedly, but quite justifiably, had no idea who I was talking about.

Once I had exhausted all my other Park avenues, I decided it was time to secure a pirogue. I had been advised at the Catholic mission that Bamako was a lousy place to do this: I would be better off at Koulikoro, some 30 miles downriver, where a flotilla of potential vessels awaited me.

Later that day I jumped off at Koulikoro's bus stop. The little port was nothing more than a mile-long line of higgledy-piggledy shops and shacks; but the Niger was far more lively here than at the capital. Piles of firewood, like giant crow's nests, lined the river front, while donkey carts groaning with sand and dried dung trundled back and forth.

I looked out over the river. Wooden boats, many loaded with pyramids of potatoes and melons, butted against each other in the soft current. Apart from the odd tiny dugout, hewn from a single tree, the rest of the fleet were pirogues, each at least 15 feet long and fused together in segments. Many of the boats were works of art, with elegantly pointed prows and hulls painted with psychedelic splotches.

Strangely, much of this motley armada was not owned by the Bozos. The Bozos, master fishermen who thought of the Niger as home, dominated great swathes of the river but not Koulikoro, which acted as a springboard for the Bambara people to trade their wood and vegetables up and down stream.

One such Bambara man was combing the river banks during my visit. He approached me in his Leeds United football shirt, his face lit up with a Cheshire cat grin.

'*Bonjour, monsieur, je m'appelle Karim,*' he said, extending a hand. '*Je suis Bambara. Tu aimes un bateau?*'

When I told Karim I wanted to buy a pirogue, he laughed. He said it would cost a fortune, in the region of CFA 500,000. What's more, because I was a *toubab* I would struggle to resell it for even half the price. Karim suggested he act as my guide. His father was Bambara, but his mother was a Bozo, so he knew the river intimately.

Karim revealed he had once ferried three Spaniards a hundred miles to Ségou but, other than this, very few tourists ever visited Koulikoro. Oh, and by the way, he added, there was also the *harmattan*, the fierce desert wind that whips south through the Sahara about now. This would be directly against us.

I insisted that I still wanted to paddle to Mopti, even though it was twice as far as Ségou, and that I would be accompanied by '*un grand ami*' (trying to make James sound more like a great friend than a huge one).

'*Comme tu veux, Thomas, pas de probleme.*' Karim slapped my back and ushered me on to his pirogue. I jumped across the hull into a foot of inky water. At least Karim wasn't attempting to disguise anything. Look, he was saying, this is clearly no fancy, sleek-hulled thoroughbred. No, this boat is a workhorse, bruised, scratched, perhaps even a little incontinent, but hey, she's sturdy, lived-in, full of character.

Karim explained James and I could paddle together at the prow, while he would steer with a pole from behind. We would camp wild or stay in Bozo villages, shop in local markets and cook over a camp fire. The journey should take about two weeks, possibly a bit more, and he would charge CFA 200,000 all in – a top deal.

After our negotiations, Karim lit a fire at the stern of his boat using some dried straw as kindling. He then took a stick and held a little can over the flames, which sent up a plume of black smoke. I imagined he was blessing the canoe, working up some positive karma before launch off.

Having known I wanted to travel by canoe in Africa I had done some homework before departing England. I knew many other cultures worshipped their canoes. The Mukogee Indians of North America, for instance, believe one of their gods descended by canoe from a hole in the sky, whereas the ancient Olmecs in Mexico were convinced the canoe was a celestial vessel, a link between the earth and the sky, enabling them to speak to their ancestors. These beliefs are not only tribal. To this day some Scottish trawler men remain fiercely superstitious, banning the colour green on deck and insisting their wives never use a washing machine the weekend before sailing out, as it might wash their souls away.

But with the Bozos, I drew a blank when it came to boat lore. I had read many other things about them though. That they lived in Egypt before settling on the Niger's banks some 5,000 years ago; that they still worshipped crocodiles and hunted hippos with poisoned spears; that they were neither stooges to Christianity nor Islam, maintaining a spiritual independence and that they were fishermen to the core, disdainful of those who worked on the land, so much so that they have a proverb: 'If you see a Bozo bent over, do not think he is working the earth, he is throwing up.'

It seemed the Bozos respected their river and the animals within it, more than their boats, and certainly more than dry land. Even so, having heard Bubakar's incessant prayers, seen a dead frog thrown down a well and witnessed Mamadou's 'Mali, Mali' toast, I was convinced Karim's little fire must symbolize something.

'Oh, it's a not magic fire,' said Karim, amused by my suspicions of *ju-ju*. 'I'm heating up some tar to plug up the leaks in the boat. Then I'll make some tea. Do you want a glass?'

Soon we were sitting on the pirogue's gunnels, sipping our tea. It was wonderfully quiet, the silence almost thickening as the sun fell over the water.

Before I left, Karim told me he needed to let his family know about our plan. All going well, he should be able to meet the following evening.

Karim proved as good as his word, although he did bring along an extra passenger, his wife, Fatima. I proved as good as my word too, although I not only brought along James (the heaviest I had ever seen him), but Raph, who had tired of drumming lessons and wanted a few days on the river.

Whatever happened, it was going to be one very crowded pirogue.

CHAPTER 12

TILTING AT WINDMILLS

ARMED ONLY with cowrie shells and waistcoat buttons Mungo Park was in no position to buy a canoe while traipsing up and down the Niger in 1796. Following his ambush by bandits near Bamako, even these were snatched from him, and he was left with nothing but his shirt, trousers and 'magical' hat. It was only thanks to his never say die attitude that Park continued to stagger west towards the Atlantic.

Ironically, it seemed the farther he peeled away from his beloved Niger (which forks south at Bamako) the easier his journey became. The night after his ambush he was warmly greeted by a village chief, who even promised to track down his pilfered belongings. Sure enough, a few days later, while resting in the nearby town of Wonda, Park was reunited with some of his clothes.

This generous act was all the more remarkable considering Wonda was suffering from near famine conditions. Being the rainy season with the harvest still many months off, hunger was rife. Things were so bad that Park witnessed women selling their sons off just to obtain food, while other families were forced to live on stewed maize blossom.

Moving on through the waterlogged landscape, Park finally reached the village of Kamalia, where he was put up by an affluent Muslim slave trader, Karfa Taura. His new host, who had never seen a white man before, not only supplied Park with a hut and two meals a day, but offered to let him accompany his slave caravan to the Gambia River once the rains had stopped. In return Park would have to repay Taura about £20 – the going price for a slave – when they reached the coast.

Park had the sense to realize he was on to a good thing. Taura even regularly visited the explorer's hut to check on his health. Other traders became jealous of Park's treatment and ugly rumours about the white man began to circulate. Months passed, Ramadan was celebrated and still the caravan stayed put. Park spent much of the time in a state of high anxiety, worried all the poisonous gossip would tarnish Taura's view of him. But the trader remained friendly and, by 19 April 1797, the caravan, including dozens of slaves, six singing men, a clutch of scholars and a world-weary Scottish explorer, headed off.

Despite his long rest, Park was still in a pitiful, run-down state. As the caravan slowly snaked towards Gambia, the slaves, despite all their own sufferings, sympathized with the barefoot explorer, who was struggling to keep up. Some of them even brought him water, or collected branches for his bed at night. Park was touched by their compassion.

The plight of a female slave called Nealee left an especially strong impression on him. Nealee had been lagging badly for days. She had made one escape bid but had collapsed, exhausted, in the grass. Whipping did not speed her up, and when she was tied to a donkey, she repeatedly fell off.

'*Kang-tegi, kang-tegi,*' shouted some of the other slaves in the caravan, 'Cut her throat, cut her throat.' This brutal request was actually a plea for compassion, to kill Nealee quickly and avoid her suffering a protracted and painful death. One slave hurried back to kill her, but returned having not gone through with it. Nealee was instead left by the roadside, where, Park imagined, she would soon be finished off by wild beasts.

The caravan finally pulled up near Pisania on 10 June, the very spot Park had set off from some eighteen months before. The explorer's arrival was greeted with much surprise and delight, as he had long been feared dead, killed by the Moors at Ludamar.

To thank Karfa Taura for his kindness Park paid him (on loan from Dr Laidley) double the amount he initially agreed. Taura was 'overpowered' by Park's kindness and impressed by the European-run trading station, especially the schooners on the Gambia River. At one stage he sighed: 'Black men are nothing,' and seemed incredulous Park had even bothered to explore 'so miserable a country as Africa'. He was equally amazed when Park shaved off his long beard, thinking the explorer had morphed from a man to a boy. Park was, after all, still only 26 years old.

Park did not have to hang about for long. On 15 June, an American ship, the *Charlestown*, docked on the river, loaded with 130 slaves. The *Charlestown* was bound for Carolina, but, due to heavy leaking, was forced to anchor in Antigua, a little over a month later. Eleven slaves had died in the crossing. Park caught a connecting ship, and arrived in Falmouth on 22 December, 1797. After two years and seven months Mungo Park was home.

* * *

On my own Niger journey all was going to plan. James had flown in to Bamako the evening before; pale, disoriented and surrounded by wannabe guides. Despite the 'what the hell am I doing here' look in his eyes, there was also a spark, an excitement, I hadn't seen in him for quite a while.

To be fair, I had only given James about 30 seconds to acclimatize before whisking him off to Koulikoro and now, early the following morning, we stood on the Niger's banks waiting for Karim. We were surrounded by food – rice, spaghetti, tomatoes, onions, garlic, papayas – recently bought from the local market.

Raph, sporting a red bandanna, soon joined us. He looked like an extra from a kung fu movie with a woefully slim budget. '*Ça va*, gentlemen?' he said, putting down his belongings, all rammed into a knapsack no bigger than a supermarket bag. He sat on his haunches and threw a stone into the Niger. A circle of ripples pulsed across the water, clear and symmetrical as tree trunk rings.

'Have you got enough stuff?' I asked Raph. 'A tent, for instance?'

'It's okay, *mon ami*, I have a mosquito net.'

'What if there's nothing to hang your net from? No trees or bushes, just sand.'

Raph laughed at the idea: 'Easy, I use the canoe paddles.'

In contrast to Raph, James hefted a monster rucksack, the sort even Atlas might have thought twice about taking on. Having discarded his stressful London life my friend had clearly decided to lift a different world on his shoulders, one bursting with every type of snakebite gloop and camp fire gadget known to man.

'What have you got in *that*?' I asked, pointing an admonitory finger at James's back.

'Oh, you know, the usual. Clothes, medicine, water filters, iodine, Deet, fire-starters, bin-liners, a book on how to do cryptic crosswords, oh, and this,' James unsheathed a long, rusty bladed machete from his belt.

'Phew, what's that for? Peeling mangoes?'

'Very droll, Tom, but if the tent breaks and we need to make some alternative shelter, don't come running to me.'

'But you've got a decent tent, haven't you?'

'Of course, a three-man one, so we can fit our kit in it too.'

'The size you are, my corpulent friend, you'll be lucky to squeeze yourself in. Let alone that beast on your back.'

'What does corpulent mean?' interrupted Raph. 'Is it big?'

'It's a polite way of saying fat. Very fat.'

'Shut up, Fremantle, you anthropological throwback,' James retorted. 'Your problem is you are several centuries too late, with your stout shoes and worsted shirts. Oh yes, you love all this Don Quixote, tilting at windmills stuff. And here I am about to paddle down the Niger with you, like bloody Sancho Panza.' We both looked at each other and began to laugh.

'Oh—my—God,' Raph said, his eyes wide as a lemur's. 'And I thought I was fluent in English.'

* * *

Before long we were all aboard Karim's pirogue, drifting slowly away from Koulikoro. Karim, standing at the stern, piloted his boat using a bamboo-like pole which, with its metal tip, looked like a dandy's cane. His wife Fatima sat at his feet dying her toes blue, her beautiful, melancholy face shielded by a baseball cap. James and Raph paddled in unison near the front, while I balanced on the prow, trying to pole in time with Karim using a wooden stake that was half lance, half caber.

All our baggage was stuffed in the middle of the canoe, suspended on wooden pallets to avoid it getting soaked. Bailing was a near full time job. The 20-foot boat's linked segments were stitched together with strips of baobab bark. Fountain-like leaks would jet out without warning, needing to be plugged with rags. At times we were sunk so low it felt we were more *in* the Niger rather than *on* it.

Still, we were in better shape than Mungo Park. On his second expedition to Africa in 1805, he spent much of his time in a vessel which had been cobbled together from a couple of rotten canoes donated by King Mansong. Of the party of 43 Europeans who travelled with Park to Africa on his return visit, three-quarters were dead by the time he even reached the Niger. It was to be a tragic journey.

But it was impossible to doom-monger about Park's fate on a day like this; it was simply a joy to be here. The sun shone, the wind was on our backs, kingfishers dive-bombed the shivering water and the crews of passing boats (none of them with engines), all waved and smiled when they saw James in his Crocodile Dundee hat, Raph in his bandanna and me struggling with my Excalibur of a pole.

The river soon fanned out into a band of silver studded with grassy islands. The islands had flocks of sheep on them, the Niger hemming them in better than any fencing. Up ahead the clouds flowed in some strange current of their own, making pale, flat-bottomed armadas across the horizon.

As night fell, Karim steered us onto a deserted sandbank. We had covered 20 miles. Karim and Fatima stretched out on a groundsheet and wrapped themselves in blankets. It was late February and, although the days were mercury-busting hot, the nights were still cool. James erected his domed, bright orange tent, while Raph, sure enough, hitched up his mosquito net using the paddles.

Using my head torch I set about trying to find some wood. This was a frustrating task, as, being on a sand bank, timber was not in ready supply. I picked up some twigs of driftwood and one sodden log. With much blowing and coaxing, Raph and James sparked up a reluctant fire. We brewed up some spaghetti, which barely got to boiling point, before James drained it and added some sooty tomato sauce.

We all ate from our mess tins, cross-legged around the dying fire. Raph sniffed his portion suspiciously. Sand flies whirred about, landing in the food and tickling our faces. Frogs chirruped and burped. Karim and Fatima ate a little and fell asleep under a bright slice of moon.

James and I troughed down our spaghetti, saying things like: 'Ahh, what a great feed', 'top belly-filler' 'a fine sauce'. Raph did not share our enthusiasm. He chewed, solemn as a food critic, and poked at his congealed, half-eaten pasta, with a tiny two-pronged fork.

'You English,' he said softly, but with great passion, 'have no fucking taste buds at all.'

* * *

By the second day we were working much better as a team, our poles and paddles striking the water in harmony. Some of the crews coming towards us had hoisted makeshift masts. Attached to them were sails, made from patchworks of hessian sacks, shimmering blue, white and yellow in the breeze.

We passed Bozo settlements; nothing more than thatched huts on the sand. Karim told us they were temporary homes set up in the dry season that would be washed away when the rains came. The Bozos then either retreated to permanent villages further inland or took off downriver for a few months. Karim joked that Bozos were hopeless with their land and gardens; the river was their only true home.

Around noon we always docked at one of the villages. Here we would fill our jerries from the local water pump and stock up on food. Hordes of children always joined us, holding our hands and chattering like starlings. '*Tubab, tubab,*' shouted some of the more confident ones. '*Cadeaux, cadeaux.*' We ate lunch under the shadiest trees: a combination of sardines, tinned meat, crackers and mangoes.

Despite his meagre belongings, Raph boasted a GPS navigation system. This was a yellow device, the size of a large mobile phone, with which he could plot our exact location. Karim became obsessed with it, asking every few minutes how many kilometres we had clocked up. But Fatima, rather like Ali with Mungo Park's compass, eyed the GPS with a mixture of awe and distrust, clearly suspecting it of possessing hi-tech *ju-ju*.

In the evenings we continued to anchor the pirogue on sandbanks, then set up our tents and make a fire. Karim and Fatima always ate separately. Karim, who was 38, had only recently married her. She was his second wife, some 15 years younger than him. His other wife, the mother of his two teenage children, had stayed in Koulikoro. It was clear Karim and Fatima, though never unfriendly, liked their space. Karim explained it was nice for them to have time together, as back in the village there was never any privacy at all.

'Africans are never alone,' Karim told us, revealing a seriousness I hadn't seen before. 'Wives, children, brothers, sisters, cousins, friends all come in and out of each other's houses. Sometimes I feel most lonely when I'm around so many people. I only want to be with one wife, or one child or friend, or even just with myself.'

After our evening meal James and I would put time aside to write our diaries. We would sit in the sand as the sun set, flocks of white egrets flapping leisurely overhead. Raph avidly read my copy of Park's diary and picked up on several things I hadn't, such as the explorer's fondness for *tomberongs*, which I knew as coogoo, the small, yellow berries I had eaten so often with Bubakar. Park also liked *nitta*, the seeds of the baobab, and once tried butter made from the nuts of the still prevalent shea trees.

The mosquito menace hadn't changed much in 200 years either. Park writes of 'amazing swarms . . . which rise from the swamps and creeks in such numbers as to harass even the most torpid of the natives'. He was to spend many sleepless nights fanning himself with his hat, blistered and feverish from so many bites. Armed with tents, Deet and mosquito coils we had it soft.

Perhaps the most glaring difference, though, was Park's famous description of his first sighting of the Niger at Ségou, 'as broad as the Thames at Westminster': but to me it now looked less than half that distance. It was also very shallow and just before pulling up at Ségou harbour, Raph, losing his footing while poling, fell in. At first I thought he might be in trouble (in the wet season he would have been) but then saw he was only submerged to just over his knees.

It was a beautiful night, the fullish moon already as high and clear as a star. Lush gardens fringing the river bank were tended by bare-breasted women carrying calabashes of water. They moved as quiet as ghosts, through the plots of onion and maize.

We all grabbed our belongings from the pirogue and slumped down on some grass, bats flitting above us. A muezzin echoed in the distance, the deep haunting yodel like a noise from long ago: a noise Mungo Park would have heard many times.

* * *

Before Park's near miraculous reappearance in England the African Association, believing him to be long dead, had sent out another Niger-bound explorer. This was Friedrich

Hornemann, a confident and scholarly 25-year-old German, who had recently graduated in theology with flying colours from Gottingen University. Hornemann had been fascinated by Africa since reading books about the continent as a boy. He later learned of the African Association through one of his teachers, Johann Blumenbach, a famous ethnologist and long time friend of Sir Joseph Banks.

In 1797 Hornemann travelled to London and impressed the members of the African Association's selection committee. He was offered a salary of £200 and became the first explorer whose next of kin the Association agreed to help out in the event of his death. Like Ledyard and Lucas, Hornemann was to have a crack at the Niger from the northern route, his instructions to travel from Cairo to the desert capital of Murzuq, some 1,000 miles south-west, and then down to Katsina in present-day Nigeria.

It was an ambitious plan from the outset. The Napoleonic Wars were raging and that summer the French navy had wrested control of the Mediterranean. Being neutral, however, Hornemann was able to sail through to Cairo unharmed. Here, he met Joseph Frendenburgh, a fellow German, who spoke fluent Arabic and had visited Mecca three times.

Perhaps through Frendenburgh's influence, Hornemann decided it would be a good idea to disguise himself as a Muslim. This way, he hoped, he could blend in seamlessly with any westbound caravan. Hornemann hired Frendenburgh as his side-kick and began learning Arabic.

The Germans' caravan was hindered by delay, first due to a plague, shortly followed by Napoleon's invasion of Egypt. On 21 July Napolean triumphed at the Battle of the Pyramids, devastating the silk-robed, scimitar-wielding Mameluke cavalry with superior fire power. When the shooting stopped some 1,000 Mamelukes lay dead: the French casualties were less than 30.* Cairo was now in a turbulent state and restrictions were imposed by the new occupiers. Hornemann, using all his considerable charms, managed to meet up with Napoleon, who was so impressed by the adventurous German that he granted him a special pass, some funds and even offered to forward his mail to the African Association in London.

By 31 August the caravan was ready to leave. Riding on camels, Frendenburgh and Hornemann (who now called himself Yusuf) posed as Mameluke merchants. Their disguises were unconvincing from the outset and on the first evening an elderly Arab accused them of not helping prepare dinner, something all young Muslims would usually do. When they reached the oasis at Siwa, in the heart of the Libyan desert, Hornemann sparked suspicion again when he sketched a temple, a radical breach of Islamic etiquette.

A few days later the caravan was joined by a hundred armed nomads marshalling a herd of donkeys. Frendenburgh overheard some of the nomads talking. Clearly in a state of panic, he told Hornemann the nomads suspected them of being Christians and that they would be 'assuredly put to death'.

But Hornemann, full of courage and *sang-froid*, confronted the nomads head on. Displaying mock outrage, he insisted that the nomads had witnessed him and Frendenburgh reading the Koran and told them: 'Dost thou not know that it is a great sin to tell one of the Faithful that he is a Pagan?' Frendenburgh

---

* Wildly one-sided battle casualties such as these became increasingly common, especially during the Scramble for Africa in the late 1800s – early 1900s. Despite some heroic stand offs against the European powers, local armies were often heavily outgunned, causing Hilaire Belloc to write, a full century after the Battle of the Pyramids, the grimly comic lines: 'Whatever happens we have got, / The Maxim gun and they have not.'

then recited some Koranic passages in his faultless Arabic. The bluffing worked and the two Germans were never again accused of being infidels.

The caravan reached Murzuq, the capital of the Fezzan, in mid-November. It was a hot, enervating place and Frendenburgh soon fell sick and died of fever. Hornemann stayed on for seven months, observing the various tribal customs, including the 'wanton manners' of the women and the prevalence of venereal disease and haemorrhoids, the latter 'no doubt greatly increased by the immoderate use of red pepper'. As there were no southbound caravans, he later struck out north to Tripoli, where the timid explorer Simon Lucas was still English consul.

After a short hiatus Hornemann set off again, hoping to reach Katsina and Timbuktu. His last letter to his sponsors was written from Murzuq in April 1800, assuring Banks there was no connection between the River Niger and the River Nile. Members of the African Association waited in hope for Hornemann to return, in the meantime publishing his journal and sending a copy to Napoleon. But, unlike Park, there was to be no triumphant reappearance.

It was only some twenty years later when two other British explorers, George Lyon and Joseph Ritchie, arrived in Murzuq that Hornemann's fate was revealed. Apparently he had made it to Katsina, then travelled south into the kingdom of Nupe, where he had died of dysentery just 300 miles from the Niger delta.

'The people became greatly attached to Hornemann,' Lyon was told by a man who had travelled with the German, 'on account of his amiable deportment and skill in medicine, and he was generally considered a Marabout (a holy man).'

Hornemann's journey was certainly on a par with Park's. In many ways he was a more impressive traveller, passing off as a

Muslim, using his medical skills (Park never did this, despite being a trained doctor), and winning the hearts of local people. 'I hope to do better than him [Park],' Hornemann had boasted in Cairo, hinting that the Scotsman would have got further down the Niger dressed as a Muslim rather than in his breeches, boots and frock-coat.

But history can be cruel. Despite Hornemann's extra-ordinary feat his scant, posthumously published notes sparked little interest and it was Mungo Park, with his readable, fresh off the press diary, who was to become the Niger's first *bona fide* celebrity.

Chapter 13

SLOW BOAT TO MOPTI

MARKET DAY and Ségou was humming. Dawn bathers, lathered in soap, created frothy eddies on the Niger's surface. Behind them a team of labourers hefted mud bricks on to an ox cart, while old women touted baskets of chilli and papaya. Further up children, sleek as otters, splashed and frolicked in the shallows.

The harbour was the busiest to date, with lots of dugouts and *pinasses* – three or four times the size of a standard pirogue – anchored in disorganized ranks. From a distance it looked like their hulls had been painted by Jackson Pollock. Passengers spewed out of the bigger vessels, as relentless as insects through a crack in a wall.

Mungo Park had been impressed when he visited Ségou in the summer of 1796. Even though King Mansong didn't allow him into the centre, he still noted the thriving population, the large boats, the prosperous countryside and wrote that Ségou 'formed altogether a prospect of civilization and magnificence, which I little expected to find in the bosom of Africa'.

Raph, James and I were suitably impressed by Ségou's wide, tree-lined streets and easy-going charm too. After a day of meandering about, stocking up on food and dodging the souvenir touts, we dined at a restaurant overlooking a square that, bar the dust and donkeys, would not have looked out of place in Provence. The restaurant was teeming with aid workers. There was a gaggle of young Dutch nurses, some German agronomists and a French couple dripping with ethnic jewellery.

It was Raph's last night. Over the last week his face had sprouted a mass of tiny red pustules. I had treated them with iodine that morning and he now looked like the victim of some terrible medieval pox. Raph, with his diseased visage, said he didn't want to socialize with anyone except our team. I could understand this, we'd had fun clocking up the miles over the last five days. We'd miss having him around. 'Mali, Mali,' James and I toasted him and before long Raph was due a long stint of carnal abstinence.

'Why should I worry about celibacy,' said Raph, swigging on a Coke bottle. 'My girlfriend won't want to touch me now.' He gestured to his spotty face. 'Ah, what a future. No sex, my busy job, my cellphone, my crazy world. God, I'll miss the river. It's so peaceful. The egrets, the paddles, the drum beats.'

'You can still play your drums,' suggested James.

'And you can carry on reading Mungo Park's diary,' I added. 'I need my copy, otherwise you could keep it.'

Raph nodded his head. 'Yes, I need to know what happens.'

'Well, if you must know, Mungo Park dies of a rash of tiny red pustules. Tragic really, and terribly painful.'

'Oh, ha ha, English. Hopefully these spots are contagious and then you'll die too.' Raph lifted his bottle and toasted us, wishing us luck on the next stretch of the journey. 'Come on then, tell me what really happened to Mungo Park. I've read to the end of his first journey. Once I'm in France I may forget about him. So tell me, what happened when he got home.'

* * *

It was still dark when Mungo Park's stage coach pulled up in London on Christmas morning, 1797. To kill time before calling at the home of James Dickson, his brother-in-law, Park decided to wander in the grounds of the nearby British Museum. By chance Dickson, who tended the museum gardens, had risen early. When he saw Park approaching, the distinguished botanist could not believe his eyes. Was this really his relative, or some sort of ghost?

Mungo Park's presence was all too real and within a few days he was the talk of the town. Sir Joseph Banks was over the moon. Park's return was a triumph for the African Association: the explorer had solved the riddle of the Niger's flow, got within a canoe-ride of Timbuktu and, most important of all, lived to tell the tale.

Banks wasted no time prompting the press. The story was soon splashed over various publications, including *The Times*, which claimed sensationally (and entirely falsely) that Park had discovered Hausa, a city on the Niger's banks that was twice the size of London.

Before long Mungo Park, the humble son of a Selkirk tenant farmer, was thrust into the full glare of London's social spotlight. At first the glitterati couldn't get enough of him. Britain was in need of a hero, a distraction. The Royal Navy was close to mutiny over lousy conditions and the Army was still struggling in the war against Napoleon. Things had got so bad that in February 1797, a force of 600 French soldiers had landed at Fishguard on the Welsh coast. Although the invaders were soon rounded up – some by a pitchfork-wielding cobbler called Jemima Nicholas – there was still a general feeling of unease across the country.

Park's story acted as boon in these troubled times. The celebrated hostess, Georgiana, Duchess of Devonshire, even wrote a song glorifying the explorer's arrival at the Niger. But Park soon tired of all the froth and attention, and it showed. Lady Holland thought the returning hero 'has neither fancy or genius, and if he does fib it is dully'. Another prominent party-goer noted 'strangers who looked to him for animation and lively conversation found instead considerable coldness and reserve'. The invitations soon dried up.

But an empty social diary was no bad thing, as Park, urged on by Banks, still had his own travel diary to write up. Park was provided literary assistance by Bryan Edwards, an MP and the Association's new secretary. Although an accomplished writer, who had penned a critically acclaimed history of the British West Indies, Edwards was an unusual choice. For all his establishment cachet, he was known to enjoy dancing with tinkers' wives and owned some large Jamaican estates that relied heavily on slave labour.

At first Edwards struggled with Park's prose, finding some of the early chapters repetitive and unexciting. But by the time Park reached Ludamar his pen had taken flight and Edwards called some of his work 'equal to anything in the English language'. *Travels into the Interior of Africa* was published in April 1797 and sold out its first 1,500 copies in a week – a runaway bestseller. It has rarely been out of print since.

'A plain, unvarnished tale' is how Park, quoting from Othello, described his story, and this is what made it such a hit. The reading public were fed up with boastful or lascivious travellers' tales. Dr John Hawkesworth's *Voyages*, an account of Captain Cook's travels in the Pacific, sold well but was ridiculed for dwelling too much on titillating subjects such as the tattooed buttocks of Tahitian women. *Travels to Discover the Source of the Nile* by James Bruce was also savaged by critics. Bruce showed a baleful lack of modesty, depicting himself eating lions, shooting an arrow through three shields and blood-letting a harem of naked Abyssinian women.

In contrast, Park made himself out to be almost goofily incompetent. He is prepared to admit that many Africans see him as a freak, that he is afraid of lions and useless at fixing guns. When it comes to women, Park always acts the perfect gentleman, never coming across as superior or haughty.* His lack of power lends him qualities rarely displayed by many later, more imperious, Africa explorers. Park's poetry is in his innocence, of seeing a place for the first time, and all the fear and wonder that goes with this.

Park also managed to steer clear of controversy over slavery. Reading between the lines it is clear Park, a sensitive man, is often appalled by the cruel way he witnesses slaves being treated. Yet, he remains wishy-washy on the subject, possibly due to Bryan Edwards' anti-abolitionist influence.

Discussing a potential ban on slavery Park writes: 'the effect would neither be so . . . beneficial as many wise and worthy persons fondly expect' and he sees slaves' minds as being still in an 'unenlightened state'. Park's words come across as uncharacteristically patronizing and were later latched on to by the pro-slavery lobby. Fortunately the abolitionists found much to highlight their cause in his diary too. Park, realizing slavery to be an explosive issue, may have taken this ambiguous stance in order to avoid kicking up a fuss.

---

* In this respect Park was much more disciplined than several other high-profile explorers. Even Dr David Livingstone, in a letter to his friend G.E. Seward in 1866, admitted to many sexual conquests in Africa: 'I had like Solomon three hundred wives princess [sic] (but don't tell Mrs Seward),' wrote the legendary missionary.

Indeed his diary seemed to please almost everyone. Even the most mordant critics spared him. *The Gentleman's Magazine* was spot on with the view that: 'Few books of Voyages and Travels have been more favourably received.' Only one question now remained. What would Mungo Park, farmer's son, surgeon, botanist, explorer, diarist, turn his hand to next?

* * *

Before Park even finished his diary Joseph Banks had begun tempting him with a fresh expedition, this time to Australia. Initially, Park had jumped at the idea but then got cold feet, citing that the proposed salary of 10 shillings a day was too low. Banks agreed to up the wages and kept on pressing Park to commit, but he remained reluctant.

Sir Joseph, at the time plagued by gout, was furious at Park's attitude and described him as 'a fickle Scotsman'. But he softened when he heard from the botanist James Dickson, the real reason for the explorer's keenness to stay put.

'I have found out from his sister,' Dickson wrote in a letter to Banks, 'which is my wife, that there is . . . a love affair in Scotland, but no money in it. What a pity it is men should be such fools that might be of use to their country.'

Sure enough, back in Selkirk Park had become smitten with a local girl, Ailie, the daughter of his old mentor, Dr Thomas Anderson. They married in the summer of 1799. Within a year Park had become father to a son, another Mungo, and settled down in the quiet town of Peebles working as a country doctor.

Life in Peebles* was not without its distractions. Park enjoyed his pipe, the odd glass of strong beer and 'a look

---

* Peebles, roughly the same size as Selkirk, must have had a somewhat dour reputation. The lawyer Lord Cockburn famously quipped: 'As quiet as the grave – or Peebles!'

through Mr Oman's telescope'. He clearly doted on his family and had some interesting friends, including the novelist Walter Scott. However, it was all far removed from the day to day thrills and struggles he faced in Africa. Inevitably, within a couple of years the hero of the Niger became restless again.

Walter Scott sensed his friend's frustration. One day he spotted Park dropping stones into the River Yarrow. Scott joked: 'This appears but an idle amusement for one who has seen so much shining adventure.' 'Not as idle as you suppose,' replied Park, explaining that it was the way he measured the depths of rivers in Africa. The Niger had clearly returned to the forefront of Park's mind and he later admitted to Scott that he 'would rather brave Africa and all its horrors than wear out his life in long and toilsome rides over cold and lonely heaths and gloomy hills'.

With the Australian journey no longer on the cards, Park wrote to Banks hinting he would be interested in any fresh assignments. Sir Joseph, concerned with growing French domination, now had a more imperialistic approach to West Africa. Two years earlier, at the annual meeting of the Association, the ambitious statesman, after congratulating Park on his travels, had grandly imagined British troops manning trading stations all along the Niger's banks.

This idea was never acted on, and a later plan, mooted by Lord Hobart, to send out a gun boat full of redcoats to build a row of forts between the Gambia and Niger rivers, was also jettisoned. All further projects were put on hold when the new, tight budgeting prime minister, William Pitt, took office in 1804. Park, having waited in London for further instructions, returned to Scotland. He did not return alone though, and the Park family now had a new house guest, Sidi Omback Boubi, a government-sponsored Arabic tutor.

Omback Boubi clearly caused as much amazement in Scotland as Park had done on the Niger. The young Muslim refused to drink alcohol – berating Park on one occasion for serving a brandy pudding – and insisted on slaughtering all his own meat. That said, the initially suspicious locals eventually warmed to him and he enjoyed his sojourn with the Parks, later sending a letter to Ailie: 'I will never forget how happy I was at Fowlshiels . . . I never in my life will forget you.'

By autumn of 1804 Park was back in London. Lord Camden, the new Secretary of State for War and Colonies, was keen for Park to make 'a journey of Enquiry' into Africa rather than a blatantly military foray. Park claimed he could rustle up 30 soldiers and carpenters (to build boats) and sail down the Niger, which he was now convinced ran south into the Congo.

Major Rennell, the geographer who had drawn up a map of Park's first journey, believed the trip would be suicide, but Banks still gave the go ahead, despite conceding it posed 'the most frightful hazards'. Walter Scott also pleaded with his explorer friend, now a father of three (and Ailie pregnant with a fourth child) not to go, but to no avail. Shortly before Christmas 1804 a timetable was hastily drawn up. If Park left early in the New Year, he could be on the Niger, his boats built and ready to go, within six months. Timing was paramount to beat the rains.

The journey was the first ever to be sponsored by a British government, but due to paperwork wrangles Park did not set sail from Portsmouth until 31 January: a fatal delay. Also on board was Park's brother-in-law, Alexander Anderson, as his second in command, and a Selkirk friend, George Scott, conscripted as a draughtsman. Park – who had been given the honorary rank of captain for this trip – boasted they were off on 'certainly the greatest discovery that remains to be made in the world'.

This may have been true but Mungo Park was a changed man. His courage was still intact, but he had lost the patience and humility that had served him so well on his solo voyage ten years before. This time, Mungo Park, the celebrity explorer, believed he was invincible.

* * *

With Raph gone, we pushed on westwards. The fecund gardens fringing the river bank soon petered out into sand as we neared Sansanding. Pied kingfishers, ibises and yellow wagtails flashed in and out of sight, as did the other pirogues, their sails punched by the erratic wind.

James had been in Africa for about two weeks now and he was thriving. His skin, a milk blue colour on arrival, was now darkening and he had sprouted a convict beard. After struggling to keep up, he now attacked the paddling like Davy Crockett. When he had the chance he snapped photos of random subjects: flocks of white ducks, Bozos casting fishing nets and the mud mosques, as symmetrical and elegant as any Oxford college.

Fatima, so quiet until now, also came to life. At Ségou market she had bought herself a charcoal burner, and insisted on doing all the cooking. Her kedgeree-style lunches made a welcome change from the unvarying gruel James and I had produced. Although she still refused to join us for any meals – Karim said this was common for women in his village – I sensed she now felt part of the crew.

At Massina, the largest town since Ségou, our visit coincided with a football match. The two competing sides were girls' school teams and we turned up just in time to see the final goal and the cup presentation. A crowd surged around the eleven victorious girls, ululating crazily, as the glamorous, frizzy-haired captain acknowledged all the applause. She was then hefted up on to her team-mates' shoulders.

The atmosphere was high-octane, but under control. Then a motorbike pulled up and the mood shifted. The crowd let out a collective scream of adulation, and charged towards the suited biker. In the mayhem the triumphant girls' captain lost her balance and was thrown to the ground. The crowd trampled over her, as unthinking as a herd of cattle, leaving her curled up like a foetus, her nose blooded and her cup nowhere to be seen. Her outraged team-mates tended her, stunned by the sudden reversal in their captain's fortune. This ugly scene had taken place in less than a minute.

'This man on the motorbike is a famous footballer,' said Karim, ushering me through the riotous throng. 'He once played for Mali. He is very popular. They love him here, they all want to meet him.'

'But that girl,' I replied, barging forward. 'One minute she was a heroine. Then he turns up and she's ignored, run down.'

'Girls don't play as much football here.' Karim said, amused by my reaction. 'It's a game for men. I think it's a silly game whoever plays. Let's get back to the river.'

* * *

In the evenings we continued to camp on the sand, often next to Bozo villages. Wide-eyed spectators would watch while James pitched his tent or '*La maison orange*', as Karim called it. Before the light waned, we played catch or tag with the children. Many of them were desperately hungry, and would nibble away at the skins of our mangoes after we'd discarded them. But for all the distended stomachs and hacking coughs, there was always laughter.

But at one settlement beyond Sansanding there was no

laughter. With its shabby, lopsided huts and wastrel dogs, it looked like a plague or typhoon had just swept by. Some children surrounded us, many of them coughing wretchedly. One little girl, with bush-baby eyes and consumptive cheeks, was spewing blood. She had flies hop-scotching over her face and her ribs flickered with tight, raspy breaths. By some wretched irony, her skirt was decorated with little aeroplanes: 'PARIS!' read their contrails.

The girl's hang-dog father stood nearby. He implored (with Karim acting as interpreter) for us to hand over some medicines. James had brought an extensive medical kit, but this was out of his domain. Raph, who had once attended a Red Cross course, had been very anti distributing any medicine at all. He had said, probably correctly, that villagers believed white man's medicine could cure anything and handing out even basic supplies would cause confusion.

With Raph gone, James and I decided to play by our own rules. We agreed that, as long as Karim was able to translate for us, we would distribute, when needed, such essentials as Savlon, rehydration salts, bandages and small quantities of aspirins, but that was it: no strong stuff, no prescription drugs.

After applying some Savlon to the sickly girl's sores and shooing the flies off her face, there was little left to do. 'She needs to go to hospital now, right now,' said James to Karim. 'Tell her father we are terribly sorry, but we don't know what to do. It looks like she has TB or something. She must see a doctor.'

Karim translated this to the father, who nodded, his eyes sad, resigned, weary. He picked up his daughter and smiled down at her, before walking back to the huts. After the children had dispersed we all sat in silence.

'Why can't she be helped?' said James, angry. 'We are near a river. There should be some sort of ferry going up and down with medicines. A hospital boat! Look at the state of those children, it needn't be like this.'

'There is little money here,' replied Karim. 'Some Bozo people do not want to travel to a hospital. Have no money to.'

'But these are children!' James shouted. 'It's just fucking terrible.' Regaining his composure James looked up at Karim. 'I'm sorry. It's just that I used to live in Africa as a boy. In Kenya, until I was 16. My father was a pharmacist. He used to visit all these remote areas, distribute medicines. I idolized him. He loved his job but sometimes he'd come back and say there was nothing that could be done for the people.' James paused and kicked the sand. 'When your hero says nothing can be done, you can't believe it. But I can see what my father meant now.'

'Africa is sad sometimes,' said Karim.

'But the thing is something can be done here. I know it can. We're by a river which has access to all these little villages.' My friend's face lit up. 'This is what I want to do, Tom. I want to set up a boat service here distributing medicines.'

'I hate to tell you, James, but you've spent the last 15 years working with trains.'

'That's over now. And come on, mate, I often felt I made as much impact in London as I would pissing in the sea. But this hospital boat would be something so positive. I'm an engineer, and I love boats, always have.'

'What about the money?'

'I could find it, Tom.' My friend was excited now, his flow of words jumpy, staunchless. 'Coming to Africa for me feels like coming home. I'd forgotten how much I love this place, the people here. I feel so alive. Back in England I'd watch news reports about civil wars and famines, but that wasn't the Africa I'd known. It struck no chord. Remember I was here in post-colonial times. But now I'm here again, I realize it wasn't just my gilded childhood, my rose-tinted youth, it was Africa itself. That's what I loved! The space, the sounds, the smells, it's all coming back. That little girl tonight, Tom, I've never seen anyone like her. Let's not kid ourselves, the chances are she'll die and I'm sorry, but that just can't be right. I want to help.' James fell on his back and looked up at the stars. Now that his words had run out he became pensive.

We all looked up at the moon: bright, gorgeous, fullish. A shooting star popped off in a wild trajectory, as if one of the planets had just given birth. The night skies were so clear here in Africa. There was no haze, or fuzz, or veneer; you could not help but be awed by your own insignificance. But with that came a wild and terrible freedom, where anything was possible.

'Oh, I'm probably bullshitting,' James said after a long pause. He was spent now, the zip in his voice gone. 'I'm just star-gazing. I'll get back home and conveniently erase this night from my memory. The hospital boat. That little girl. Join the 'there's nothing we can do in Africa' chorus.' James closed his eyes and sighed. 'But, hey, isn't it nice to dream.'

* * *

The day we were due to reach Mopti, the normally calm Niger came to life. The *harmattan* gradually whipped up the current into a roiling broth. Before long the river was unrecognizable. It had become more like the sea, white-tipped waves lashing against our waterlogged hull.

Soon we were the only boat on the river with Karim battling to keep us on course as James and I paddled and Fatima bailed. The fact all the Bozo fishermen had docked their boats was not a good omen, and soon we were forced to pull over on the sand. The wind was wild, sending spirals of gold and grey into the murky air. We covered our faces to defend against any high speed dust and hunkered down.

Above the haze of the horizon, mare's tails fringed the blue. We waited for two hours, three, four, as the *harmattan,* whistled and whooshed around us. The word *harmattan* derives from the Arabic for 'evil thing', and it certainly boasted sinister qualities that day. I decided I preferred the more poetic Tuareg name, the Hot Breath of the Desert.

The Hot Breath certainly has a very long reach. Each year the swimming pools of St Tropez and Nice become caulked in gritty Saharan dust and in 1989 the *harmattan* was so strong that fully grown grasshoppers had been swept across the Atlantic and dropped on the sugar cane fields of Antigua five days later.

In earlier times one member of the French Foreign Legion gave this rousing assessment: 'that terrible wind that carries the Saharan dust a hundred miles to sea . . . as fine as flour, filling the eyes, the lungs, the pores of the skin, the nose, the throat, getting into the locks of rifles, the works of watches and cameras, defiling water . . . rendering life a burden and a curse'.

Things were not so bad for us. We were on the river, where the wind was cooler, and we were under cover. That said, the Niger's current was now decidedly against us. We had been battling the wind for the last week, but nothing on this scale. Still, Karim knew exactly what he was doing and Mopti was only a matter of miles away; it was simply a case of soldiering on.

We finally pulled into Mopti's harbour as the sun vanished from the bruised, violent sky. On the river front a line of women walked passed balancing buckets on their heads. '*Toubab,*' one shouted, and they all laughed.

'How do they balance those buckets in this wind?' I asked, but no one could hear me.

We squeezed between two tar-black *pinasses* and roped up to them. Our canoe was now almost a third full of water, and James and I bailed wildly as Fatima and Karim salvaged all the belongings. We took over an hour before we were satisfied the boat would be safe. All of us were drenched. Laden down with kit, we trudged over the stony river front, up a set of steps and onto a deserted street.

The acacias quailed against the wind and a metal sign, warning of AIDS, rattled on its hinges. Random cows wandered by, lit up by jinking hurricane lamps. We feasted at a street stall where a hawker was still gamely grilling fish *brochettes*. Revived by the food, we stumbled on to a soulless white concrete hotel, where we secured two fiver-a-night rooms. James and I laughed at our beardy, dust-caulked faces in the mirror, then collapsed gratefully on rickety beds. Hours later I woke, dazed and shivering. Outside the wind was still howling.

CHAPTER 14

DESTINY'S DIARY

MUNGO PARK was slowly slipping off my radar. On his first Niger journey the exhausted Scot never made it as far as Mopti and on his return trip his last diary entry was in Sansanding, a village James and I had canoed past over a week ago.

But, limited though it is, Park's second diary still makes for illuminating reading. We know his troop ship, the *Crescent*, dropped anchor off Gorée Island in late March 1805, where he recruited some soldiers from the British garrison there. They were a rag-tag bunch, many of them convicts, deserters or victims of the press-gang, but the lure of double pay and potential discharge from the military was enough to hook them in.

Park, upbeat as ever, was thrilled with his new team and in a letter home calls them 'the most dashing men I ever saw'. He went on to rave: 'they jumped into the boats in the highest spirits, and bade adieu to Gorée with repeated huzzas.' In reality, it is likely the men were eager to do anything to escape the hard, monotonous and sickly life they currently endured.

And so, early in April, accompanied by his brother-in-law, Alexander Anderson, his Selkirk friend, George Scott, his 36 soldiers, five carpenters (all navy convicts found in a jail in Portsmouth docks) and 40-odd donkeys, Park set off down the Gambia River. His one disappointment had been failing to 'prevail on a single Negro to accompany me'.

Three weeks later Park reached Pisania and, after recruiting an English-speaking Mandingo guide, Isaaco, and buying some more donkeys, his motley caravan headed into the bush. Right from the start Park's diary is peppered with phrases such as: 'very fatiguing and troublesome' or 'in a constant state of alarm'. It becomes clear he finds leading a team of callow soldiers and recalcitrant donkeys far more taxing than taking to the road solo.

The caravan of white men soon began to deteriorate. The new soldiers struggled to keep up, fell sick and lost their way; donkeys became bogged in swamps or threw their loads; temperatures topped 100°. Throughout May progress was sluggish. Isaaco was briefly kidnapped by natives, a swarm of bees killed six donkeys and, most worryingly, a soldier named John Walters suffered a chronic fit and died.

On the night of 4 June the first rains lashed down, which even a serial optimist like Park heralded as 'the beginning of sorrow'. He was to be proved only too right. Before long soldiers were dropping like flies, fever and dysentery running rife. When possible Park tried to tend his dying troops but often they were abandoned where they fell in the bush, only to be stripped naked by scavenging robbers. Few knew the dignity of a grave, including Park's old friend, George Scott.

Word spread through the villages about the pathetic state of the *toubab* party and thieves became increasingly tenacious, at one point snatching a musket out of Park's hands. On another occasion the explorer shot a fleeing bandit in the leg.

Despite the havoc, Park's courage never fails him. He negotiates with village chiefs, repacks broken saddlebags, spurs on his men and even remembers to toast George III on his birthday. He straps dying soldiers on the backs of horses, scares away lions that attack the livestock at night and at one stage crosses a stream sixteen times, hauling supplies, leading donkeys and piggy-backing his sickly brother-in-law, Alexander Anderson. Isaaco, the guide, proves equally unfazed and heroic. On 4 July he is attacked by a crocodile and escapes after jabbing the animal in both eyes with his fingers.

For all the horrors the woebegone party endure, on 19 August there is a glimmer of hope: the first view of the Niger. Cresting a hill near Bamako, Park wrote that he saw the river 'rolling its immense stream along the plain'. Still, it was hardly time for celebration: of his initial party only ten men were left alive, not one of them a carpenter. Surely now was time to admit defeat, or at least hole up in Bamako until the rains ceased.

But Park was in a death or glory mind set. His diary entries at this juncture give little inkling of vulnerability. He comes across as a man in denial about his wretched situation, blinded by self-confidence. He even has the bravado to suggest that if the same journey had been made in the dry season only three or four men would have been lost out of 50. Statistics don't come much more wildly rose-tinted than this.

Having hired some canoes in Bamako, Park and his band limped downriver towards Ségou. Men continued to die en route, one corpse being dragged off by a wolf before it could be buried. Even ever robust Park fell sick, weakened by a brief bout of dysentery.

The canoes pulled up at Ségou on 19 September. Mansong, the ruler who had given Park 5,000 cowrie shells on his first journey, was still firmly in power. As before, he was wary of meeting the white man face to face and sent one of his ministers instead. During the meeting Park discussed the possibility of

Mansong trading direct with Europe, rather than using greedy Moorish middlemen. He then presented the minister with some silver-embossed pistols and other gifts for the king.

Mansong was still clearly spooked by Park's presence but, keen for the white men to move on, promised to donate some canoes and provide them safe passage as far as his kingdom stretched. After a few days there was still no sign of any canoes. Park decided to move downriver to Sansanding and wait there. To kill time profitably the explorer sold some of his surplus supplies at the market in exchange for cowrie shells. He struck up a roaring trade and writes that he was: 'forced to employ *three tellers at once* to count my cash'.

But while he was raking in the cowries, Park was still losing men. Early in October two further soldiers died, one of the bodies later devoured by a hyena. Park's biggest blow came when his brother-in-law finally 'bid adieu to the things of this world'. Alexander Anderson had already been sick for weeks, often carted around in a litter. It is clear from his diary that Park was devastated:

'No event which took place during the journey,' he wrote, 'ever threw the smallest gloom over my mind till I laid Mr Anderson in the grave. I then felt myself as if left a second time, lonely and friendless, amidst the wilds of Africa.'

These words show a strangely callous side to Park, as there had been plenty to be gloomy about prior to Anderson's death. But the now obsessive Scot had no time to mourn as King Mansong's canoes finally appeared: just two, both of them half-rotten. With his four surviving soldiers (one named Abraham Bolton proving especially helpful) Park set to work. In less than three weeks the canoes had been cobbled into His Majesty's Ship *Joliba*, a 40-foot (mostly) watertight schooner equipped with bullock skins to protect it against spears and arrows.

On 16 November 1805, Mungo Park wrote his penultimate diary entry:

'All ready and we sail tomorrow morning, or evening.'

* * *

The wind was still blowing furiously in Mopti the following morning. Grey, foreboding clouds swirled above the harbour and the boats stayed docked; not one Bozo out braving the turbulent current. The only sign of life was a bearded fellow in a blue robe washing his lorry. He had reversed it into the river and was sponging down its grubby flanks. In the distance the towers of a mosque in the old town prodded the dismal morning sky.

James, Karim, Fatima and I breakfasted on bread rolls at Bar Bozo, a well-known riverside haunt. We were now over-looking the Bani River, not the Niger, Mopti lying on a swampy stretch between the two. This was our last meal together, but the first time Fatima had joined us to eat. James and I were delighted. She was shy and awkward at first, but then flashed a supremely happy smile. After over a fortnight on the river it finally felt like we had won her confidence.

Karim had arranged for his pirogue to be strapped to the side of a motorised *pinasse* to speed up his journey home. It left in an hour. Sipping our coffees we watched the harbour come to life: boat-builders hammering and sawing, a potter at his wheel, a young girl chasing a guinea fowl with a stick. The air smelt pleasantly pungent, of fish, salt, oil and smoke.

'Our *pinasse* goes as far as Massina,' Karim told us, gesturing to a huge wooden boat painted with flowers, butterflies and crescent moons. 'After that the river is too low for an engine, so I will have to pole. But the wind will be with me and Fatima. But not with you two. You are heading north, it will be right in your faces.' Karim laughed at the thought. 'You will go very, very slowly.'

He was absolutely right, and it was something that had been on my mind. I still wanted to travel like Mungo Park, but now the *harmattan* was up, canoeing long distances would be nigh on impossible.

'We could take a motorized boat too,' said James, knowing full well this was against the rules. From Koulikoro to Timbuktu, I had laid down that we would follow the Niger as Park might have, the internal combustion engine strictly forbidden.

'A motor! Tssk, tssk!' hissed Karim. 'This is the dry season. The river is still very low in places, there are few motor boats heading north.'

'That's good,' I replied. 'In the wet season I bet there're boats revving everywhere. It's better like this, more peaceful.' Nearby a donkey let out a plaintive bray. I paused, hit by a sudden brainwave. 'What about donkeys? We could walk to Timbuktu with a donkey cart.'

'Whoa, whoa,' James implored, as if trying to rein in a bolting horse. 'What do you mean, donkey cart! And more importantly what do you mean, walk!'

'I've used donkeys before, mate, north of Bamako. They were great.'

'Whoa, whoa!' James clearly sensed the bolting horse galloping out of his control. 'You told me we would be canoeing. I hate walking. Hate it. Remember!'

'You can sit in the donkey cart. I'll lead it.'

'Now that sounds more like it.' James conceded, his horse now under control, but not quite back in the stables.

'Tssk, tssk,' said Karim. 'If you are carrying James you don't want a donkey. You want a bull! A bull has more force. You will need to take lots of water for you and the animal. Lots of food. It's going to be dry, sandy, very hot.'

'You're right, Karim. Spot on. A bull it is. And maybe a donkey too. The wind will be against us, but that's fine when we're walking, it will help cool us down.' I looked over at James. 'What a plan, hey, mate?'

James lowered his head and rubbed his forehead very hard with his fingers. 'A bull, a donkey and 300 miles of wilderness,' he whispered. 'Holy mother of God. I should have stayed with London Underground.'

* * *

After waving off Karim and Fatima it was time for a new plan of attack. Before seeking out some suitable beasts of burden for the long march north, I suggested a brief break from Mungo Park's route. In Mopti we were near the city of Djenné, a place often described as 'an African Venice'. I thought a visit there might help take James's mutinous mind off strong winds and donkey husbandry for a while.

From Mopti we caught a *bache* – an elongated van with ranks of wooden pews – early on Sunday morning. The idea was to sleep the night in Djenné, ready for the town's famous Monday morning market.

After three hours we pulled up outside Chez Baba, a Djenné guest house, where a poster of Christian Velten (L'ETRANGER PERDU) hung above reception. We dumped our kit at the rooftop dormitory, drank some tea and meandered off towards the Great Mosque.

It's sometimes a mistake to see a city's main attraction before anywhere else. The Great Mosque is Djenné's Taj Mahal and the largest mud-walled building in the world, the sort of architectural gem that is always splashed on Malian travel brochures. But unlike the Taj Mahal, which up close surpasses all its photographs, the Great Mosque was to my mind, initially at least, a bit of a let down.

Sure, it was nice to see a truly organic building, simple as a giant sandcastle, without any steel, plastic or concrete. Sure, the three 40-foot towers, each one topped with an ostrich egg, made an impressive façade. Sure, the fact the walls all had wooden beams sticking out of them, like some sort of architectural acupuncture, gave it a distinctive air. But something was wrong, the mosque just didn't look, well, grand enough.

It was only after wandering around the town for a while that Djenné grew on me: the school children on the street, watching with grown up eyes, as their teacher drew on a blackboard, the old men dozing under the passion fruit trees, the exotic Moroccan window shutters, the dugouts gliding on the River Bani, the donkeys, the hustlers, the call of the muezzin. None of this would have changed since Mungo Park's day. Indeed the settlement of Jenné-Jeno, less than two miles from Djenné's centre, supposedly dated back to 300 BC.

That evening I saw the mosque in a different light. Rather than being taken as a single entity it was a building that beautifully complemented its surroundings. It certainly looked grand now, the falling sun gilding its walls the colour of honey, as the faithful flocked to its gates. All violence had drained from the sky and the breeze was now gentle and refreshing.

Outside, the market traders were busying themselves ready for the morning. An ox cart groaning with watermelons bundled by, one of the fruits bounced off, rolling through the dust like a great green cannonball. Women in dazzling dresses balanced buckets of vibrantly hued spices on their heads, while a fetish salesman began to unwrap his monkey skulls, cobra skins and a quiver of porcupine quills.

'This Big Jerry,' shouted a cocky boy named Mohammed 5, who had recently tagged on to James. He pointed into the crowds. 'You meet Big Jerry.'

178

Big Jerry was heading towards the mosque, dressed in a fez and a grey *boubou*. He was certainly big, both tall and heavily paunched, but still with a lightness in his step. He looked like a cross between Falstaff and a friendly genie.

'Big Jerry is American,' said Mohammed 5, introducing us and wiping a tendril of snot from his nose. 'He live here three years, he help teach me English. He is Muslim man now.'

'Excuse Mohammed 5, he's a good boy but very pushy,' said Jerry, shaking our hands. 'I'm on my way to the mosque to pray. I'd invite you but, as you probably know, only Muslims are allowed in. It's a shame because it's wonderful.' Jerry beamed a beatific smile. 'Nearly 5,000 people can fit in the mosque, that's almost half the population of Djenné! Such an atmosphere. Tourists used to be able to visit, but not any more. Apparently a European film crew used the mosque to shoot some semi-naked models. It upset the elders and they've banned tourists.'

Jerry went on to explain that the current mosque only dated back to 1907. The original had been built in the thirteenth century – when Islam had first been brought to Djenné – but was later destroyed by a religious zealot named Cheikou Ahmadou, who believed the town had become too decadent and didn't deserve such a beautiful building. Story has it Cheikou ordered the air holes in the mosque roof – normally shut off during the rainy season – to be left open and the building soon became flooded and collapsed.

'What I love about this mosque is that it's re-plastered with mud at the end of every rainy season,' said Jerry. 'Those wooden beams sticking out of it are used for climbing up. Everyone in the town joins in. Those not plastering on mud, make tea or cook. It is a great communal event.' He stopped to look at his watch. 'Oh my, I must go now. Prayers start any minute. Let's meet tomorrow. How about it? Mohammed 5 will show you where I live.'

And with that Big Jerry marched off, the muezzin still echoing around the mud walls that all Djenné had so dutifully helped to build.

* * *

Mohammed 5 appeared at Chez Baba early the following morning, sporting a baseball cap. He led us through a series of narrow, zigzagging streets into a courtyard lined with red plastic chairs. In the middle of the yard was a fig tree and, to the side, Big Jerry's mud home.

Big Jerry was waiting for us with a tray of tea glasses. He had no fez on today, his grey hair shaved into a buzz cut. We all sat down around the fig tree, except Mohammed 5 who peeled away to play table football with some friends. Black hornets buzzed lazily in the torpid air.

'So I guess you fellas want to know what I'm doing here,' said Jerry finally, having handed out the tea. 'Well, three years ago I was really fat. I'm still fat, but back then I could hardly move. I was pushing 50 and working as a preserver of historical buildings in Washington. I knew if I didn't change my life I'd be dead before too long.

'I'd been to Djenné before and fell in love with the place. So I decided to follow my dream. Jacked in life in America and bought a one-way ticket. The change was amazing. In America I ate burgers and never walked anywhere. Here I eat rice and dates and walk everywhere. I've shed dozens of pounds. I'm like a new man.'

'But what work are you doing here?' asked James. 'How can you survive?'

'Oh, you don't need a lot to survive here! No, no. I've no wife and kids, just me to care about. I've saved up enough in America to see me through several lifetimes in Djenné. The only work I do here is unpaid. I teach English to kids, take them on trips, organize a youth club. And I'm writing a diary of my time here. Destiny's diary I call it. I want to include all the Djenné folklore I can. In Africa most things are passed on by telling stories, not in books. I think it's important for me to provide a written history.'

'What sort of things?' I asked.

'Well, just the other day, one of my youth club boys swapped the muezzin's tape at the mosque. So instead of the normal chant that evening all of Djenné's faithful heard Bob Marley singing "Buffalo Soldier". "Buffalo soldier, dreadlock rasta, fighting on arrival, fighting for survival." It was very funny.'

'Did the other Muslims find it funny?'

'Oh yes,' said Jerry, shooing away a hornet from his face. 'Muslims are not as joyless as you imagine. Particularly the West African Muslims. They're not as austere here as in the Middle East or North Africa. Some are positively lax. But faith is still vital to their lives.'

'Are you strict?'

'Well, I pray five times a day, but I'm not as strict as some. Last year one of my neighbours went on the *hajj* to Mecca. There was a stampede and he was killed. I was very upset but everyone here was happy for him. They said that dying at Mecca was the ultimate, an honour. That sort of thing can be hard to get your head round.' There was a lull in the conversation while more tea was poured by Mohammed 5, now back from his football.

'So what do you miss out here?' said James.

Jerry rolled back his head and laughed. 'The thing I really miss is pork. Oh, man. As a Muslim there are only two ways in which you can eat pork without jeopardizing your religion. One is eating it without knowing what it is, the other is if it's the only food available in someone else's house. Once a year I visit my sister back in the States. I always tell her to make sure there is nothing in her house to eat except pork. Man, oh man, I look forward to that day.'

'Do you ever get lonely?'

'Nah, I was more lonely in the States. Here everyone knows me, helps me out. Soon after I arrived I came down with malaria. It was terrible. There's no hospital here, just a little clinic. Besides, I was too weak to get to Mopti or Bamako. The fever did me in. I lost six of my teeth in two weeks.' Jerry opened his mouth to reveal his ruined dentistry. 'But the people here were amazing. I'd be dead without them. I'd much rather be killed off by an illness here than spinning out my days in some glum old nursing home in the Washington suburbs.' Jerry took off his glasses and looked up to the sun.

'Yup, I don't really miss anything about America except my family and pork chops. This is my home now, not some passing phase. The imam at the mosque keeps insisting I must find myself a wife! That would be nice. An old guy like me. Whatever happens, I'm not moving. This is where I want to be laid to rest. This is where I'm happy.'

* * *

Later Jerry led us through the market. Every square yard was covered with produce: sacks of maize, gooey nut pastes, hard balls of soap, pyramids of sheep offal and buckets of fish or honey. Herds of goats and a pair of camels were being ushered across the shallowest point of the river. Jerry explained the river is what made Djenné special.

'Djenné has resisted almost a hundred sieges in its history,' he told us as we walked along a street fringing the river. 'The Bani surrounds it like a moat. That's what makes it so unique. But,' he pointed to a gutter filled with scummy water, 'there are disadvantages to being this remote. The sewage system is awful and there's too much litter. That's something else I'm trying to improve.'

We walked on through a jam-packed section of the market that seemed to boast every foodstuff known to man.

'Yes, it's a big market,' said Jerry, sensing our amazement. 'One of the biggest in West Africa, but remember we're by a river. Away from the river the scanter the markets become. As you get towards Timbuktu it's less fertile, so mostly the same old stuff, nuts, dates, rice, the odd vegetable, but not as much.'

'Is there anything you can't buy here?' asked James.

'Ha, good question. There is actually. Egret feathers. In the nineteenth century feathers were all the rage for the la-di-da ladies to decorate their hats. The trees were thick with birds. Then there was a massacre. As you can see, egrets are thin on the ground here now.'

Once we were away from the main throng Jerry pointed to a cluster of children under a mango tree. They were listening to a man dressed in a white robe. He looked like he had been on the road, his robe badly stained with dust.

Jerry explained that Djenné was a very religious town, with over 40 Islamic schools. Marabouts (holy men) with supposedly magic powers travelled from village to village picking up children to bring to Djenné. Some of the children were as young as five when they arrived, often with little or no money. They survived off their wits and any donations. He said marabouts varied, many were kind and gentle but some could be very hard. A marabout from near Ségou had recently taken a party of children to Djenné and a young boy had died of hunger on the way.

'If you think children have it tough today though, think again.' Jerry stopped and gestured to a small, unremarkable looking mud hut. 'This little place, my friends, is where a young girl was buried alive in the ninth century. Story has it she sacrificed herself to the gods in order to save Djenné from collapsing. Only her innocence could cure the immorality of the town.'

Jerry nodded his head and gave some CFA notes to an elderly man who was guarding the hut. 'People come here to give donations and to pray for this girl,' said the big American. 'To thank her. I often come and pray for her too. The way I see it, without her Djenné would not be here. She has given me a great new home.'

* * *

Unlike Jerry's genuinely upbeat diary, the diary of Mungo Park's second journey to Africa, was full of bogus optimism. Indeed, even the explorer's penultimate entry* on 16 November 1805 – 'all ready and we sail tomorrow morning, or evening' – proved incorrect. Park ended up stuck in Sansanding for several more days.

During this time he sensibly handed over his journal to Isaaco, with instructions to take it back to Pisania. He recruited a new guide, Ahmadi Fatouma, who claimed to know the next stretch of the Niger well, insisting no danger would occur until Timbuktu.

Park also wrote some letters: one to Lord Camden explaining that only four of his men were still alive, and on 19

---

* Park's very last jotting in his journal was made the same day 16 November, a titbit about the local botany: 'There are no shea trees in Kong or Gotto, and very few in Baedoo.' This is typical of Park's second diary – rushed, bland and impersonal – but considering his predicament, it is incredible the explorer managed to put pen to paper at all.

November, his last recorded letter was to his wife, Ailie. After bemoaning the sad death of her brother he writes, clearly with strained levity: 'the healthy season has commenced, so that there is no danger of sickness . . . I do not intend to stop or land anywhere, till we reach the coast . . . You may be sure that I feel happy at turning my face towards home.'

The mood was perhaps better summed up by one of the surviving soldiers, Lieutenant Martyn. 'Thunder, death and lightning – the Devil to pay,' was the opening line of his letter to a friend on Gorée Island. Martyn then hints that Park is not himself, lists the horrors the party have endured to date, compliments the Sansanding beer and describes giving a Moorish drinking companion 'a damn'd good thrashing'.

On 20 November, 1805, Mungo Park and his sorry posse paddled off from the Sansanding shore. Not another word was heard from them. Even today the final chapter of Park's story is ripe with conjecture and hearsay. Only thanks to his guide Isaaco are we able to fill in some of the gaps.

Five years after Park's disappearance Isaaco volunteered to head inland and search for him. The enterprising Mandingo managed to track down the only man who could truly shed any light on the matter, the other guide, Ahmadi Fatouma. On seeing Isaaco, Ahmadi wept uncontrollably and stated: 'They are all dead.' It is through Ahmadi's story that the complex puzzle of Park's final weeks can be partly pieced together.

The journey was clearly no picnic from the start. As Ted Morgan (writing as Sanche de Gramont) so pertinently put it in *The Strong Brown God:* 'He [Park] was taking a makeshift boat pieced together from two rotten Bambara canoes down an uncharted river whose banks were occupied by Christian-hating Tuaregs and rapacious blacks.'

Park's refusal to stop and pay fealty to any chiefs and his insistence on arming the *Joliba* with 15 muskets exposes his paranoia. Perhaps the cruelties meted out to him by Ali's henchmen in Ludamar were still haunting him. The once confident explorer glided down the middle of the river, avoiding contact with the locals at all costs, and only sending Ahmadi ashore if fresh supplies were needed. It seemed the local tribes he had so diligently written about on his first journey stirred no interest this time: his only focus was the Niger's mouth.

The *Joliba* must have stood out a mile. According to Ahmadi she could comfortably hold 120 passengers. Inquisitive tribesmen paddled out in canoes to inspect the strange vessel, huge even by today's standards. On several occasions Park, rather than explain his presence, simply ordered his men to open fire on any converging boats.

Lots of blood was spilled. Near Kabara, the nearest river port to Timbuktu, Ahmadi revealed: 'we were again attacked by three canoes; which we beat off, always killing many of the natives' and then further along in the kingdom of Gotoijege: 'we counted sixty canoes coming after us, which we repulsed, and killed a great number of men. Seeing so many men killed, and our superiority over them, I took hold of Martyn's hand, saying, "Martyn, let us cease firing, for we have killed too many already" on which Martyn wanted to kill me, had not Mr Park interfered.'

Following this carnage in the Moorish-occupied land around Timbuktu things seem to have calmed down. Other than the odd close shave caused by surfacing hippos, the beleaguered *Joliba* traversed the Niger bend and plied on southwards unscathed into present-day Nigeria.

The one place we know Park did briefly berth is in the Hausa state of Yauri, now in western Nigeria. This was where long-suffering Ahmadi was dropped off, his contract having run its course. A village chief gave Park some food, including a bullock and a sheep and, in return, the explorer handed over five silver rings and some powder and flint, all of which he asked to be passed on to the local king.

The village chief urged Park to travel overland from there on, and offered to provide some guides. But the explorer remained suspicious, believing it better to carry on downriver despite the threat of rapids and hostile tribes. On the plus side, Park had lots of fresh supplies and must have realized by now that the river would soon hit the sea.

From Yauri on, reports are conflicting. The most convincing theory is that Park died at the rapids of Bussa, either late in 1805 or early in 1806. Whether he simply fell in or was attacked by hostile tribesmen, nobody will ever know. Ahmadi Fatouma,* despite not seeing the fate of the explorer first hand, gave the following vivid account:

> The people began to attack him throwing lances, pikes, arrows, and stones. Mr Park defended himself for a long time; two of his slaves at the stern of the canoe were killed; they threw everything they had in the canoe into the river, and kept firing; but being overcome by numbers and fatigue, and unable to keep up the canoe against the current, and no probability of escaping, Mr Park took hold of one of the white men and jumped into the water; Martyn did the same, and they were drowned in the stream in attempting to escape.

* After Park's departure from Yauri, Ahmadi Fatouma told Isaaco that he had been put in chains and released three months later. He claimed to have heard about Park's death from a slave who had survived the attack on the *Joliba*.

For all the vainglory of the second expedition, not to mention its scientific pointlessness, it was still an extraordinary logistical feat. Park was, after all, less than 350 miles from the Niger's mouth when he drowned. Had it not been for his comeuppance at Bussa, he might well have scraped home. It was a tragic end, but perhaps an apt one, Park hurling himself, like a semi-crazed Narcissus, into the waters that so bewitched him.

But Mungo Park's story was still far from complete. Over the following decades dozens of other explorers continued to strike out in search of Timbuktu and the Niger's mouth. Through them, and a host of other far-flung sources, information kept filtering back about the lost explorer. To a lesser extent it still does today. As for my own Niger journey Mungo Park would catch up with me far quicker than expected, and as for his diary, it would never really let me go.

CHAPTER 15

HOGON IN THE DOGON

THE NIGHT AFTER leaving Djenné, James and I found ourselves sleeping under the stars once more. Instead of ending up where we should have been – on the banks of the Niger haggling for a bull – we were now over 80 miles south of Mopti, having been gulled into a three-day trek in the mysterious Dogon Country, or *Pays Dogon*, as the French more eloquently call it.

At Djenné, Big Jerry had raved about the Dogon, a unique tribe, who for over 500 years have stayed largely cut off from the rest of the world. Despite forays by slave raiding parties, zealous Muslims, Christian missionaries, not to mention dozens of French anthropologists, the Dogon have doggedly clung on to their own distinctive culture.

Big Jerry urged us to bus across to the town of Bandiagara (over 100 miles west of Djenné), find a Dogon guide and head for the cliffs to the south. He said, rather dramatically, that we would never forgive ourselves if we didn't. We followed his advice and now our dapper, English-speaking guide, Mamou, snored alongside us on our roof-top dormitory in the splendidly named village of Djiguibombo (Ji-ji-bombo).

189

Once again we had deviated from Mungo Park's route, Jerry's lush description of the Dogon proving too enticing. Besides, I convinced myself, Park, at least on his first journey, would never have skipped an opportunity to meet a new tribe. It would also be a valuable warm up before our long march north to Timbuktu and watching James lug his generous girth up and down craggy slopes would be worth every CFA.

Our first morning was disorientating. As we had arrived in the village long after dark we still had no idea of our surroundings. Yawning from our roof-top beds, we peered out on a ravaged land, the sand and rock like ancient skin, full of wens, gashes and pockmarks. All familiarity fell away, no rivers, no signs, no fences: a moonscape of bleak and savage beauty.

After several cups of belly-warming tea – dawn was noticeably cooler here – Mamou showed us around Djiguibombo. He explained it was one of several hundred Dogon villages dotted along the 120-mile swathe of scrubland that lined the Bandiagara Cliffs, now rising up to our east.

Mamou, we were rather alarmed to learn, was not a Dogon at all. He had been born in Mopti but, having mastered French and English from the tourists, had moved to Bandiagara to work as a guide. To be fair, he seemed to know his stuff. As we wandered around the thatched, alien-looking huts, some made of stone, others sun-dried mud, he gave us an arresting commentary.

The hut with antlers and monkey skulls hanging from its roof, Mamou told us, was lived in by a hunter, whereas the one with the red door was where the village women retreated during menstruation. We moved on to the tall, lean, pepper pot-shaped granaries, all elevated on stones, and divided by sex. The male ones were solely used for storing millet, whereas the women's were divided into compartments for rice, beans and peanuts, with an additional nook to secrete their valuables.

The most distinctive building was the *togu-na,* a round, squat structure rendered with *banco* – a mix of straw, dung and rice husks – where the elders gathered to spin yarns and make decisions about village life. Mamou explained the low ceiling was to prevent any fierce arguments, the idea being if people couldn't stand up they couldn't hit each other.

'They should try it at Westminster,' quipped James. 'John Prescott would love it.'

After presenting some kola nuts to the village chief, we shouldered our rucksacks and trudged off along the rock-strewn plateau. It was a wonderful day for hiking; the nascent sun still gentle and the sky the colour of faded denim. At the village of Kani-Kombole we passed a mud mosque, much smaller than Djenné, but with a true fairytale quality. It looked like an elaborate termite mound fringed by a palisade of earthen fingers: I half expected Gandalf to appear from its shadowy interior.

In fact the whole area was other-worldly. There were trees with bundles of straw embedded in them like strange fruit, hunters with flintlock rifles that looked as if they hadn't been fired since Waterloo and electric blue Abyssinian rollers flying over head.

Mamou told stories as we walked. How the Fulani herdsmen are allowed to graze their cattle on Dogon land during the dry season in exchange for milk. The Fulani use cow dung for making fires in the evenings, tut-tutted Mamou, as if manure was a class A drug. He conceded that the Dogon got on fine with the Fulani but distrusted the Bobo people, who lived on the Niger delta and had a reputation for surliness and eating dogs.

At the village of Teli we hiked up a steep rock face to ogle at the most extraordinary buildings to date. Lining the escarpment was a rank of smooth earth towers sheltered by a massive overhang of rock: a miniature Manhattan sculpted from mud and clay.

'These are the lowest buildings, only five hundred metres up,' said Mamou. He pointed further up the cliff. 'Look there.' I arched my neck and saw several other fragile dwellings honeycombed into the sandstone.

'How can anyone get up that far?' panted James, slumping against a boulder.

Mamou explained that the cliff houses had been inhabited by the Tellem – a pygmy race able to climb like monkeys – as long as a 1,000 years ago. The Tellem sensibly lived high up for protection but still were flushed out when the Dogon – thought to have stemmed from the Nile valley – first appeared about 400 years later. The huts were now largely deserted, as were the small dank caves behind them.

As we descended down to Teli, Mamou stopped to point out the village's mosque and church. He explained that the 300,000 Dogon along the Bandiagara escarpment were of varying religion. A large village like Teli catered for several faiths and was split into different quarters – Muslim, Christian and animist – but with Dogon being the lingua franca.

'The most traditional villages are in the far north of *Pays Dogon*,' said Mamou, as we hit the flat again. 'They are all animists and want to be left alone. I cannot take you there. They do not like tourists.'

I told Mamou that in Mopti I had met a Catholic missionary who thought animists were the easiest converts whereas hard-line Christians or Muslims would never change their faith.

'Like anything, Tom, you have strong Christians, strong Muslims and strong animists. Some animists never change too. They like what they have. They don't bother anyone, and want to be left in peace.'

192

'Fair enough. But are tourists that much of a threat? We've hardly seen any so far.'

Mamou grinned. 'Just wait until tonight.'

* * *

Later that evening we walked into a sprawling village called Ende. Almost immediately we were pounced on by a young Dogon salesman with a shaved head and a gold stud in his ear. He wore a T-shirt reading: NO MONEY NO HONEY. He was charming and funny, if a bit repetitive, offering us baggy Dogon shirts (all dyed with indigo) and Dogon headgear – pointed hoods with dangling tassels to fend off flies.

We resisted and moved on to our camping spot, another courtyard surrounded by flat-roofed buildings to sleep on. This time we were not alone. There were parties of French and Dutch, a Japanese couple and a lone Mexican. I had met very few backpackers on my West African travels and looked forward to mixing with them.

The atmosphere was not great though; everyone seemed to be comparing prices. The French party had paid more for their three days than the Dutch, and were haranguing their guide about being ripped off. The Japanese were both ill and the Mexican man, Marco, after sharing some tea with us, unleashed his many woes.

'I have a guide called Chicken,' said Marco, a spry, simian-faced man with a wisp of goatee. 'He keeps getting drunk and losing the way. He is hopeless. I know you are supposed to have a guide, but this guy.' He jutted his jaw in the air. '*Hijo de puta*! I'm better off alone.'

Marco said he had paid Chicken half his fee but refused to hand over the rest. What he didn't realize was that Chicken was sitting in the corner with some of the other guides, playing a sort of Malian backgammon. Mid-rant Marco caught sight of him and stood up. Chicken stood too, a rangy, bug-eyed man with tribal scars on his face. He pointed at Marco and started laughing, he had clearly been boozing.

This was too much for Marco and he homed in on Chicken, barking abuse, his fists raised. Chicken backed off and two of the other guides pulled Marco away, whispering for him to calm down. Chicken continued to giggle nervously.

Mamou, who was turning out to be a trooper, tried to defuse the situation. After half an hour of negotiation there was a fragile truce. Marco agreed that Chicken could still guide him, but he would have to stay silent and accept half price. They begrudgingly shook hands before the still gnarly Mexican walked away, cursing quietly in Spanish.

'Well done, Mamou,' said James. 'I see what you mean about tourism now.'

'Yes,' he replied, 'of course tourism is great too. It brings in jobs, money and shows the world our beautiful country. Foreigners have helped Mali a lot. There are Dogon schools and clinics funded by all sorts of places. Canada, Japan and Saudi Arabia. But there are problems, as you see tonight. Tourism is new to the Dogon, and things are changing too fast. Greedy tourists have taken away lots of the original Dogon art – the masks, the wood carvings – to keep or sell in their own countries. This is a big problem, history is vanishing fast.'

I remembered Big Jerry mentioning this about Djenné too, how some of the ancient carvings and pottery in Jenné-Jeno, had been sold for millions of pounds by exploitative dealers and collectors. Stuff that would be invaluable to Mali now on show in obscure European galleries.

'Tourism is important, but not everything,' said Mamou. 'Now you can see why some villages keep to themselves.'

That night as I climbed to my roof space on a Dogon stepladder – a log with foot-holes hewn out of it – my insides liquidized. Bugger it, too much chilli with my dinner. I clambered down, my head torch emitting a dull lance of light. Most West African toilets are simply a hole in the ground: nothing fancy but clean and effective. The one at this camp, though, had been modelled on Western design (obviously without the flush). It looked like a war zone, reminding me forcibly of the loo Ewan McGregor vanished down in *Trainspotting*. Some things are better not tampered with. I shut the door and trudged off into the bush.

* * *

The following morning I was woken by pounding noises below. I looked down from the roof and saw a dozen women armed with wooden poles pummelling onions into a white mulch. The onions – a major crop here – gave off a sharp, invigorating aroma that stung my eyes.

Mamou was already up and we shared some coffee and a baguette. He asked me if I wanted to see the Hogon, the head man of the village, who welcomed visitors in his cave on the escarpment that towered over Ende. I jumped at the offer. James, nursing sore feet, said he would prefer to stay below and take some pictures of village life.

'But James, you are strong man, very big man,' said Mamou. Many Africans respected James for his weight, seeing him as a man of 'great force'. It annoyed me intensely.

'He's a fat ponce,' I said, although I had to admit James, once a brilliant rugby player, had been putting 100 per cent into his walking.

'Slave driver, Fremantle! Colonel bloody Blimp! Remember, I'm supposed to be in a canoe right now.'

Mamou set off up the rocks at his usual brisk pace. I shuffled along in his wake, sweating in the early sun, grabbing at boulders and tree roots to haul me up. Within half an hour we were at the entrance of the Hogon's high-rise cave. Mamou called out to make our presence known and an elderly, hunched man in a blue cape appeared. He sat on a mud throne embedded with sheep's teeth and puffed on a small bone pipe. Tugging at his silver beard, he resembled a poet caught in the thrall of some insistent muse.

He stayed like this for some time, then looked at us, smiled, and rang a bell. The bell was nothing special, the sort of bell rustic hotels keep at reception or goats wear around their necks in Crete. Mamou said I must refer all questions to him, and he in turn would ask the Hogon. I was never to address the Hogon direct.

Feeling rather humbled I told the Hogon how much I liked the *Pays Dogon*. Mamou grinned, perhaps thinking my opener a bit toadyish.

'The Hogon says it is more beautiful here in the wet season. Then there are waterfalls in the rocks, and the land is green.'

I asked about all the different symbols. The sheep's teeth were apparently a reminder never to take livestock for granted – to thank them for keeping hunger at bay. Mamou added that sheep or goats were still sometimes sacrificed to heal rifts or feuds within the village. Only the Hogon could perform the sacrifice, always up in the cliffs. He used to drink the blood of the animal but this was not compulsory now. The Hogon's family home was down in the village but he regularly visited his cave to pray, contemplate and receive people.

The most striking of all the symbols was a large serpent, carved in the wall to the side of the Hogon's throne. Mamou explained the snake was sacred to the Dogon. Legend had it that a snake cleaned the Hogon by licking his face and body, but if the Hogon was a bad man, he would be bitten instead. At 80 years old this Hogon was clearly a good egg.

The Hogon was voted in by the village, but often the position was hereditary. The last Hogon in Ende, this man's brother, had died in the year 2000 after holding the post for several decades.

The old man put down his pipe and held up a couple of wooden masks. One showed a rake-thin figure, with his eyes downcast and the other a woman with her hands over her face. They both looked very severe, as had all the Dogon masks I had seen to date.

'Masks are very important to the Dogon,' said Mamou, translating the Hogon's quiet murmurs. 'There are many mask festivals. These two masks show humility to the gods. The Dogon are supposed to act as messengers between the heaven and the earth.'

I had read about one mask ceremony, the *Sigui*, which was celebrated once every sixty years. It took place only when one of the – usually invisible – moons of the star Sirius appeared in the night sky, something the Dogon latched on to long before any Western astronomers. The *Sigui* mask was kept locked away in a special hut until this date.*

Mamou then attempted to explain some of the Dogon cosmology. It was all relentlessly complex and fearsome. Suffice to say that Dogon animists believe in one god, Amma, who created the earth by hurling a ball of clay into space.

According to my guide book the earth then took the shape of a woman with a termite mound acting as her clitoris. For Amma to make love to the earth, he had to remove the clitoris. In many Dogon communities both girls and boys (the foreskin being seen as the feminine part of a man) are compulsorily circumcised. Once Amma and the Earth had made love, they gave birth to a jackal, then a set of twins (half-human, half-

---

*The next *Sigui* is due to be held in 2027.

snake), before finally humans were created. And that's when things got really complicated.

I thanked the Hogon for his time. In some ways he was just as I had pictured him, wise, quiet, patient, smoking on his pipe. I handed over six kola nuts, leaving them in a box at his feet and followed Mamou back down the escarpment. In the background I could still hear the soft chime of the Hogon's bell.

We camped that night on a dramatic shelf, hemmed in by outcrops of caramel rock and the next day walked on to Dourou, the village where we were due to be picked up. The last few hours of our trek were especially lovely. We passed gardens, luminous with onion plants, watered by chattering, barefoot women. We paddled in a lily pool and traversed gorges thick with scented weeds. At Dourou we played catch (James had packed a tennis ball) with the village children, dragonflies whirring all around.

At one point during the game James stumbled up to me. He looked as happy as I had ever seen him, sweaty, weary, but very content. He really was thriving in Africa and it was great to see. All that morning he had been talking excitedly to Mamou about his idea for a hospital boat on the Niger. He clearly hadn't let it slip just yet.

'Tom,' he said urgent, breathless. He was holding his tennis ball. 'You're not going to believe this. It's so great. I did something this morning I haven't done for ages.' He paused, gasping, against a sweeping backdrop of sand, rock and scrub. 'I ran! I bloody ran. No, not ran. Sprinted! Ah, ha! How about that! Thank you, *Pays Dogon*. Thank you, Mamou!' He thumped my back. 'Come on then, Fremantle. Let's get back to Mopti and I'll race your skinny arse to Timbuktu.'

* * *

After Mungo Park's death, the quest for Timbuktu and the

Niger's mouth intensified. Indeed, even before Park set off on his final 1805 mission, another African Association explorer had fallen by the wayside.

Henry Nicholls, having read Park's *Travels*, sailed off in November 1804 to the slaving station of Calabar on the Gulf of Guinea. He was the first Association explorer to have a crack at the Niger from the southern approach. Ironically, he had no idea that his starting point was near the Niger's mouth, his goal.

Even so, Nicholls's journey began well. He cleverly pandered to the vanity of the local chiefs – one with the impeccable name of Ego Honesty, King of Ebongo – by claiming he wanted to write about them. It made little difference. Like so many before him, within three months of setting foot in Africa, Nicholls fell sick and died.

The heady days of Mungo Park's triumphant first expedition were long gone, and the cash-strapped African Association was struggling. Even its leading light, Sir Joseph Banks, dogged by poor health and distracted by his myriad other duties, could not save it from gradual extinction.* No one with his flamboyance or energy was waiting in the wings. The baton of exploration in West Africa was now thrust into the hands of a much bigger player – the British government.

---

* After the deaths of Park and Nicholls the African Association's flow of explorers to the Niger dried up. Its one major coup (before being absorbed into the Royal Geographical Society in 1831) was talent spotting the great Swiss traveller, scholar and writer, Jean Louis Burckhardt. From his recruitment in 1808 up until his death in Cairo in 1817 his achievements in Egypt and the Middle East were manifold. Not only did he discover the ancient city of Petra (in present-day Jordan) and the pharaonic temple of Abu Simbel, but journeyed further up the Nile than any known Westerner before him.

But things did not improve. In 1815 Major John Peddie set off on an expedition in Park's wake. His orders: to recruit 100 men from the Royal Africa Corps and hasten 'the discovery of the mouths of the Niger'. He died within days of arrival. Captain William Gray and Staff Surgeon Dochard assumed command. Assailed by fever and shunned by the King of Ségou, the survivors limped back to the coast. The cost was high, both human and financial. Not only did dozens perish but the budget radically exceeded that of *all* the other West African expeditions to date.

It was time for a fresh tack. Perhaps the Niger segued into the Congo? Park thought so, so did Banks, and now, more importantly, John Barrow,* the ambitious Second Secretary of the Admiralty, thought it might too. Barrow sponsored an expedition in 1816 led by Captain James Kingston Tuckey. Tuckey and his 53 men struggled less than 300 miles up the Congo. Only 19 of them survived: Tuckey was not one of them.

The 1818 expedition of Joseph Ritchie, George Lyon and John Belford to Tripoli was equally fruitless. They were an unlikely trio: Ritchie, the wholly unsuitable leader, was a shy, moody doctor and a friend of the poet John Keats (he had promised to throw a copy of *Endymion* into the Sahara), Lyon was a cheery young navy lieutenant and Belford, a shipwright, recruited to build a boat once on the Niger.

---

* John Barrow, a future head of the Royal Geographical Society, fought tirelessly to finance sponsored missions to Africa. The only child of a Lancashire farmer, he was a highly focused, well-travelled man with a sniff of the imperialist about him. When Sir Joseph Banks died, gout-ridden and exhausted in 1820, it was Barrow, more than any other statesman, who pushed initiatives to solve the riddle of the Niger.

They left Tripoli disguised as Moors, part of a caravan of 200 men and as many camels. Over a month later they reached Murzuq, where the German explorer Friedrich Hornemann had stayed some 20 years before. The climate was just as unhealthy. Within a fortnight Belford had become deaf, Lyon weak with dysentery and Ritchie palsied with a bilious complaint which eventually killed him.

Ritchie had already squandered most of the trip's funds on useless kit: lead, bottles of arsenic, corks to preserve insects. Lyon and Belford, destitute by this stage, retreated north across the sands and sailed home. Lyon, despite never getting anywhere near the Niger, told Barrow he was convinced that it ran into the Nile. Apart from a camel brought back as a gift for King George IV, the journey had produced nothing but heartache and skewed information.

* * *

Only one expedition in the 1820s, despite being far from harmonious, shed more light on the Niger. The three men involved – Major Dixon Denham, naval officer Hugh Clapperton and Dr Walter Oudney – were instructed by the Admiralty to travel to Tripoli, then south across the Sahara to Lake Chad.

Despite several false starts they finally set off over the sand in the spring of 1822, backed by a substantial caravan and the Pasha of Tripoli's blessing. The going wasn't easy, at one point Denham noting 'more than one hundred skeletons', near a dried up well. But what threatened the expedition most was the bristling feud between Major Denham and the two Scots.

Indeed, relations between Denham and Lieutenant Clapperton disintegrated to the extent they stopped speaking, their servants forced to run caustic, handwritten notes between the two men's tents. But for all their pride and dire behaviour Denham and Clapperton were both up to the job, and after three months had successfully reached Lake Chad.

The lush Eden-like environment acted like balm, helping improve the party's frayed dynamics. Denham waxed happily about the tall reeds and the 'biblical profusion of wild-life' including 'spoonbills of snowy whiteness, widgeon, teal, yellow-legged plover'.

Two weeks later they moved on west to Kukawa, the capital of Bornu, where the local ruler sent out several thousand cavalry in suits of medieval-style armour to welcome them. The white men, awed by Bornu's might and sophistication, were now breaking new ground, no other Europeans being known to have reached this far.

Despite all this serendipity Denham and Clapperton were soon at each others throats again. Any scrap of goodwill between the two men soured irreparably when Denham, who enjoyed romping with local girls, sparked a rumour that Clapperton was a homosexual. At the time this was a damning, even jailable accusation, which the Scot (once rumoured to have proposed to a Huron princess) vigorously denied.

The party split. Denham wanted to circumnavigate Lake Chad to find out if the Niger flowed into it, while Clapperton and Oudney headed west towards the city of Kano (now in northern Nigeria). The two Scots soon faced an unexpected adversary, the cold. It was now well into winter and Clapperton noted their water skins froze 'hard as boards'. On 12 January 1824, frail, consumptive Oudney already sick for months, dropped dead while trying to mount his camel.

Clapperton soldiered on to Kano, an opulent city of some 40,000 in the kingdom of Hausa. The explorer donned his naval uniform on arrival. Being six foot tall, red-haired and freshly primped, Clapperton might have caused quite a stir.

Not a bit of it. Kano had already witnessed countless foreigners passing through. The Scot noted, perhaps a tad ruefully, 'not an individual turned his head round to gaze at me'.

The restless naval officer soon moved on west to the equally prosperous Hausa capital, Sokoto, where he hit it off with Sultan Muhammad Bello, the powerful and scholarly ruler. Before long though, the weary explorer fell sick and made his way back to Lake Chad. Clapperton looked so wan and wasted on his return Denham did not recognize him.

Denham's reconnaissance around Lake Chad had proved equally action-packed. At one stage he had been captured by Fulani warriors, stripped naked and escaped as his captors squabbled over his clothes. While fleeing he tumbled down a ravine, landed beside a boa constrictor and sprinted through woods until finally bumping into some sympathetic natives from his original travelling party.

Denham and Clapperton returned to England in June 1825 after three and a half years away. Their mission was deemed a success, having provided valuable information on Lake Chad and the elusive kingdom of Hausa. Both of them were lionized and received promotions. Denham wrote a popular if self-aggrandizing book about the journey and in 1828 was appointed governor of Sierra Leone. He died of fever within a year of returning to Africa.

Clapperton, now convinced the Niger flowed into the Gulf of Guinea, was back in Africa within three months, landing at Badagri, near present-day Lagos. He had fresh fire in his belly, knowing that a new recruit, Major Gordon Laing, was already surging his way down towards Timbuktu from Tripoli. No one was going to steal Clapperton's thunder: the race for the Niger's mouth was back on.

CHAPTER 16

CHINA AND CHE

BY THE end of the interview in Mopti's Bar Bozo, I was convinced Yusuf would be the right guide. With his rakish looks – silver ear stud, scented hair and megawatt grin – he seemed older than his 22 years. His English was good and he knew all about donkeys, having steered them around building sites as a teenager. He had also come lavishly praised by Mamou, whom both James and I liked and trusted.

Although Yusuf was a Dogon, he said he knew the road to Timbuktu well. He recommended travelling with a donkey cart until the village of Konna, some 50 miles north of Mopti. From there on it would be sand all the way and we would need a bull too. Once at Timbuktu, Yusuf assured me, we could easily find a buyer for the cart, the bull and the donkey.

'Price of bulls in Timbuktu very good,' said Yusuf. I smiled at the strangeness of his sentence: not one I was likely to hear twice in a lifetime.

Once I had struck a deal with Yusuf, the pair of us rushed around haggling for food, charcoal, candles and millet for the animals. We had left James recuperating at the guest house, loose bowelled as a calf after our Dogon adventure. He was steeling himself for an early start the following morning. It was mid-March now and the heat stifling. The wind, although not as severe as during our stormy paddle into Mopti, was still very evident, the palm trees nodding wildly on the river front.

The wagon was easy enough to find. There were dozens to choose from, and I plumped for a sturdy contraption with rubber tyres and two large wooden forks on which to attach the donkey. It cost CFA 75,000, about £75. Yusuf assured me, with a raffish wink, that the donkey would cost about the same, but that I should leave that up to him.

'I see you outside your room,' shouted Yusuf, as he vroomed towards the market on his moped. 'Be ready by four in the morning. We go before the sun.'

* * *

Yusuf turned up bang on time and together we packed the wagon in the meagre moonlight. Apart from all the usual desert paraphernalia Yusuf had brought along a huge ghetto-blaster, powered by a car battery.

'I thought we were only taking important stuff,' said James, shoving his rucksack on the wagon. 'Food, water, tents, that sort of thing. I doubt Mungo Park was a fan of hip-hop.'

'Music very important, James. Good for heart.' Yusuf passion-ately thrust his hand over his rib cage, as if struck by a spear. 'On the road no women. If no women, I must have music.'

'But you'll only be away for two weeks!'

'Two weeks without woman. Oh, no, no, no. I will die. Only music will save me.'

'Hey ho,' said James. 'Let's get this circus on the road.'

Together we approached the newly purchased donkey, now lurking in the shadows, a look of thinly veiled *froideur* on his

205

face. He seemed in good shape though, his grey coat glossy and clean. He also proved very biddable as we harnessed him to the wagon's forks.

We made off through Mopti's trafficless streets, the swamps glimmering under an icy lozenge of moon, the churring of cicadas all around. Yusuf sat on the edge of the wagon, tapping the donkey with a stick. 'Pussky, pussky,' he hissed, or something like that.

At one stage Yusuf's gentle 'pussky, pussky' ceased to have much effect. To save face he let rip with a lone 'PUSSKY!' while waving his stick like a conductor in the final throws of the *1812 Overture*. Our 'still under warranty' beast didn't like this much, whinnying and lashing out with his front hooves, he veered off fast to the left. James and I, who had been walking behind, charged after the wagon, now randomly spewing out kit.

The donkey sawed round towards a white concrete building where a man sat on a mattress, brewing tea in the half-light. He stood up, a look of grave concern on his face. Once he had acknowledged a runaway jackass clipping towards him, his grave concern shifted to outright terror.

'Oh, shit,' whispered James. 'I recognize this place, it's where I came to get a visa extension. It's the bloody police station.'

Sure enough, the man wore a yew-green uniform with blue epaulettes. The donkey scrunched to a halt in front of him, as if suddenly sensing his rank. Stunned into silence, the shaken lawman looked not as if he had just spotted a lone donkey, but the Four Horsemen of the Apocalypse. Yusuf jumped off the wagon and supplied a quickfire apology.

The policeman remained far more decorous than he should have. No bribes were demanded, no fines, no confiscations, just a polite warning to use head torches until the sun was up. He even fed the donkey a handful of sugar: animals have a great way of breaking down barriers sometimes.

'Good start,' said James, attaching his torch to his forehead as we moved on. 'This donkey has a definite rebellious streak. Let's call him Che.'

As the early traffic began to pass us, Yusuf steered the wagon off the road onto a dirt track running parallel. Before long dawn broke, exposing a parched landscape studded with sheep and thorn bushes. A shepherd slept on the hard ground. His spread-eagled limbs, contorted in the oddest manner, made it look as if he had been dropped from a great height.

At the town of Sevare we repacked the wagon after its near destruction during Che's break for freedom. A crowd converged on us, offering coconut chunks, bananas and fried plantains. At first Che became skittish but after munching on some millet stalks began to relax.

When we got going again, Yusuf, reclining on a foam cushion, reggae pumping from his stereo, looked in his element. He waved at the children running alongside like a benign but decidedly decadent monarch. Before long James had begun to limp and jumped up next to him. The two of them smoked James's roll-up cigarettes and chatted while I walked behind. Even with James on board Che trotted along at the same pace.

After nooning it under a mango tree while the sun was at its zenith, we pressed on to a village by a lake, clocking up 25 miles over the day. While James and I set up camp and filled our water jerries, Yusuf bought a chicken, a squawking, consumptive-looking bird, which he killed with my penknife, blood spurting across the sand by our bonfire. We cooked it, stirring the meat into a pot of rice. Ravenously pawing at the food, we all grinned at one another. It was good to be on the road again.

* * *

Next morning we breakfasted on bananas before cracking on

towards Konna. We made it by mid-morning, by which time Che was flagging, his usually perky ears drooping like autumn leaves. It was clear we were going to need a bull to share the load.

Yusuf handed the reins to James and jumped off the wagon. 'I look for a farmer,' he said, disappearing into a labyrinth of corrugated shacks. A hawker roasting a sheep over an open fire stood near us, smoke and fat permeating the air. James, desperate for a pee, handed Che's reins to me. He slid off the wagon and headed for the bush. As he walked away I noticed a rip in his trousers.

'What happened to your strides, Jim?' I asked.

James looked over his shoulder and ran a hand down his leg. 'Holy shit,' he shouted. 'They've disintegrated, and the back of my shirt.' It was as if his clothes, all good quality desert gear, had been doused in acid. It turned out to be a spot on analysis.

'It's that car battery, it's leaked all over me.' He rushed back to the wagon and smelt his seat. 'Acid! Bollocks! They're the only trousers I've got! They were supposed to stand up to anything – heat, cold, crocodile bites.' James threw his hat on the ground. 'But battery acid is taking the piss.'

He stomped off into the distance fumbling with his ruined wardrobe. Later, when he returned, he put on a pair of knee-length shorts, and went in search of a tailor.

Soon Yusuf reappeared struggling with a colossal cream and brown Brahmin ox.* Despite its mangy hide and errant horns, it looked in reasonable shape, with plenty of visible muscle. I inveigled Che from the wagon, tied him up and helped Yusuf

* The Collins English Dictionary describes an ox as: an adult castrated male of any domesticated species of cattle, esp. used for draught work.

and the farmer reverse the ox in his place, its fleshy hump prodding up between the wagon's two forks.

'No problem,' said Yusuf, vaulting back on his perch and waving his stick in the air. 'Pussky!' Clearly the word had lost none of its impact as the ox launched off, keranging the wagon into the side of a baobab, and sending a posse of turbaned on-lookers running for cover. James, fresh from the tailor, watched the runaway wagon yaw past him, Yusuf pulling impotently on the reins. He shook his head and walked back to Che. Finally I caught up with the ox and grabbed the lead rope.

'No problem,' repeated Yusuf, unconcerned by his disastrous trial run. 'When we are away from the village the bull is fine. Right now, he is crazy.'

Sure enough, the flighty ox did seem to relax the more Yusuf drove him away from the crowds. James, who adored Che, suggested buying another donkey instead. I was tempted but Yusuf insisted we should alternate the ox and the donkey: one pulling in the morning, the other in the afternoon. I took the plunge and bought the ox for CFA 200,000, hoping we could match that price in Timbuktu.

James looked the heavy beast up and down, as if an expert on livestock feng shui. 'That animal,' he said 'has as much chance of walking to Timbuktu as I do.'

* * *

Before we set off from Konna, James put his engineering skills to good use, and repacked the wagon to avoid more acid spillage. I paid the farmer and flicked through Francis Galton's *The Art of Travel* to remind myself what the great Victorian wanderer said about pack-oxen.

'"Oxen require less tending than any other beasts of burden,"' I read to James. '"They were also the first animals used to cross the Sahara as far back as 1000 BC, well before camels."'

'Well that's something,' he replied, pulling a bungee over the wagon's tarpaulin.

'"In all cases oxen prove unruly at the beginning of a journey."'

'We already know that.'

'Sshh. "Oxen are coarse, gross, and phlegmatic beasts,"' I continued to read. '"When the ox gets up, he is sulky and ferocious by turns; and kicks, jumps, and bellows."'

'Dear God, we can still get a donkey, you know.'

'"The first time of mounting an ox to break him in is a work of almost certain mischance: for the long horns of the ox will often reach the rider. All oxen's horns should have the tips sawn off."'

I paused. 'Have you got a saw blade on your Swiss Army penknife?'

'No, only a file,' aid James, wrapping the car battery in a bin liner. 'And ox pedicures aren't my thing.'

'Don't worry,' I replied, 'the book ends on a positive note. Listen to this. "To make oxen quiet and tame, scratch their backs and tails – they dearly love it – and hold salt in your hands for them to lick. They soon learn their names, and come to be caressed when called."'

'I'm buggered if I'm caressing him,' said James. 'In fact I'm not even touching him. You can do all the ox affection stuff. But we need to christen him. His Malian name sounded like China, let's call him that.'

'China it is. It suits his delicate nature.' Holding China's lead rope I rubbed his neck. The languid beast looked up at me, then bellowed mournfully and tried to shish kebab me with his left horn. 'Steady boy, steady now.' I backed away, a craven matador.

'Maybe you should try the salt licking trick instead, Tom. Let's face it, your ox-caressing, well, it needs work.'

* * *

China set a cracking pace for about two hours, Yusuf not having to utter a single PUSSKY. We all congratulated ourselves on a wise investment. But the going had been easy and once we hit the deeper sand, China slowed radically. James took hold of Che while I tried to tease along the flagging ox with the lead rope.

When we hit our first incline China wasn't having any of it. With a plaintive groan his legs fell from under him. I looked on in horror. At first I was terrified China had suffered some sort of terminal seizure. But on inspection he looked fine; breathing a little laboured perhaps, but not on his last rasp just yet.

Yusuf circled China, occasionally prodding his ribcage or feeling his snout. He whispered PUSSKY, bellowed PUSSKY, cooed PUSSKY but China was unbudgeable, anchored to the sand. Having worked on farms I remembered one technique used to rouse a fallen cow. It involved grabbing hold of the animal's tail and gently yanking it upwards. I tried this on China, a series of tentative tugs. He looked round at me nonchalantly and continued to slurp at the water bucket we had put in front of him.

'There's only one thing for it,' said James. 'We'll barbeque China in the next village and buy another donkey.'

'No,' replied Yusuf, outraged. 'He is good bull. Much force. This sand is too deep. We fine if we stay on hard ground.'

At this stage an unlikely guardian angel materialized over the scrubby dunes. He shimmered gradually into view like the first shot of Omar Sharif on his camel in *Lawrence of Arabia*. Rather than a camel, he was astride a Thelwell-like horse, comically undersized in relation to its rangy rider. The stranger was turbaned and swaddled in a white robe, his grey eyes the only visible part of him.

He leapt off his mount and weighed up the scene: one collapsed ox, one sleeping donkey, one hysterical Dogon, two sunburnt Englishmen, all in the middle of nowhere. There was humour in his eyes as he started talking to Yusuf.

'He says the bull is fine,' said Yusuf. 'He says he is just lazy. We are too gentle with him.'

After circling the stricken ox a couple of times, the tribesman picked up China's tail. He held it delicately, as if it was a dodgy electrical lead, and slowly massaged it. We all watched, transfixed. Still holding the ox's tail, the tribesman hunkered down and grasped it harder, holding it up to his chin like a weightlifter. China turned around, clearly panicked.

Our new friend, the ox whisperer, lifted the tail to his mouth, paused, then bit down hard, as if into some delectable fruit. China, lowing horribly, sprung to his hooves and plundered on up the slope. He had suffered the bovine equivalent of being goosed.

'That man just bit China's tail,' said James in disbelief. 'Poor old beast. Fresh ox-tail or what.'

'Yes,' I replied. 'Very harsh but at least he's up and running.'

I grabbed hold of Che's halter and jogged after the newly recharged China. He was going great guns, the wagon now cresting the incline and about to head downhill.

Yusuf, standing on his wagon perch, was yahooing with delight. 'The man say this bull no fall down now,' he shouted back, exhilarated. 'China no fall down until Timbuktu.'

* * *

Major Alexander Gordon Laing, a reckless, iron-willed Scot was the next great hope for exploration in West Africa. Laing sailed from Falmouth to Tripoli in the spring of 1825, just as Clapperton, his future rival in the race for Timbuktu, was returning from his ground breaking journey with Dixon Denham.

Major Laing had already set eyes on the Niger, having almost discovered its source on an expedition three years earlier while with the Royal Africa Corps in Sierra Leone. Despite Laing's commanding officer claiming that his military exploits were 'worse than his poetry', John Barrow decided to take a chance on the brave but undeniably precocious young officer.

At Tripoli Laing spent several months preparing for his journey into the interior. He still found time to woo Emma Warrington, the daughter of the British cousul. The young lovers married on 14 July 1825, just before Laing lit out for Timbuktu. On the insistence of Emma's imperious father the marriage was to remain unconsummated until Laing's return.

Despite the hazardous nature of his journey Laing had no doubts he would succeed, seeing himself as a man of 'enter-prize and genius'. What with the intense summer heat (at times nudging 120°) and the woeful supplies of food, Laing's journey south was punishing. But the robust Scot could handle hardship, as was evident in late January 1826, when he was set upon in his tent early one morning by thieving Tuaregs.

Considering the extent of his wounds it is incredible Laing survived. With gory precision he described his condition: 'five sabre cuts on the crown of the head and three on the left temple . . . a musket ball in the hip, which made its way through my back . . . five sabre cuts on my right arm and hand, three of the fingers broken.'

And yet within 20 days the gung-ho officer was back on his camel and heading south. He didn't make it far though, and at the next village was struck down by a plague, 'similar to yellow fever'. Despite the disease killing his faithful West

Indian manservant, Jack Le Bore, and several others in his caravan, Laing was able to shrug off the illness, and carried on towards the gates of Timbuktu.

Even before Laing began struggling through the Sahara various other European explorers converged on the Niger. An old Africa hand called Mr Bowitch, who had been in France studying astronomy, threw his hat in the ring late in 1824. He died within days of arrival on the Gambia River.

Perhaps the most colourful candidate was the Italian archaeologist, Giovanni Battista Belzoni, a man mountain and one-time actor who had starred not only in the circus but as the giant at the end of Jack's beanstalk. In 1816 Belzoni and a team of workmen had dragged the bust of Ramses II from Luxor to the Nile, and then excavated the newly discovered temple of Abu Simbel. In 1824 the eccentric Italian set off for Timbuktu: dysentery killed him within two weeks.

But nothing could quash the spirit of adventure and in 1825 the Geographical Society of Paris promised a 10,000 franc reward for the first man to reach the fabled Timbuktu and return alive.

The biggest challenger to Laing was now Hugh Clapperton, who had spent less than three months back home with his family, before sailing to Africa again. This time he was accompanied, not by haughty Denham, but a respectful 21-year-old Cornishman, Richard Lander. Clapperton and Lander anchored off the Gulf of Guinea in November 1825, confident the southern approach to the Niger was the right one.

By spring they had travelled north as far as Bussa, where Mungo Park had perished. They visited the rapids where Park had capsized but when Clapperton quizzed the local people about it they stayed tight-lipped, which he took to be evidence of their guilt.

At the nearby village of Wawa the two men fended off the

advances of a wealthy and highly sexed widow, Zuma (the Arabic word for honey). Lander turned her down point blank, calling her 'a moving world of flesh, puffing and blowing like a blacksmith's bellows'. Having been shunned by the younger man, Zuma threw herself at the equally resistant Clapperton, who described her as a walking water butt but later conceded she might once have been a 'very handsome woman'.

Fleeing Zuma's amorous demands the two men made it to Kano by July. After a period of illness, Clapperton left Lander to guard their scant belongings and moved on north to Sokoto, hoping to pave the way for an advance on Timbuktu.

* * *

On 13 August 1826, Major Gordon Laing, exhausted, battle-scarred but undeterred, limped into Timbuktu. He had been on the road for over a year. But gone was the Xanadu in the desert, its streets paved with gold and its courts full of philosophers and poets. In fact, the Timbuktu Laing witnessed was more likely a very ordinary mud-brick town ravaged by the sun and the desert winds; its halcyon days long forgotten.

For all this, Laing displayed no disappointment, writing to Warrington in Tripoli that Timbuktu 'completely met my expectations', adding that his new bride, Emma, had been 'uppermost in his thoughts'. The letter was sent at the tail end of his 40-odd day stay in Timbuktu. He left the city on 22 September, part of a small northbound caravan, having been warned by the local sultan that his life might be in danger.*

---

* Laing's safety in Timbuktu may have been jeopardized by the legacy of Mungo Park: 'the Christian who made war upon the people inhabiting the banks of the Niger'.

Thirty miles north of Timbuktu, on the second day of his journey home, Laing was attacked by Tuaregs again. This time there would be no Lazarus-like recovery, no reunion with his chaste and adoring bride. Laing was strangled with a turban and then beheaded, his body left to the vultures.

Clapperton fared little better. Despite a friendly welcome in Sokoto on his first journey, relations had now soured and Sultan Bello, the local ruler, had become suspicious and hostile. Clapperton fell sick. Lander, still holed up in Kano, travelled north to visit his ailing master. By the spring of 1827 Clapperton, plagued by malarial nightmares and acute stomach pains, knew he was fading. He died on 13 April, cradled in Lander's arms.

Lander, wracked with fever and paying his way by writing charms (as Park had done some 20 years before), made his way south. After nearly drowning and narrowly avoiding the spear of a Yoruba tribesman, he made it to the coast at Badagri. The six-month journey hadn't been all bad. The Emir of Zaria had presented Lander with a young slave girl who not only washed his feet but rubbed his temples with lime juice and fanned him to sleep.

At the coast though, Lander's luck ran out. Thinking him a spy, the King of Badagri ordered him to swallow a bowl of poison, squeezed from the bark of the toxic red water tree. Lander gulped it down and retreated to his hut where he forced himself to vomit. He survived, and the astounded king, believing he must have some sort of divine powers, spared him.

Lander stayed on in Badagri for several months, repulsed by all the cannibalism and human sacrifices. One day he witnessed a group of prisoners of war bludgeoned to death, their hearts cut out, then stuck on the tips of tall spears and paraded through town. He was finally picked up in February 1828 by an English brig and returned home to a hero's welcome.

Like Mungo Park before him, Richard Lander would soon be lured back to Africa. Could this brave, happy-go-lucky Cornishman, the grandson of a Land's End wrestler, be the one to finally reveal the Niger's mouth?

* * *

Our own road to Timbuku was not without its troubles. Walking through semi-desert with three men, an ox and a donkey it was hardly surprising. Our main concern was water. We could carry 60 litres, but at times this was stretched dangerously low. The heat was still incredible, the shade paltry. There were days when we didn't see another donkey cart, let alone any overland vehicles. Despite following a route loosely parallel to the Niger, we were still several hours from its banks.

James was a stickler about water, whereas Yusuf and I were more relaxed. But after our first close shave, badly misjudging the distance of a remote village, I wised up. I agreed with James that we needed to fill up any chance we could, however much it slowed us down. Now we were on sand, not dirt or bitumen, our progress was sluggish, often only managing 15 miles a day.

We resembled a small and shabby circus. Yusuf steered while I walked with whichever animal was not hitched to the wagon. James alternated between the two or us, sometimes walking, sometimes on board.

Relations with Yusuf frayed badly one evening. He was a great one for using the word 'definitely', when 'probably' or 'not a chance in hell' would have been a safer option.

'There will definitely be a water pump, James.'

'The village is definitely only one kilometre, Thomas.'

He had told us 'definitely' that a village called Sare was only ten minutes away. It turned out to be more like three hours and our water supplies drained to nothing.

When we arrived it was dark and the village water pump was broken. James flipped. 'Yusuf, you told us definitely! Definitely! Definitely! That means without a doubt. We are all going to die if you keep doing this. Come on! You're the guide. You seem more interested in your music than the animals or the water.'

'Just say if you don't know, Yusuf,' I implored. 'Definitely is the wrong word.'

'Okay, okay,' said Yusuf, angry. 'I will not say the word definitely. I say I don't know. But I do know. You ask me to guide you. I know this area, you don't. This trip is difficult for me too, you know. I no travel like this before.'

The villagers led us to a well, where we hauled up rubber buckets full of dark, brackish water. We watered the animals, then filled our own containers. Village pumps, some funded internationally, were a source of clean water, whereas wells were considerably dirtier. After we collected the water Yusuf kept his distance from James and me. It dawned on us we had been applying our own interpretations of 'definitely', without sympathizing with Yusuf's.

He was a 22-year-old, leading us on a journey that he had only ever completed before in overland vehicles. Despite the enervating conditions he had always stayed cheery and upbeat. James and I realized we had been acting like desert divas, expecting Yusuf to know the road to Timbuktu as if it were the M4.

'Yusuf,' said James, walking up to him. 'I'm sorry I shouted at you. It was wrong. This journey can't be easy for you. You are a good man.'

I apologized too and we all shook hands and slapped backs. This boosted Yusuf's confidence, as did a party at the village that evening.

We were all invited to a wedding dance. The assembled throng were dressed to the nines. The women were heavy with jewellery, their costumes brocaded with gold lace. They looked the very definition of elegance, even those with baby papooses on their backs. The men sported spotless robes, two of them holding guns, which they clacked together in the same way Morris Men do sticks. It was a visual treat, all the dancers at one with the rapid pulse of drums. James and I were pulled into the crowd, the villagers shrieking with laughter as we tried to respond to the urgent rhythms.

'What does this all mean?' I shouted over to Yusuf, who was dancing with a pretty village girl, the jewels in her hair winking in the lantern light.

'I don't know,' he said. 'I can't speak this language. But the dance is great.' He flashed a smile. 'I think this girl loves me, Thomas.' She certainly was eyeing him up. 'You walk too much with China, Thomas. You too tired for girls. Too old. But all girls love Dogon boys,' Yusuf boasted happily. 'I have sexy time with many African girls, and some others. Once I get sexy with an Australian woman. She was 52!'

'Fifty-two!' I said. 'Are you sure?'

'Of course, Thomas!' Yusuf tossed his head back proudly like a bird in a courtship ritual. 'Definitely!'

* * *

The wedding party had lifted our spirits and the sharp exchange of words between the three of us had cleared the air. But despite good team dynamics progress remained miserably slow. Several days later we were still nowhere near halfway to Timbuktu. This was nobody's fault, I had simply been far too optimistic in my timetable predictions.

One morning in the village of Ngorkou I woke, rolled out

of the tent, only to find Che missing. He had been hobbled by Yusuf the night before but must have broken free. We spent a desperate morning asking around, scouring the barren landscape, running madly after any Che deadringers. At midday one of the village elders appeared holding a familiar-looking donkey. We all whooped for joy. We had lost the morning but found Che.

We lived off rice, sardines, dates, nuts and, when available, mangoes. We walked over sand, dirt and scrub land, the hot wind in our faces. Sometimes we passed small forests, or clusters of coconut palms, providing shade and lush green respite from the endless beige, grey and gold. Sometimes the wind would be cool, the sky bruised, but usually the heat just beat down on us, day and night, melting our resolve and bodies.

In the morning we always popped malaria tablets, dripped iodine in our water bottles and shook our boots to check no insects were in them. One morning James and I lifted our tent and two ghostly pale scorpions scuttured clumsily over the sand. With a brief, instinctive flourish Yusuf stabbed one with a stick and scrunched the other with the heel of his plimsoll.

'We have to kill them,' he explained, flipping the pale corpses on the embers of last night's fire. 'They are bad animals. My brother was bitten once. It did not kill him, but he was very sick.'

'Scorpions are one of the oldest unchanged living creatures,' said James. He was constantly displaying flashes of knowledge like this, picked up from his past African life. 'Scorpions are the same now as they were hundreds of years ago, haven't evolved at all. Bit like Fremantles really. Amazing, heh? They have a great mating dance too. Obviously they have to be very careful! Oh, and after sex, the male is usually eaten.'

Unable to come up with a single item of scorpion trivia, I consulted the ever enlightening Francis Galton. He

A fetish stall at Djenné, items for sale include cobra skins, crocodile teeth and monkey skulls

Women carrying firewood near to Djiguibombo, Dogon Country

Dwellings in the cliffs, Dogon Country

The Hogon in the Dogon, sitting on his mud throne

Camel stuntman near Sare

Practising my ox whispering skills on China on the road to Timbuktu

James holds on to China, while Yusuf sits
in the cart. A bemused Che trails behind

The author leading China past a solitary and strangely irrelevant
sign in the sand. There was no right turn: and no road

Yusuf nursing an eye patch after his heroic but
wholly misguided attempt to cut it as a rodeo rider

With James and Yusuf, jubilant after making it to Niafounke

The peace monument in Timbuktu with a caravan
of camels languishing in the foreground

Ali, smoking on his pipe, north of Timbuktu

Crossing the border into Niger with my fellow Askia Transport passengers

Some of Niger's rare and beautiful giraffes having a siesta south of Niamey

Plaque on the monument honouring Mungo Park and Richard Lander at Jebba, Nigeria. 'BOTH DIED IN AFRICA FOR AFRICA'

A ravaged but still proud Mungo Park, sketched shortly before his second fateful journey to West Africa

recommended rubbing a scorpion sting with pipe tobacco, but other than that to treat it like a snake bite.

'And what does he say about snake bites?' asked James. 'Snakes are timid animals. We'd be very unlucky to come across one on open ground like this.'

'Just as well,' I said, flicking through *The Art of Travel*. 'Galton suggests sucking the poison. He says if this can't be done in time, to explode gunpowder in the wound, or else burn it out with a white hot ramrod. He says to use the utmost cruelty to prevent lethargy in the patient.'

'Gunpowder would certainly put pay to lethargy,' agreed James. 'But I think techniques have moved on since then.'

Back in medieval times Ibn Battutah had mentioned desert nomads thrusting snake-bitten limbs into the guts of a freshly killed camel. As we had no camel I saw little point in bringing this up and sacrificing either Che or China with a Swiss Army penknife was unthinkable.

The only other animals we saw in profusion, apart from the ever-present mosquito, were locusts. At the village of Sarafere we camped under a tamarisk tree, near to the water pump. After setting up the tents I walked over to Che and China with some millet stalks.

Whump something pelted me in the face. 'Jesus, what was that!' *Whump, whump, whump.* It was as if I was under attack from a squadron of impish bats. I heard Yusuf and James letting out similar cries of alarm. I shone my head torch down on my T-shirt and saw a long tawny locust, the length of a finger, perched near my navel.

Several of the village girls, who had been pumping water at the well, came over to investigate the commotion. The oldest of the group, a wild-haired girl in her early twenties, chattered with Yusuf for a while.

'Should we move our camp?' I asked Yusuf. 'The locusts are right by us.'

'No need.'

'Don't the villagers want to scare them away? They'll damage the land.'

'Sometimes, yes, but not these ones, they are too few. The village people are happy they are here.'

'Happy?' asked James. 'Why?'

Yusuf looked at us both as if we were beyond help. 'Because, my English friends, they will eat them. Yes, eat them! If they are still here in the morning we can eat them too. Locusts for breakfast. Much better than sardines or bananas.'

* * *

By morning the locusts had flown on. We peeled open another can of sardines and brewed some coffee. It was decision time. At Sarafere we had reached a crossroad, either we made a beeline straight for Timbuktu, in about another week, or walked west for two days to the river town of Niafounke and completed the journey down the Niger in another pirogue.

It was late March now, the mercury cranking off the scale. We had been on the road for 12 days, with Che and China both working furiously. They had been well fed and watered but another week might be asking too much. We were a good team, fit and happy, but time was ticking. James needed to be back in Bamako in two weeks to catch his flight home. My Nigerian visa expiry date was looming and Yusuf was longing for a reunion with the women of Mopti.

We decided to strike out for Niafounke, our penultimate day proving the biggest test to date. The landscape was spellbinding. One minute we would be in a spinney of white-barked eucalyptus, the next lost in a wasteland of bleached earth, prodded by sepulchral termite mounds. As the day drew to a close we fell upon some mud huts fringing a river tributary.

'Don't worry,' said Yusuf, after chatting with some locals. 'There's a ferry.'

We tagged on with a group of villagers, their faces barely visible in the moonlight. The lead man, a blue-turbaned hulk, shone a lantern on the river.

'You've got to be joking' I said to Yusuf, looking down on the small wooden boat, about the size of Karim's pirogue. 'That's not a ferry, it's a canoe!'

'No problem.' Yusuf was irrepressible. 'We unload the wagon, put the stuff on board. Then we take the animals across.'

'Okay, you're the guide.'

Fumbling about in the gloaming, we loaded the pirogue with rucksacks, millet bags and the still weeping car battery. A space was left in the centre, where the wagon was upended; its forks sticking up towards the opal crescent of the moon.

James and Yusuf boarded while I stayed on the bank holding on to Che and China. Within fifteen minutes the pirogue returned. The blue-turbaned man jumped off, decisively grabbing China's lead rope and tying it to the boat's prow. He then manhandled a hyper-resistant Che on board.

Before I had a chance to protest the crew were pushing the boat off from the bank. I splashed on board, amazed to see China swimming alongside, peaceful as a swan. Che continued to struggle, our little boat on the verge of rolling. By mid-river the angst-ridden donkey burst free from his handlers and sploshed into the water.

'God, no, he'll drown,' I shouted, thrusting my hand into the cold. Che resurfaced and I grabbed his mane. The villagers laughed as I struggled to keep hold. Soon it was clear Che was a champion swimmer and broke free. All I could see of him now was his head forging through the water like a crocodile. I let him go, laughing too, my heart pounding so hard I thought I might throw up.

At the other end James and Yusuf had already loaded the wagon. I manoeuvred China between the wooden forks and, led by the lantern-wielding villagers, we powered on through the tall grass. I felt very lost, but excited too, as I gazed around, drunk on the beauty of it all.

Out here there was only the simple rhythm of nature, the groan of China's harness, the wind soughing through the acacias, my jinking money belt, the dainty *thup thup thup* of Che's hooves, the moon and fireflies. It was a scene Mungo Park might have recognized, one without any past or future, just right here, right now in the African wilderness. Fleeting yet timeless. This is it, I thought, this is why I came here.

* * *

We reached a glade in the grass and set up camp, tethering the beasts to a thicket. We invited the villagers to eat with us, but they smiled shyly and made for home. While James chopped onions, I dealt with the animals. As I emptied water into the plastic buckets I heard China shriek. I shone my torch, only to see Yusuf leap-frogging on to the tired ox's back.

'What the hell are you doing, Yusuf?' I shouted, not unreasonably, but rather too late.

As our guide grappled for his balance on top of China, the horrified ox reared up like a rodeo bull and lashed back with his horns. Yusuf flew forward, China's right horn making brief but sickening contact with his head. Like a high jumper he landed on his back in the grass. James and I rushed over. Yusuf was groaning, befuddled, not quite sure where he was, or what he was doing, blood trickling down his face.

James ripped open his rucksack and fossicked around for his medical kit, while I tried to speak to Yusuf.

'What were you doing, Yusuf?'

For what must have been thirty long seconds he said nothing. Then a slow smile spread across his face. 'I wanted to ride China,' he whispered. 'I can ride Che, so why not China. It is our last night, my last chance.'

'He's an ox, Yusuf,' I laughed, glad to see he hadn't lost his consciousness or his sense of humour. 'He's never been ridden in his life. It was a brave move, I'll grant you that, but bloody stupid.'

James returned with a medical bag that would have done a St Bart's paramedic proud. He pulled out a plastic phial of saline water, gently squirted it in the gammy eye, before applying a gossamer patch which, if possible, made Yusuf appear even more rakish than usual. I was impressed with James's medical flair: the best I could have offered was Optrex.

We ate some spaghetti and onions; Yusuf fell asleep soon after. He had been lucky, China's horn missing his eye by less than two inches. When he woke the following morning his eyelid was swollen and blood clogged, but his vision good. He stayed well away from China; and China well away from him.

* * *

We trundled into Niafounke late the following day, having crossed the Niger on a ferry, this time a substantial vessel with several other wagons on board. Niafounke was by far the largest place we had visited since leaving Mopti two weeks ago. Although really nothing more than an extensive mud village we managed to track down a *campement* with a dormitory, and a quiet courtyard for the animals to rest.

We were told the *campement* was owned by Ali Farka Touré, a well-known Malian musician, who lived on a nearby farmstead. Yusuf was a fan and had played some of his music on his ghetto-blaster. He wanted to meet him but during our visit the local hero was out of town, recording a new album in Paris.

Having dealt with the animals, we threw our stuff in the dormitory and sat out in the courtyard, our table fringed by bougainvillea. A barman appeared with three ice cold beers. We cheered. We'd drunk nothing but lukewarm water since Mopti. We all raised our bottles and toasted Che and China, Yusuf's eye, his girlfriends, his future, James's shrunken girth, Timbuktu, Mungo Park and Christian Velten, whose poster, once again, was stuck to the walls. We ordered three more beers, and three more, all of us exhausted but ecstatic, another slice of map complete.

Just before turning in a child, shaven-headed, sinewy, about 10 or 11, sprinted past us. He was being pursued by a pot-bellied man with a crew cut, holding up a stick. At first I thought it was some sort of game, perhaps a father and son playing together. But then the man cornered the boy, yards from where we sat, and began to beat him viciously.

Once the stick, frail as bamboo, had shattered on the boy's back, his thuggish attacker began to punch and kick at him. Woozy with drink, we all rose up, but already two of the bar staff had rushed over and were pulling away the boy. The attacker was enraged, thrashing out at anyone near him while the boy sat cowering, shaking, and holding back tears.

The thug finally backed off. Still ranting and cursing he marched off into the night. One of the bar staff gently helped the boy up. He limped past our table, shaking but still tearless. I noticed his feet, like so many children in West Africa, looked like an old man's, the skin hard and fissured. The boy glanced at us, his eyes guileless yet drained of all youth, his face knitted with a fragile dignity. Yusuf looked like a child in comparison – we all did. Then the barman took the boy's hand and led him back onto the deserted street.

CHAPTER 17

AMONG THE TUAREG

WE NEVER did discover what happened to the boy. Yusuf asked around but didn't unearth much. He tried to persuade James and me that it wasn't such a big deal, this sort of thing happened. He'd probably stolen the man's wallet or watch. What could we do anyway? He was right, of course, but it was hard to accept someone could beat the living daylights out of a child and get away with it.

Up until now I had seen so much affection showered on children in Africa that this incident just didn't fit. But then I thought back to Big Jerry's story of the boy dying on his way to Djenné with the marabout. I thought of the girls' football match in Massina, the boisterous crowds at the horse race in Nara, Mohammed's bursts of anger in Banjul, the death of Robert's brother in Sierra Leone; how violence could flare up in even the most tranquil of settings, the gentlest of hearts. It made me realize how little I understood of Africa. After two months I hadn't even scratched the surface.

James and I now only had one goal: to reach Timbuktu. Niafounke was pleasant enough but little different from any other remote Sahelian town. As promised, Yusuf helped us to sell Che, China and the wagon. We held a mini-auction in the courtyard of the *campement*. The eventual buyer, an elderly farmer with a white fez and a Rasputin beard stumped up just over half the price. This was a woeful loss, but it was clear the only *toubabs* in town – unless they wanted to travel home with two very high maintenance pets – had no choice.

The farmer handed me over a brick of CFA and briskly walked away with Che and China dragging the wagon side by side. They had been admirable beasts of burden, and still looked in great shape. I wondered if we had done the right thing.

We were soon back on track after meeting two Bozo fishermen who owned a hireable pirogue. With the four of us poling and paddling they anticipated us reaching Timbuktu within four days. We said our farewells to Yusuf and gave him a healthy tip. His lack of navigational skills had been more than compensated for by his upbeat nature and ability to make friends with villagers. The morning after our livestock auction we waved him off in a motorized *pinasse* bound for Mopti.

'James, Thomas, I see you in England one day,' he said. 'Definitely, okay!'

We sailed soon after. The two Bozos hardly said a word throughout our time on the river. They spoke no French, English or Bambara, but they poled with grace and energy, our prow spanking the waves as we battled against the wind. The insipid river scenery – sand banks interspersed with near identical villages – did little to stir the soul.

Occasionally a surfacing hippo or dive-bombing kingfisher would break the monotony. James tumbling overboard after losing his footing was another highlight, as was watching the dextrous ease with which our Bozo crew cast their fishing nets. The fact one of them wore a sweatshirt with 52 CHICAGO on it only slightly jarring the sense of place.

After three nights camping, on the fourth we docked in Korioume, a languid port south of Timbuktu. We still had an hour until dark. Once in Timbuktu my self-inflicted spell of motor-free travel would be over, but for the remaining 12 miles I had to stay true to Park. For this reason James hired a donkey cart and trotted off with the bags while I marched behind.

Gum trees flanking the road rattled in the breeze while the sky, full of brindled cloud, soon darkened. I flipped on my head torch. Odd traffic passed us: a Land Cruiser, a cyclist, four Tuaregs on camels. When we reached the gates of Timbuktu, marked by a strangely dowdy white arch, we shot a couple of photos and ploughed on.

Soon we pulled up at a breeze-block building called Camping Tombouctou (the French name for the city). It was nothing much, but the staff were friendly and it had plenty of sleeping space on the roof: always the best spot. There were no other guests. We ate a bowl of spaghetti, drank a beer and sat on the roof-top admiring the stars. God, it felt good. Having harboured so many doubts and fears about this journey, it now made perfect sense. The road to Timbuktu was complete.

*   *   *

The view from the roof in the morning was less impressive than the star-spangled night had been. Directly below us was a clutch of lopsided huts covered with rattan and black plastic. A ragged man prodded at the embers of a fire, but, other than the baying of a faraway dog, there were no other signs of life.

After breakfast – bread, jam, dates, coffee – I left James washing his clothes and took a stroll through the sand to Timbuktu's decrepit heart.

For all the poverty, malaise and 100° heat, there really was still something special about this city. Tourists might now be able to fly in and out on lightning tours but it was, after all, still a place of pilgrimage. One could forgive Gordon Laing, who had stumbled over hundreds of miles of perilous terrain and been pummelled to within an inch of his life, for putting on his gold-paved spectacles and refusing to admit Timbuktu's shoddy reality.

Though absurd to compare my jaunt through West Africa to Laing's, I still liked to think it had been quite a safari; two months of leaky pirogues and bullet-strafed jalopies, runaway donkeys and collapsible oxen. That first night in Banjul and my dance with Naya now seemed many memories away.

Reaching this city of legend, this byword for all things exotic and remote, this home to 333 saints (as one sign announced), I could not believe my luck, nor help but have a spring in my step. Millions fantasize about Timbuktu as a magic land, a faraway sanctuary, but so few have the chance to find out. I hoped my journey had been true to at least some of those dreams.

Later, back at Camping Tombouctou, James and I were converged on by dozens of touts saying things like: 'Trust me, my name is Ali Baba' or 'I am Mustapha, the best camel driver in the desert.' Now that it was early April the sledgehammer sun was keeping most sensible tourists well away. As the only *toubabs* in this part of town James and I were easy prey. We finally conscripted a mullet-haired guide called Little Mohammed. He was 15, spoke good English, and impressed us with his ambition to be a doctor. He was in sharp contrast to Yusuf: serious to the point of dourness, but clearly determined to make something of his life.

Little Mohammed wanted us to see it all. He showed us into the Djinguereber Mosque, built in 1327, a relic of Timbuktu's heyday, a time when the great King Mansa Musa still led gold-laden caravans across the desert. Inside the mosque – the first

I had been able to enter in West Africa – it was wonderfully cool. Barefoot, we chicaned our way through the hundred or more columns supporting the solid mud walls.

In one alcove Little Mohammed stopped and pointed to some names inscribed in the mud. 'These are women's names,' he said, frowning into a shaft of sunlight. 'Women too old to have children. Clean women. Only they can come into the mosque.'

As we walked Mohammed rhapsodized over Timbuktu's rich past, the fact it had not only been a religious centre but a melting pot for scholars and princes. Even now Timbuktu boasted libraries full of books on the city's golden years. For all its diminished glory it was good to see this studious teenager was clearly still proud of his home.

'Everything was fine until the Moroccans attacked in the sixteenth century,' said Mohammed, as we put our shoes back on outside the mosque. 'Then the city was ruined. The trade stopped. Now the sand and the wind blow south and take away a bit more of Timbuktu each year. Within a hundred years it will not be here any more.'

Sobered by Mohammed's observation, we continued through a narrow street hemmed in by beautiful Arabesque shutters. We stopped to eat some bread – warm, doughy and delicious – from one of Timbuktu's many al fresco ovens and slugged back a couple of cups of cold yoghurt. After a game of bar football, we threaded on past some stately mud houses, one of which the German explorer Heinrich Barth had stayed in during his African travels in the 1850s. It had now been converted into a museum in his honour.

Barth's achievements were nothing short of remarkable. Travelling five years on the trot in West Africa – eight months of this spent in Timbuktu – he clocked up over 10,000 miles. The German's stamina and scholarship were both formidable, and his observations of the local people sensitive and far ahead of their time.

He eluded death on several occasions, one time drinking his own blood to slake his thirst and another when a flash flood prevented some bandits pursuing him across a raging river. But for all this, Barth was not lionized on his return to Germany. Despite becoming professor of geography at Berlin University, his travel journals were turgidly written and poorly reviewed. He died aged 44, prematurely burnt out, bitter and isolated, albeit with a trove of inimitable memories.

The next house Little Mohammed pointed out was that of Gordon Laing, the only indication of the doomed officer a faded metal plaque above the door erected by the Royal Africa Association. This was only a stone's throw from the home of René Caillié, the Frenchman whose extraordinary journey across the desert in the mid-1820s secured his place in history as the first European to reach Timbuktu and return alive.*

* * *

By the time René Caillié had Timbuktu in his sights he was already a well-seasoned traveller. Born into poverty in rural France and spurred on by the story of Robinson Crusoe, the

---

*This title may have belonged to an American sailor, Robert Adams, who claimed to have been shipwrecked off West Africa in 1810 and enslaved in Timbuktu. Although much of Adams' story rang true there were some inconsistencies, such as his description of Timbuktu as being the size of Lisbon. Whatever the case, Adams, who had been carrying no scientific equipment with him, shed little light on the mythical city. His adventures, even if plausible, were soon deemed irrelevant. It should be remembered Mungo Park, obsessed with reaching the Niger's mouth, sailed right by Timbuktu in 1805.

coltish young adventurer first sailed to West Africa at the age of 16. After some initial forays around Dakar, he took a side trip to the West Indies where he read Mungo Park's diary.

Further animated by Park's adventures, Caillié returned to Africa, but fell sick after a gruelling journey into the interior. On his return to France he worked at a Bordeaux wine merchant for four years. By 1824, the year the French Geographical Society offered a prize for the first man to reach Timbuktu and get home again, Caillié had drummed up enough funds to travel once more.

With no government sponsorship or grand scientific goal, the self-possessed Frenchman sailed out to Sierra Leone. On arrival Caillié lived the life of a Muslim ascetic, learning Arabic and how to navigate without a compass. He toughened himself up by walking long distances in the midday sun and secured a job in a Freetown indigo factory to boost his finances.

By March 1827 Caillié was ready. Sporting Arabic robes, he took on a new identity, calling himself Abd Allahi, an Egyptian-born Arab, who had been captured during Napoleon's invasion, taken to France and sold as a slave to a West African merchant. All he wanted to do now was return home to Egypt and see his family. It was a convincing story and a brilliant disguise: to all intents and purposes René Caillié no longer existed.

From Freetown Caillié travelled north-east, reaching the River Niger at the port of Kouroussa within three months. The Africans treated him kindly, but joked about his long nose, as they had done with Park 30 years before. After shrugging off a bout of malaria Caillié joined up with an eastbound caravan. By now his shoes had fallen apart and he walked barefoot.

Near a village called Tieme, Caillié fell sick with scurvy. Plagued by excruciating pain and reduced to a skeleton, he wrote: 'One thought alone absorbed my mind – that of Death. I wished for it and prayed for it to God.' Had it not been for an old lady called Manman, Caillié might not have pulled through. As it was, toothless but good-hearted Manman prepared him a potion made from boiled red wood. It saved his life.

Caillié reached Djenné in March 1828, and was told it would not be possible to travel overland from there on as the Tuaregs owned the desert. Instead the Frenchman boarded a pirogue laden with rice, millet and cotton. He was given a berth in the bowels of the boat, amidst some slaves. This hiding place was to protect him from pirates who regularly ambushed the boat and demanded payment.

The pirogue pulled up at Kabara on 20 April. After a year of unimaginable hardship Caillié finally walked into Timbuktu. Unlike Gordon Laing, he was sorely disappointed.

'Everything was enveloped in a great sadness. I was amazed by the lack of energy, by the inertia that hung over the town . . . a jumble of badly built houses . . . ruled over by a heavy silence.'

Caillié was only in Timbuktu for a fortnight, lodging in a mud house close to the one Laing had stayed in. During his visit some Moors led him to the spot Laing had been beheaded. Caillié shed a quiet tear realizing 'no monument will ever be reared on the spot where he (Laing) perished'.

Other than some sketches of the mosques (which he performed secretly, while pretending to read the Koran), Caillié had little to keep him in Timbuktu. He left in May 1828, joining a caravan of camels, ferrying gold, slaves and ivory to Morocco. It was a hard, 2,000-mile slog across the Sahara: temperatures nudged 160°, wells were few and the Moors hostile, but Caillié was a survivor and after three months reached Tangiers.

The explorer's return to France caused only a mild frisson of excitement. It was not until the British press* began to mock Caillié's claim that the French rallied to his defence. The Geographical Society honoured him with their prize, the French government awarded him a pension and King Charles X made him a Chevalier of the Legion of Honour.

But, like so many explorers, Caillié's moment in the spotlight was brief. His 1830 book, *Travels Through Central Africa to Timbuctoo*, failed to spark the interest it deserved and his honest, if less than flattering, description of the fabled city was not what the reading public wanted. Before long he was suspected of being a fraud; even his pension was stripped.

Caillié died at the age of 39, broke, dejected and still plagued by ailments from his African travels. For all his shining achievements the white man who finally succeeded in reaching Timbuktu and living to tell the tale, must have wondered if it had been worth all the trouble.

* * *

That evening, as we sat eating mutton at a street stall, Little Mohammed introduced us to a Tuareg called Ali. He was tall, well over six feet, and enshrouded in an indigo *tagelmoust*, a traditional Tuareg robe. His owlish face was his only visible feature. Ali spoke quietly, his English extensive and precise. Occasionally he stopped to take a drag on his bone pipe and puffed out a cloud of fragrant blue. He told James and me he wanted to take us to a Tuareg encampment north of Timbuktu, a half day's camel ride away.

* John Barrow, keen to defend Laing's achievement of reaching Timbuktu first, lambasted Caillié, cynically disputing the Frenchman's every word.

So far the other Tuareg in Timbuktu had been relentlessly hard sell. Little Mohammed had dismissively waved them all away, implying they were fakes and charlatans, who no longer lived like nomads and didn't know one end of a camel from another. Ali, however, he assured us, was the real thing, a Tuareg, a blue man. He certainly looked it, his indigo head-dress having bled onto his face, turning it a dark navy.

'I will see you tomorrow,' said Ali solemnly. 'Little Mohammed will bring you. The camels are ready.'

Sure enough, by mid-afternoon the following day James and I were each perched on a camel and lolloping off into the sands. It was surprisingly comfortable, my cushioned saddle not dissimilar to sitting on a sofa, albeit during a mild earth tremor. Judging from the agonized groans emitting from James's beast, it clearly thought its rider had drunk far too many pints of Guinness in his lifetime.

Camels are the ultimate Timbuktu transport, able to plod along without water in blistering conditions for a full five days (or in winter a fortnight or more). With their thorn-resistant foot pads, their double-lidded eyes and nostrils that can shut off the sand, they are made for the wilderness. As Archibald Robbins, an American sailor shipwrecked off West Africa early in the nineteenth century put it: 'were it not for the camel, the immense desert called the Zahara must be whole [sic] deserted by human beings.'

This isn't quite true because oxen and horse-drawn chariots were used to cross North Africa, albeit painstakingly slowly, back in 1000 BC. The camel made its inaugural performance in the Sahara around the third century, and there's been no turning back since. I'd read somewhere that the ultimate expression of love for a Tuareg was still to kill a camel, cut out a hunk of its best, bloodiest meat, and present it to his lover.

'Yes,' said Ali, when I asked him. 'That is true. Camels are sacred to the Tuareg. Without them we cannot survive.' He explained camel humps were carved on Tuareg jewellery, while camel skin was used to make wallets and water bags. Almost every part of the camel – hair, meat, milk – was put to good use.

But, for all the romance associated with them, the Tuareg themselves hadn't always garnered such favourable reviews as their humped friends. Ibn Battutah called them a 'rascally lot' and Heinrich Barth described some Tuareg nobles in Timbuktu 'swaggering through the market-place . . . pushing aside the blind and the halt'. One rattled nineteenth-century traveller went as far as saying: 'the scorpion and the Tuareg are the only enemies you meet in the desert.'

They certainly could be brutal. In the summer of 1869 Alexandrine Tinne, a 33-year-old Belgian heiress, who was attempting to become the first woman to cross the Sahara, was murdered by her Tuareg guides. As they charged towards her she held up her hand, which one of them lopped off. Another shot her in the heart. Tinne was easy pickings but the Tuareg could show great heroism too, mounting some of the fiercest and most sustained resistance against the French colonizers in the 1890s.

More recently, following a period of drought in the early 1990s, the Tuareg rebelled against the Malian government. Struggling to survive on the remote edges of the Sahel, the blue men appealed to the government for more autonomy and financial aid. When nothing happened they raided a military outpost some 200 miles east of Gao. Soon a full scale war was sparked, further fuelled by race issues, the olive-skinned Tuareg believing themselves the aristocrats of the region, innately superior to the blacks. Partly as a consequence of all the unrest the corrupt leader Moussa Traoré was overthrown, while hundreds of thousands of Tuareg refugees fled for Burkina Faso, Algeria and Mauritania.

The region remained tense until 1996 when a peace agreement was signed, followed by a communal burning of weapons in Timbuktu by both sides.

When I quizzed Ali about the rebellion, his mask of gentility crumpled. He turned on his saddle and looked me in the eye. 'If anyone threatens our freedom, we will fight, fight to keep our lives,' he hissed, as we rode up a dune, the sand glowing pink in the setting sun. 'Soon there may be no Tuaregs. Our children now play football instead of riding camels. This is not right. They must learn to understand the desert. It is our future.'

* * *

When we reached the camp I saw what Ali meant about the fragility of Tuareg life. A barricade of thorn bushes surrounded a circle of down-at-heel rattan huts. Twig fires flickered and spat. Several pot-bellied children stared up at us, one of them coughing horribly. We dismounted our camels, James's beast letting out a whinny of relief as he tumbled from his saddle.

A group of men in indigo, one with a silver-handled sword in his belt, helped us unload the kit. We were then ushered over to a straw palliasse in a bunker of sand. Overhead a lone, leafless tree clawed at the sky. We were soon presented with a bowl of unidentified bones. They were disgusting, gristly, hairy and bitter, with barely any meat on them at all.

All the time we had been with Ali, James and I had snacked on biscuits, bananas and dates. Even now, rather than gnawing madly, Ali nibbled delicately at the bones and sipped on his sweet tea, elegant as a society hostess. For all this he was clearly the possessor of an outrageous, sinewy strength. I could now understand the saying: 'Unless a man is reaped by the sword he lives forever in the desert.'

After dinner several other blue men arrived on camels. They jumped off and hobbled their beasts, speaking in heated Tamashek, the language of the Tuareg. Before long they spilled some hand-made wares on the palliasse in front of James and me. It was clear they would not leave before some deals had been clinched. We had a jolly haggling session during which James bought a Tuareg headdress and I opted for a couple of crescent moon amulets.

Pleased with the sales, they backed off and told stories amongst themselves. Ali joined in, pausing occasionally to translate for us. One of the stories centred on a wealthy Tuareg elder whose fortune had been made in the 1950s during French rule. All his money was in francs but due to the isolation of his home (50 miles north of our camp) he had heard nothing about the advent of the Euro. Now his outdated francs, his family's fortune, were as worthless as grains of sand. It was a sobering reminder how cut off the Tuareg were from the rest of the world.

Once the salesmen had dispersed, James and I were approached by a weathered lady wrapped in a black shawl. Ali told us she was worried about her young son and asked us to follow her.

She led us to a circular hut, its sandy floor as hard as tiles. The child was three or four years old and desperately thin, lying on a rattan mat, the air around him trapped, curdled with sickness. From what we could understand from Ali the boy had suffered diarrhoea for weeks. James rustled up a weak rehydration mix of salt and sugar, but promised nothing, urging the boy's mother to take him to see a doctor.

'There is no doctor,' said Ali, simply. We returned to the palliasse and sat in silence for a while. A herd of goats frolicked nearby. Ali's wife, an attractive woman with caramel skin and bright, blue-grey eyes joined us. She hunkered down at a discreet distance, cradling their young son. Ali and she exchanged affectionate eye contact. He told us that he, like most Tuareg, had only one wife, but hoped to have three or four more children.

'But it's so hard for children here,' said James. 'What about their health, their education. Wouldn't it be better in Timbuktu?'

'Children are the only way for us to survive.' This was a line Ali used repeatedly. A world without Tuareg was unthinkable to him. As he spoke now in defence of his life his words achieved a strange fluency.

Ali explained that if his son spent too long in Timbuktu, he would become soft. He would play football, eat too much, drive a moped, or fall for a non-Tuareg girl. He said that if he became used to this wilderness, this dry place, he would not pine for the city. He would get to understand the camels, the thorn bushes, the sand and even the desert beetles that survive by drinking only their own sweat. And that in time, rather than looking out on a landscape of severity, boredom and fear, he would see only a place of wonder: a map of his own heart.

Exhausted by his explanation Ali yawned and stretched out on the palliasse. Soon he was asleep. All was silent bar the breathing of the camels and the cries of a nearby baby.

*　*　*

As we approached Timbuktu the following day we stumbled on a caravan of a dozen camels, all roped together in single file. Like ours, they were single-humped dromedaries, but carried substantially heavier loads. Strapped to their backs were tablets of salt, no longer white, but stained a dirty grey by their travels. Commentating from his saddle, Ali explained each of the blocks weighed up to 50 kilograms. Some camels carried only two, while others had four, the equivalent of nearly a quarter of a tonne.

'They probably came from Taoudenni, a salt mine north of here,' said Ali. 'They travel maybe a month or more.' Little Mohammed had already told us of Taoudenni, a remote oasis over 400 miles north of Timbuktu, near to where he had been born. Until the late 1980s Taoudenni was notorious as a sort of Saharan Siberia, where criminals and political undesirables were banished. Even now, it has yet to fully shake off its sinister reputation.

'This is not proper desert here.' Ali urged his camel on by prodding a bare foot into its neck. 'There are still some thorn bushes. You need to travel at least another week before the Sahara starts properly, where the sand is pure.'

We followed the caravan until the camels had pulled level with the *Flamme de la Paix*, a concrete peace monument on the fringe of Timbuktu, commemorating the spot where the Tuareg had burnt their arms in 1996. Onlookers appeared from the surrounding mud houses to inspect the salt tablets, each one marked with red dye to denote the owner's name.

Ali said caravans at this time of year were rare because of the heat. This was a very small one, with only a dozen beasts: normally a modern-day caravan would boast 40 or more. I tried to imagine what an arresting spectacle the caravans of the Middle Ages would have made when as many as 40,000 camels traipsed between Taoudenni and Timbuktu.

Little Mohammed, sporting Blues Brothers shades, appeared out of the crowd to welcome us back. He held our two camels as they slumped down on the bleached earth, front legs first, then back, noses held imperiously in the air. Once on the ground James and I swigged greedily on our water bottles.

'When the summer is over I will go to Taoudenni again,' said Little Mohammed. He always sounded so serious for his 15 years. 'Some of my family still live near there. This is why I want to be a doctor so I can help them. Be a doctor of the desert, a doctor for the Tuareg.' He stopped and smiled.

'Well done, Mohammed,' said James, gasping after swigging almost an entire litre of water. 'That's great. Honestly it is, really great.'

'Each January they have a music festival in the desert near to Timbuktu,' continued Little Mohammed, animated now. 'They have Tuareg music, Fulani music, many types. Ali Farka Touré played this year. And Robert Plant, you know from Led Zeppelin. He is English I think. Thousands of people come from all over Mali. They need many doctors for that. But my people, the Tuareg, they need doctors all the time.'

'Yes, Mohammed, well done,' repeated James, slapping Little Mohammed on the back. 'That's great you want to be a doctor of the desert. Yes, absolutely brilliant. You must do everything you can. Please do it. A doctor of the desert, oh, Mohammed, that is so good to hear.'

CHAPTER 18

SHOOTING SOUTH

THE FOLLOWING dawn Little Mohammed waved us off from Korioume on an eastbound *pinasse* freighted with millet sacks. We were in a hurry, James's flight a mere six days away. It was time to tear up the miles West African-style, just as Mungo Park had done at this stage of his journey almost 200 years ago, albeit with tragic results.

Now we were no longer relying on paddles, donkeys or even oxen, we hoped Gao, the next major city on the river, would only be three days away. From there James could easily reach Bamako and I could jump on any transport – bus, lorry, moped – shooting south across the sand towards Nigeria. We assumed that now we were in a boat with a motor we could work to a more predictable timetable – a big mistake.

Sure enough, the *pinasse* revved off from Korioume at a brisk enough pace. This lasted all of ten minutes before it sloshed to a halt, and drifted lazily over to the Niger's south bank. Soon the crew were hefting dozens of white hessian millet sacks onto the shore. When the relevant quota had been unloaded they held a pow-wow with the nearby villagers. This all lasted about half an hour, the *pinasse* launched off, reached the next village and the episode was repeated.

James and I soon realized that if this continued we would not make Gao in three weeks, let alone three days. It was our fault, of course. We thought it would be fun to be the only *tubabs* on a millet boat. It was fun, and cheap, just very, very slow. The fact no one on board spoke a word of French or English also made any travel updates tricky to gauge.

We sat next to an old, very dark man with a Confucian wisp of beard, who soon developed a taste for James's roll-ups. He was travelling with his two young grandsons, who I taught paper-scissors-stone to wile away the hours, while they proved expert hippo spotters.

Occasionally the buxom, henna-haired cook in the centre of the *pinasse* presented us with communal pots of rice embedded with small bony fish. I sat under a tarpaulin to fend off the sun writing my journal, showing the crew photos of my family and, when boredom really set in, reading James's *How to Do Cryptic Crosswords*. At night we all bedded down, sardine-style, amidst millet sacks.

Progress was sublimely sluggish. Not only were we stopping for trading and prayers, but occasional collisions with sandbanks, involving lots of shunting with long wooden poles to extricate ourselves again. At the end of the first day we were amazed to learn that, despite our boat's motor, we had travelled faster while paddling Karim's pirogue.

As his departure deadline loomed James became more pensive. It dawned on him he would soon be back in England. This meant family, job-hunting, dinner dates, Guinness: a whole new deck of cards. The Sunday after he returned he was even due to be become a godfather. He knew he had taken a big risk coming on this journey, and that now it was crunch time. Time to face the Homeric truth that when we travel it is the homecoming, what we bring back with us, that only really matters.

He steeled his thoughts accordingly, the sand in his Sahelian hourglass slowly running dry. Not even *How to Do Cryptic Crosswords*, including a stimulating chapter on anagram analysis, could hold his attention. He was interested in only one clue, one word, one answer: home.

We jumped ship at the remote town of Gourma-Rharous, some 70 miles east of Timbuktu. After three days and nights on the water we were still nowhere near halfway to Gao. With its exquisite lack of urgency our millet boat might well be zigzagging its way south even now. It was time for us to quit the river and head south across the sand, not on four legs this time, but four wheels, the faster the better.

* * *

Gourma-Rharous was such a tranquil, one-camel town, we worried it might not possess a single overland vehicle. Admittedly we had arrived in the heat of the day and the main drag's few shopkeepers were siesta-ing behind their counters or under palm trees. The one place that remained animated was the colonial-style police station, which, we were happy to see, had a couple of four-wheel jalopies parked outside it.

At reception sat a beige-uniformed officer, his face dominated by a Zapata-style moustache. Despite looking lugubrious as a bison, he proved a whirlwind of efficiency and within an hour had rustled up a driver – himself – and a dozen other paying passengers, many who ended up sitting on his battered Jeep's tailgate.

Before we left, James and I signed a hand-written contract. It stipulated Zapata would drive us as far as Gossi, a transport depot some hundred miles west of Gao, from where we could catch our connecting buses. As we left the police station I noticed a poster of Christian Velten on the wall. There was still no news, but at least efforts were being made to find the missing adventurer this far out.

Zapata blazed our Jeep into the wilderness like a man possessed. It was hard enough for James and me to stay seated in the front, let alone for the turbaned tail-end Charlies perched behind. Zapata swerved past acacias, skidded into dunes, thudded over bunkers, and revved wildly over ridges of deep sand. It was all highly exhilarating, especially when he screeched to a halt, grabbed a 12-bore from under his seat and fired off both barrels at what looked like a covey of partridge. For all Zapata's gun-slinging panache, the birds stayed vigorously intact.

Though the sun was falling the horizon stayed jellied by the intense heat. At one point Zapata removed his headdress, his dewy pate as bald as his Jeep's tyres. He wiped his forehead, swigged on a bottle of water, slotted in a fresh cassette of *kora* music and only then resumed his grip on the steering wheel. The road switched from hard earth to deep sand; one minute we were in a barren wilderness, the next rimmed by an escarpment of russet-coloured rock.

We pulled into Gossi, a knot of lantern-lit street stalls and mechanics' huts, an hour after dark. It had taken us five hours. It was too late to catch any ongoing buses so, after a dinner of bread, omelettes and coffee, we bivouacked on the ground near to a rank of food hawkers. As we cocooned ourselves in our sleeping bags, tantalizing smells of mutton, fried eggs and freshly baked dough wafted over us, occasionally overpowered by the snarling exhausts of night-time traffic.

* * *

Once the sun crested the horizon the next morning I took a stroll away from the road, washed my teeth, peed the usual 15 second *tubab's* trickle of viscous amber (despite drinking five litres of water the day before) and returned for another omelette. On the way back I noticed a sign with a silhouette of an elephant on it. I pointed it out to the hawker serving up breakfast. He was a small, weathered man, his stubble as bristly as pine needles. Considering he had been up all night he was remarkably chipper.

James, recently surfaced from his sleeping bag, helped me to interpret the hawker's scattergun French. Rubbing his stubble, he told us that when not flipping eggs, he acted as an elephant guide. There was a herd of some 500 of them near to Hombori, a couple of hours' drive west: perhaps the only elephants in the Sahel. Thanks to better grazing and a clamp-down on poachers their numbers were improving all the time, so much so they were starting to damage crops. He assured us this was an especially good time to see these elusive beasts before they retreated south to Burkina Faso at the start of the rainy season.

Though sorely tempted, neither James nor I had time to embark on a fresh safari. We each ordered more food and waited for our connections, James to Bamako, me to Gao.

'There's no way I'm going back to London, Tom,' said James, munching on his omelette and looking out into the bush. 'The money was good but no way. No bloody way. I'm going to live near Romsey, my family, my roots. The sea, ah, Christ, yes, the sea. I'm going to join a sailing club, find myself a girlfriend and a local job. Be part of something.'

'I give you two weeks.' I punched him on the bicep. 'Then you'll be the same stressed out fat cat. The Niger will flow off to a tributary far inside your over-pumped brain.'

But James wasn't listening.

'In the villages here they were so kind to us,' he continued, absorbed in thought. 'A couple of dickheads with a bull and a donkey! Some of their lives are so hard, so rough, but they didn't make any comparisons. They just looked at us and helped us out. Laughed, danced, showed such, I don't know, vibrancy, over the simplest of things. Tennis balls, chicken dinners, photos of our families.' He stopped and slugged on his coffee. 'I've been feeling sorry for myself in London the last few years. What a prat I've been! I'm the luckiest bastard around.' He paused and began to laugh. 'Okay, Mungo, I know I'm getting all sentimental, but, hey, honestly, I mean it. It's been one hell of a trip.'

Soon James's bus pulled over. We gave each other a brief, awkward bear hug, saying inappropriately bland things like 'Take care' and '*Bonne chance*'. James then surged in amongst the other passengers with their usual selection of vibrantly hued buckets and sacks.

I thought back to the pale, portly, slightly anxious character who had arrived in Bamako six weeks ago. Although I was sad to see James go now, I was happy his risk had paid off. Africa had been good to him. He had shed baggage physically, mentally and even that diabolically hefty rucksack of his was now much lighter. Waving from his window seat, my friend looked relaxed, at ease, the world off his shoulders. He was now ready, braced for perhaps his hardest journey yet, his 747 home.

*   *   *

Minutes after James's departure a Gao-bound bus turned up and within three hours – it would have been two without all the police checkpoints – I jumped down into the palm-fringed town square. A couple of shaven-headed children tugged at my leg. '*Cadeaux, cadeaux,*' they shouted, the first time I had heard this since Mopti.

While trying to shake them off a moped pulled up. '*Bonjour, monsieur,*' said the bespectacled rider, brushing the dust from his rumpled grey suit. He leapt from his Yamaha and politely shooed the children away. 'Don't worry, I'm not a guide.' He thrust out his hand for me to shake. 'I just like to speak to people from other countries.'

I had heard this ruse many times, but in Ibrahim's case it was sincere. When he worked out that I was English, his face lit up. 'Oh, I am happy,' he said. 'I lived in London for three years. A flat at the Elephant and Castle.'

Before we became too chummy I explained that I wanted to head out of Gao on the first south-bound bus. I needed to hot-tail it to Niamey, the capital of Niger, and then plough on down to the Nigerian border before my visa expired. Ibrahim assured me he could sort this out, and invited me to ride pillion on his moped.

We vroomed through the square, chicaning past a donkey cart, and down a narrow potholed street. After a few minutes we pulled over by a grocery shack. Without dismounting Ibrahim fired off some questions at the cashier's shadow and rode on.

'There's a bus this afternoon at two o'clock,' he said, spinning his head towards me, slow and precise as a gun turret. 'I'll bring you back. Okay? You've still got time for tea at my place. Real tea.'

When he said real tea Ibrahim meant Earl Grey, a brew he still had a hankering for from his London days. We sat in his living room sipping from our I LOVE JESUS mugs, while his two daughters watched a video called *My Big Fat Greek Wedding* in the background. The film had been dubbed but had English subtitles. One of the characters was saying: 'I have three testicles!' I decided my host couldn't be too much of a puritan.

Ibrahim's story turned out to be an interesting one. Born of well-to-do Tuareg parents, he had converted to Christianity at the age of 20 after speaking to some French missionaries in

Gao. It had been a tough decision but he had been impressed by the Bible, the sacrifice of Jesus.

'Many of my family have never forgiven me for converting,' said Ibrahim. 'Some of them refuse to be in the same room as me. Refuse to shake my hand.'

The first few years had clearly been immensely tough for him, but he stuck with it. Now his life revolved around his faith. During his time in London he fell in love with a fellow theologian, a Polish girl, now his wife and the mother of his two daughters.

'Let me show you our church,' he said, springing up from the sofa. 'It's just beside the house.' He led me through a paved garden lined by trellises of vines and blossom, centred around a pulsing fountain. The church wasn't really a church at all; just a large wooden floored hall with a hundred odd plastic chairs acting as pews. It could easily have housed another 200 or more. Posters proclaiming THE LORD IS KING lined the walls.

'The regular congregation is about 50, but we are building on it,' said Ibrahim, walking past the lectern. 'We have just started a youth section which is going well. Lots of hymns, Gospel singing, that sort of thing.'

'Is it tough,' I asked, 'being such a minority group?'

'A little. But I know I am doing the right thing. I am a Christian because it is a very clear religion, no grey areas. It is very definite.'

'Would it be easier for you and your wife in Europe?'

'My wife is happier here. I loved England, but this is my home. I made some English friends but I found the culture very different.' He laughed nervously, before adding: 'England is the only place in the world where a man tells his wife he loves her with his hands in his pockets.'

I laughed too. 'I've never heard that one before.'

'In England people have God's word all around them.'

Ibrahim ripped off his glasses and squinted at me. 'Many ignore God but at least they have the choice. Here, the people have no choice. We feel it is our job to spread God's love.' He looked at his watch. 'Hey, look at the time. We better get you to that bus.'

On the way Ibrahim pointed out some of Gao's landmarks – a sleepy museum, a market, a picturesque stretch of the Niger – but there clearly wasn't a whole lot to see. Gone were the opulent days of the Songhai Empire in the late 1500s when Gao was a trading and cultural hotspot. Through the years a combination of Moroccan ransacking and geographical isolation had drained it of all its former energy. A 'desolate abode with a small and miserable population' was all Heinrich Barth had to say in 1854.

But Ibrahim, judging from his breathless commentary, loved the place. And what did I know after half a day. I had been treated kindly here, served tea, driven around, let into some-one's life. That's what I would remember of Gao, not the dowdy architecture, the creeping malaise. It was always the people that stuck. I only hoped the Elephant and Castle had treated Ibrahim as well.

* * *

My bus south wasn't really a bus at all; it was more like a reconverted lorry or a mobile home on wheels. It was impressively overloaded, luggage slumping off its roof like bread that had risen too fast and surged out of its tin. To be fair, if I had read my *Rough Guide to West Africa* more thoroughly, I would have known what I was letting myself in for on my journey south:

> The piste is notoriously difficult (for some stretches
> there is effectively no visible track, and the bus can

get stuck for days) and this, added to the protracted
border formalities and the endless customs checks on
the Niger side, makes a challenging journey. Bring
plenty of water.

And this is what I could expect if I was travelling with the
region's premier bus service, SNTV, the best case scenario.
Sadly, I wasn't travelling with SNTV. I was travelling with Askia
Transport, who were dismissed as:

. . .very unreliable, using dodgy vehicles and
suffering long delays at control points since they take
passengers without identification papers . . . unless
you're desperate to travel on a specific date, they're
really not worth the hassle.

With my Nigerian visa countdown I had no choice but to plump
for Askia. I crammed in amongst the hundred or so passengers
in the vehicle. If this had been London, I thought to myself, there
would have been no more than 50. Some eyed me suspiciously,
especially the silver-haired old lady on my left, her lived-in
cheeks as rumpled as a walnut shell. But on the whole they were
a friendly bunch, smiling, offering around dates and biscuits. A
few were from Nigeria and spoke some English.

'Why you go to Nigeria?' said an old man directly behind
me. 'I am Nigerian. It fills my heart with sorrow every time I
go back there. Too many thieves and drunks and ooooh, bad,
bad women.' He laughed raucously at this, millet beer on his
breath. 'Those women are bad and beautiful, they will get you
and . . .' with this he clutched my shoulders and shook me,
causing uproarious laughter across the bus.

It took a while to get going and darkness fell within two
hours. I remember us stopping for a prayer session, a police

check and at one stage all of us helping to shove our venerable bus out of a sandy rut. At Ansongo, the last big town in Mali, I drank a sweet coffee while Bob Marley's 'One Love' pumped from a radio suspended from a baobab by a coil of wire. The white-bearded, kola-chewing hawker danced happily around his coffee stand.

It was a long, hot, dusty journey but no worse than any others. The scrunched up passengers were stoic and good humoured, although the jocular old Nigerian behind me did occasionally wail: 'Oh, Africa, Africa, how we suffer! You do not suffer in your country, England gentleman. Africa, it is Africa that suffers.' It was hard to disagree.

We reached the Niger border around midnight. We had been clipping along fine but it was here the wheels fell off our timetable, if not our bus. This, I was informed, is where we would spend the night. Everyone was told to disembark and bed down until the checkpoint opened at first light. I watched as my fellow passengers slumped down across the scrubland. Before long I might as well have been surveying a battlefield, the groans of the wounded substituted by snores and coughs. Nearby the River Niger purled its way south, quiet as a dream, while the burnished stars spun above.

* * *

In the morning a group of soldiers, who had been sleeping on mattresses outside the checkpoint, got to work. I was asked a few questions in French and my passport thrust into a pile of papers. While I waited for its return an argument erupted between two soldiers and a passenger from Chad, a rangy, gauche-looking youth, who was so incensed at not being allowed entry to Niger he picked a fight. The hapless fellow had no papers at all and was hauled off by the soldiers, crying, shouting and unrepentant. God only knows what happened to him.

Finally we set off again. I was in Niger now, a new country, although it didn't look a whole lot different, still flat, still fallow and with the same excruciating heat. My guide book showed a vibrant picture of some dancers at *La Cure Salée*, a festival for nomadic herders held in the rainy season near the remote town of Agadez. This looked about as jolly as it got here.

On paper Niger is a truly miserable sounding place, even by West African calibrations. It has the highest infant mortality rate in the world (one third dying before the age of five) and those who do survive average only a further 45 years. Literacy rates are less than 15 per cent (around 7 per cent for women). There is no university (it went bankrupt in 1993), no railway, few decent roads, an occasional sprinkle of rain and murderous quantities of sunshine.

Back in the late 1960s there was a spark of hope when in the remote Air Mountains uranium reserves were struck upon. After a 15-year boom the bottom fell out of the market. Now, following the Tuareg rebellion and a presidential assassination in the late 1990s, Niger's finances are once again in a parlous state, its tourist industry shattered.

Soaking up all the grim statistics, you somehow expect to see the horror all around you. But it's rarely evident on a bus, or in the street, rarely privy to the eyes of a passing stranger like me. The West African people are too proud for that. No, it's in the hidden places. The shabby camps in the back of beyond or the slums of the larger cities with their rusting tin huts and bortsch-coloured drains, in the unstoppable cough of a village child or the heartbroken eyes of loving parent. The people I rarely encountered; the invisible people.

But perhaps they weren't all invisible. During one pit stop in Ayorou, a tiny riverside settlement, I noticed children not only ate the peel of my discarded mango, but ravenously chewed the stone too. The harvest was long over and the rainy season yet to begin; this was the start of the *soudure*, the hungry period. What it was like in the remoter areas far from the river I could only guess.

One episode stays especially locked in my mind from the long journey to Niamey. We'd stopped off for prayers at a largish town called Tillabéri. Rather than watch my fellow passengers prostrating east, I drank a coffee at a street stall. While waiting I became so absorbed in writing my journal I failed to notice the bus was revving up, ready to leave.

Shouts of '*toubab, toubab*' slowly filled my consciousness. The girl who had poured me the coffee was nowhere to be seen. I fumbled in my money belt and left CFA 500, about 50p, to cover the cost and sprinted after the tooting vehicle. Apologetically climbing over several other passengers, I slumped back onto my allocated square foot of bench.

As the bus began to pick up pace, I heard a high-pitched scream from behind. I arched to look out of the window. Pedalling spiritedly alongside us was the girl who had served me coffee. She was on a clunky bicycle, struggling to keep it upright in the sand, waving her hands at the driver. She wanted him to pull over.

Seconds later we shunted to a halt. The girl, no more than 18, with long, raven-black hair, jumped off the bike and ran to the driver's window. Lots of excited chatter ensued. She handed the driver some notes and backed away, pointing at me.

The old Nigerian behind me explained what had happened. The girl was bringing me my change, he said. The coffee had only cost CFA 100 – a lot less than in Mali – and she wanted me to have my change.

'*Non, non,*' I protested to the driver. 'Tell her to keep it, please. Give it back to her. She is very kind to do this, but there's no need.'

When the driver translated this to the girl she simply smiled, backed away and returned to her bicycle.

'Oh, for God's sake,' I shouted in English, thrusting the money at him. 'Please give her the change. This is crazy.' The girl had pedalled furiously after the bus to return 40 pence. Forty pence! To a white man she would never see again. It was an extraordinary, soul-swelling gesture, especially in a country where 60 per cent of the population lived on a single US dollar a day. Judging by the tatty state of her coffee stall she might well be one of them.

'She is a very good girl,' said the old Nigerian.

'Yes, she is,' I replied, slumping back in my seat. 'She really is.' I was surprised how choked up my voice sounded. *Jesus, Tom, I told myself, don't lose it here. Come on, get a grip. You're tired, a bit run down. But, please, don't start to cry. Not here.*

'She is girl from Niger, very good, very kind.' The old man was off again. 'But the girls in Nigeria are not like that. They are bad girls. She is a good girl. Kind girl.' He spoke sincerely this time, no lewd insinuations or physical gestures, just singing the praises of the coffee girl. I said nothing, just took some deep breaths and closed my eyes. We were on a bitumen road now, the bus no longer juddering. Soon I fell asleep.

* * *

When I awoke in Niamey, Niger's capital, it felt like a city in a state of flux. Thanks to the uranium boom of the 1970s most of the roads were paved, but this did not stop donkeys still battling for right of way with mopeds and mini-buses. The odd glitzy hotel and high-rise sprouted from amidst all the mud, sand and litter, while camels padding over the river bridge across the Niger added a welcome whiff of romance.

I booked into the Hotel Moustache – apparently the owner boasted an abnormally hirsute upper lip – to the east of town. It was seedy but I didn't really care. I was only here one night before moving on to the Nigerian border. That said, one night made me a long stay client; most of the others, I soon discovered, booked in for an hour or two, having peeled away with one of the bar girls. To escape the muffled whinnying of strangers making love, I took a stroll around town.

The hungry period, or *soudure*, had affected Niamey too. At the central market hawkers beseeched me for a '*cadeau*' or to hire them as a guide. There seemed to be no other tourists at all. The touts looked close to snapping point, thrusting their heartbreakingly meagre trinkets in my face as if their lives depended on it. Some of them probably did.

The sun was no longer just a meteorological factor here; it was something more, something omnipotent, molten and psychotic, draining the people of hope. Some of them had clearly already given up. They sat in the dust, nothing to do, nothing to say, paralysed with ennui.

I peeled away from the market into Niamey's national museum. It was ramshackle but full of interesting curios including a 100 million-year-old dinosaur skeleton and a chunk of the moon given to the people of Niger by Richard Nixon.

A mini-exhibition about Niger's uranium deposits explained the chemical's devastating power. With visual aids it made clear 100 grams of uranium (about half a camera film canister) was the equivalent to one tonne of petrol or two and a half tonnes of wood. But this once triumphant display, set up in Niger's uranium heyday, now looked simply jaundiced and irrelevant.

My favourite exhibit was the famous *Arbre du Ténéré*. This stunted tree, the only visible landmark in a huge and remote expanse of the Sahara, became famous with travellers over-landing across the deserts of central Niger. Even now it is still marked on the Michelin map. Sadly, the tree was accidentally run down by a truck driver in the early 1970s. Its wounded branches now take pride of place in the museum, while a replica tree, made of steel, now sprouts from its place in the desert.

From the museum I weaved through some more hawkers to the internet café opposite. During the interminably slow email connections I got chatting to Raj, a businessman from New Delhi who was trying to sell cheap Chinese-made motorcycles all across West Africa. He had been partly educated in England – his mother was from London – and at times his voice slipped into fruity, Wodehousian vowels.

Raj looked out of place in the seething dustbowl of Niamey. He was dressed in an impeccable jet-black suit, with a cream shirt and a burgundy tie. Increasingly furious with his computer, he pecked at his keyboard with the ferocity of Jerry Lee Lewis.

'This stupid country,' he said, rapping the screen with his knuckles. 'I've been here three months. In Senegal, Mali, now here. Niger is worst. Nothing works. No one turns up for meetings. I'm here offering great deals but no one wants them. The whole place is dying on its feet.' He paused to look over at me. 'My contract here is three years. I'm not sure I'll last.'

Raj's company had picked him for the region because he spoke French. He thought he would enjoy the challenge of Africa, living a large part of each year in an alien environment, but he was already fast tiring of the heat, the mess, the corruption.

'Some people can adjust to Africa, I just can't,' he said. 'I came here to create some positive deals. But the big men rule everything. Once a man is rich in Africa he can't believe his luck. He does not want to help the poor. He becomes selfish and tyrannical. I don't believe this will ever change, not now, not in a hundred years.'

As Raj was talking a power cut darkened our room. The computers whirred to a halt. He began to laugh bitterly, raising his arms in the air as if a benign deity could pluck him away from all this.

'Colonization was terrible in Africa,' Raj continued, he clearly had a lot to get off his chest. 'Britain weren't great but the French were terrible. They only looked after number one. Oh, yes, there's lots of aid workers now trying to make amends, but what good are they doing. Nothing's really improved in 50 years. Poor Africa. All these crazy boundaries were drawn up, new countries created out of nowhere. I mean look at Niger. How much thought went into that? It's stretched across one of the most sensitive fault lines in the world, between black and Arab Africa.'

The lights pinged back on, stalling Raj's rant, and the computers began rebooting. Raj raised his fists in the air in mock celebration.

'So you see no hope at all?' I asked.

Raj smiled. It was a kind smile which took me by surprise. Raj had seemed so angry and self-pitying up until now. Perhaps he was okay, I thought, just weary, out of sorts. His better angels had now overpowered his demons, or at least briefly locked them in some sort of clinch.

'Hope, yes, a fragile hope,' he said, tapping at his keyboard again. 'You know that in the 1970s not one African ruler was voted out of office. Not one! Then in the 1980s only *one*. One in ten years. But listen, since then, 20 have been ousted. That's a huge shift, a sea change for the better. The big men won't go quietly, oh no, but they aren't invincible either. The question

is will the next set of leaders be any better. I wish I could say
yes, but I can't. Hope in Africa is always a fragile word.'

* * *

Early the next morning Raj picked me up at the Hotel
Moustache in a limo-style Toyota driven by his guide, Abdullah.
I had agreed to join him for a dawn safari. We were on our way
to see the last surviving herd of giraffe in the Sahel, thought
to be some 40 miles south of Niamey near a village called
Koure.

Abdullah, dressed in a suede jacket and movie star sunglasses, looked almost as out of place in Niamey as Raj. Still,
his knowledge of giraffes seemed more genuine than his
Raybans. He told us that only a decade before there had been
hundreds of giraffes. They had once grazed near Tillabéri (the
same spot the coffee girl chased my bus), but due to poaching
and erosion the animals had moved south. Now there were
thought to be no more than 80 of them. Abdullah made it clear
we might not see any, although Raj insisted: 'We're talking
about giraffes. Come on, Abdullah, they stand out a mile.'

We drove past villages of thatched huts, a nascent goat
market and dozens of baobabs silhouetted in the early light. A
warm, gritty wind blew in our faces. Raj stayed uncharacteristically quiet, looking out into the endless semi-desert. At
Koure, Abdullah spoke to a couple of rangers housed in a
wooden sentry box, and drove on. After 20 minutes we
swerved off left into the sand.

We bumped along, all of us straining to catch a glimpse of
wildlife. This was one aspect of West Africa that would have
been very different in Mungo Park's day. Although the explorer sees only one giraffe, or *camelopard*, as he calls it, he
comes across several lions, leopards, elephants, hyenas,

260

crocodiles and countless hippos. But today wildlife numbers have plummeted, much of it having been killed, not just for meat, but to make room for sheep, cattle and crops. Unlike the lusher eastern and southern parts of Africa, the Sahel is now almost bereft of big game.

It was all very different at the time of Alexander the Great when substantial herds of elephants roamed North and West Africa. But then along came the Romans, who not only enjoyed eating elephant trunk but loved to wear heavy ivory bracelets and necklaces (a sort of ancient bling). It was the lions that really suffered though, thousands of them being trapped and sent back to Rome to entertain crowds in huge venues like the Coliseum. In the first century the Emperor Trajan organized a gladiatorial bout during which over 2,000 lions were slain in a single day.

'Look giraffes!' shouted Abdullah, snapping me out of my bloody musings. 'Look, under the baobab tree, just there.' He cranked up the hand break. Gingerly, Raj and I crunched after him through the sand. And there they were. I counted slowly, nine of them. Some standing, some slumped in repose. My heart thudded harder as we inched closer; we were now only 20 yards from them. The giraffes could see us clearly but made no attempt to move. There were no other animals or birds, and very little vegetation: they were splendid in their isolation.

A male giraffe with dark markings leered down at us, swishing his tail, which looked near identical to a horse's. He had only one horn, the other half broken, making him look like some sort of elongated unicorn. A female sat beneath him, much lighter, almost honey-coloured, gorgeous and regal. The other seven were nuzzled together, some were dozing, others indolently nibbling at the tree. They looked utterly relaxed and harmonious and so tame, so guileless, showing they had no fear of man at all. Perhaps this was a bad thing; they would

261

make pathetically easy targets for poachers. But surely it would be impossible to shoot one of these animals and not, like the ancient mariner and the albatross, feel cursed.

I looked round at Raj. 'Whhhooooaa,' he said, letting out a constricted sigh. 'Oh, God. So beautiful.' He was captivated, wide-eyed. No longer the hard-nosed salesman, the ranting politico, just sheer spellbound. Abdullah was beaming too, happy to have tracked down his elegant quarry.

'Niger people,' he said. 'We love these animals. They make us proud.'

We all looked at each other, an unspoken camaraderie falling between us. We knew we had all shared something grand. It was one of those ineffable moments of travel, the reason you leave home, that feeling that you would rather be nowhere else.

As I sat in a mini-bus later that afternoon, zinging south to my pressing date with Nigeria, I thought back over the last few days. Two images stood out throughout my time in Niger, this parched country, this cartographer's excuse, this Saharan buffer zone, this place that, if I was honest with myself, I was unlikely ever to return to. Just two images eclipsing all others: a girl on a bicycle waving at a bus driver and nine lovely giraffes lazing in a baobab's shadows.

CHAPTER 19

NIGERIA

OVER TWENTY YEARS ago Chinua Achebe, one of Africa's most respected writers, called Nigeria, his own country: 'one of the most corrupt, insensitive, inefficient places under the sun. It is dirty, callous, noisy, ostentatious, dishonest and vulgar. In short it is among the most unpleasant places on earth.'

Everyone I met prior to my arrival still seemed to agree. On my travels I had already heard Gambians make fun of the Senegalese, or Malians criticize the Mauritanians, but no one, no one at all, had a good word to say about Nigeria. Not even the Nigerians themselves if Chinua Achebe and the old man on my bus to Niamey were anything to go by. Corruption was rife, military coups regular, urban violence widespread and the women would eat me for breakfast.

The Nigerian High Commission in London didn't exactly put a positive spin on things either, as I discovered when I turned up there two days before flying out to West Africa. Dozens of frustrated visa-hunters waved their papers at buck-passing officials. It was as if each office reflected its own country. Whereas the Malian Embassy in Brussels had been as Spartan and calm as the Sahel, Nigeria's High Commission was as animated, jam-packed and frazzled as I had expected Africa's most populous country to be.*

'You are going to be a tourist!' the matronly Nigerian lady had said to me while handing over my visa. 'You're not an oil worker? A teacher? A volunteer?'

'No, a tourist.'

'A tourist!' She had laughed, radiant, deeply amused, flashing Colgate teeth. 'Congratulations. You will be the only tourist in Nigeria!'

I remembered her words when, just before leaving Niamey, I read an email from Graham, a friend of mine who had spent many years in Africa as an English teacher. Graham had sent me a piece from *The Economist* about Somalia's tourist industry that was so comically depressing he thought it might make me feel better about Nigeria. This is how some of it read:

> Mr Jimale, Somalia's minister of tourism, admitted that his war-torn country has not had a single officially acknowledged tourist since the 1990s.
>
> 'The Sharmo Hotel advises guests to hire at least ten armed guards to escort them from the airport,' said Mr Jimale, 'and for extra protection you can buy hand grenades in the market for $10 each, or a howitzer for $20,000.
>
> 'Tourists can still go and see the former beautiful sights, but the only problem is they're all totally

*With over 120 million people, Nigeria is the tenth most populated country in the world. Lagos, the capital, now well in excess of 20 million people, is the world's fifth largest city.

destroyed. What's left of the cathedral is still very attractive, but if you go there, you must be aware of stepping on landmines. Our national parks were once very fine too, but they mainly lie in areas that the government now does not control. And unfortunately most of the animals have disappeared too, because we have eaten them.'

'If nothing else,' concluded Graham's email, 'you have to respect Mr Jimale's honesty and hope. There is greatness in what he says about Somalia. From my experience there's absolutely nothing great about Nigeria though. I hate to say this, but don't trust a soul. Good luck, Graham. PS Bribe everyone.'

And so as my bush taxi pulled up to the Nigerian checkpoint – I had spent the night before in a doss house in the Niger border town of Maradi – I braced myself for the worst. A soldier in black fatigues carrying a sub-machine-gun marched up to the taxi and pulled open my door. Here we go, I thought, reaching for my wallet. 'Hello, sir,' he said, smiling broadly. 'This is Nigeria. You are welcome.'

* * *

'YOU ARE WELCOME.' This is the phrase I will always remember about Nigeria. Not 'you're welcome' or just plain 'welcome', but every time, three clear words, often pronounced with such vigour it was as if a full stop fell after each one: 'You. Are. Welcome!'

This took me by surprise. I had not expected to be welcomed to Nigeria. I had expected to be badgered and hassled, grilled and ground down. But, no, I was welcomed with open arms. The fact there was sometimes an AK47 at the end of one of those arms made it no less gratifying. 'You are welcome' said the soldiers, the immigration officials, the taxi drivers. And I thanked them all, happy to hear my native tongue once again.

But for all the bonhomie, my opening couple of hours in Nigeria were still a shock to the system after drowsy, down at heel Niger. Once border formalities had been dealt with my bush taxi surged on south towards the ancient walls of Kano, my largest city in Africa to date. En route the landscape looked identical to Niger; the palm trees, the dust, the odd camel, but at the same time everything seemed more extreme. The traffic, the speed, the currency, the guns and the road blocks, especially the road blocks.

On the way from the Niger border to Kano my taxi was flagged down no less than 14 times. The checkpoints were often in the middle of nowhere and the soldiers manning them invariably shouldered some sort of weapon. It was clear if things turned nasty there would be nowhere to run. Although I tried not to show it, I was more than a little edgy.

Sometimes the road blocks were elaborate ranks of oil drums straddling the asphalt but others were more hit and miss affairs; a single wooden hurdle, a strand of rope suspended between two trees. My favourite was a long block of wood with nails sticking up from it which was whipped back and forth across the road by a soldier with a piece of string.

After the first half dozen checks I began to relax. Often my taxi was simply waved by and, even when I was stopped, the soldiers were jokey and courteous. I thought my luck had run out, though, when a huge beefcake in khakis marched up and shouted at me, his gun butting against the taxi's flank. I looked at him dumbfounded, paralysed with fear. Just as I was about to offer him all my wordly goods he let out a whoop of maniacal laughter. 'You are welcome!' he bellowed. Nigerian humour would clearly take a while to grasp. Out of the 14 road blocks I only ended up paying two bribes (or *dash*, as they are called in Nigeria). I considered this pretty good going, especially as they were only 200 Naira, about a pound each.

As we edged nearer to Kano all manner of flotsam lined the roads: rusted truck carcasses, plastic bags and dead dogs. Billboards cropped up, the most memorable blazing: FERTILIZE YOUR BODY – IMPOTENCE AND WATERY SPERM – WE CAN HELP YOU! NOW! Others advertised bread, milk, chocolates or else raged against calcium deficiency and AIDS. Near the centre we got snarled in a gridlock, the first traffic jam I had witnessed in West Africa. Hawkers tapped on my cracked window offering phone cards, toothpaste, onions and, in one case, a brace of black puppies peering, doe-eyed and anxious, out of a cage.

At around noon we pulled up at the Kano Tourist Camp, a series of concrete buildings festooned with ivy-like tendrils. A garden bursting with yellow blossom hemmed in the dormitory where I secured a bed for £2 a night. It was clear Nigeria was easily the cheapest country I had travelled in Africa to date. I dumped my rucksack in the long, shadowy room, fans thudding overhead. I was the only guest.

I immediately warmed to Kano but time was tight. As I wanted to leave in search of Mungo Park's monument early the following morning, I only had an afternoon to explore. I chose motorbike taxis as the best way to zip around the historic streets. Why didn't more African towns have this system? It seemed to work beautifully. Roadside punters were able to flag down all types of bike – anything from a 250cc Jincheng to a phut-phutting moped – at all times of day.

Admittedly the service was a little vague. The helmetless riders – who varied from teenage racers to hoary old pros – were at times stoned, fume-crazed or else trying to impersonate

Steve McQueen vrooming over the razor wire in *The Great Escape*. But the majority were steady navigators, able to chicane their way through Kano's chocked traffic far more easily than any standard taxi.

I shuttled my way from the Emir's palace, a sprawling, stately pile (firmly shut because the current Emir and his family were *in situ*), through one of the few surviving sections of Kano's 1,000-year-old walls and on to a sleepy museum. Inside was a photo of the Queen Mother, resplendent in an ostrich plume, visiting Kano in 1957, three years before Nigeria's independence.

The most memorable stop off was at the city's dye pits. Here, diligent men in white robes and conical hats sat dipping lengths of cloth into wells of blue and indigo. The wells were up to ten metres deep and it was important for the workers to continually dip the cloth in and out as, if immersed too long, all the material turned to black. The dippers each had a Nescafé tin full of ash, which, with the love and delicacy of a master chef, they seasoned their magical brews to help pattern the dye.

To the rear of the dye pits was a laundry area where clothes were washed and bashed into shape with the type of wooden cudgels once favoured by fairytale giants. Apart from the Nescafé tins and the odd pair of sunglasses it was a scene that would have changed little in 500 years.

To round the tour off I took my last motorbike ride – a Vespa-like machine with a cast-iron saddle – to Dala Hill, slap in the middle of Kano's old town. I scrambled my way to the top of the rocky path and within five minutes sat panting on its crest. Looking over Kano from a similar vantage point in the 1960s the veteran writer and traveller Jan Morris wrote:

The city sprawls below you festooned in heat and dignity. Somewhere across the horizon lies the

Sahara, and this is a place like Isfahan or Damascus, subtly impregnated with desert ways, with an echo of caravanserai, slave trade and pilgrimage . . . Kano looks exceedingly old from that high eyrie, exceedingly assured, exceedingly grand.

As I watched the sun dip over the fringing desert I decided Jan Morris's comments still rang true. It also dawned on me that it was the first major African city where I had almost been completely ignored. This wasn't surprising though, as despite spotting no other tourists that afternoon, I had seen many other shades of expat: Lebanese bakers, Indian restaurant-owners, Chinese wheeler-dealers and the odd flush-cheeked European in a suit, maybe a diplomat, a financial whiz, an odd-jobber, a lost soul.

With my sun-bleached hair and dowdy wardrobe I cut a very undistinguished dash. But then I reminded myself that even back in the 1820s the Scottish explorer Hugh Clapperton in all his naval finery had hardly caused a stir either. It was clear that over the last millennia Kano had seen every type of saint and scumbag walk through its gates. It was hardly surprising a traveller in a frayed lumberjack shirt and disintegrating plimsolls failed to turn heads in a place of such history.

* * *

I so liked Kano and the hassle-free environment of the camp site that I decided to use it as a base during my Nigerian travels. My next destination, the remote town of Jebba, was roughly 200 miles south-west and would put me back on the banks of the Niger. I wanted to travel very light and decided to leave most of my stuff with the friendly camp site staff. I'd only return once I'd tracked down Mungo Park's resting place.

Early the next morning I jumped in a southbound bush taxi. I was one of the first punters on board and squeezed into the back of the rusted Peugeot 504. Within half an hour all the other seats were taken. I was sandwiched against my window seat by a jolly, voluminously girthed woman, who introduced herself as Mrs Suleyman.

While waiting to drive off we were beseeched by a blind man, his eyes rheumy and pale, led by a melancholy-looking boy of about ten. The urchin thrust his hand into the taxi while the old man wailed plaintively. Mrs Suleyman handed over a mango, while I donated some coconut biscuits.

Soon we were gunning down a major highway out of the city. Gunning was no exaggeration. Our driver was a youth, no more than 18, his elbow stuck out of the window in a determined zigzag. A Marlboro hung from his lower lip and a pair of blue-tinted sunglasses perched midway down his nose. He barely looked old enough to drive a go-cart, let alone a lumbering estate car crammed with a dozen passengers.

I had read that Nigeria was notorious for wild driving. Not quite as bad as South Africa where over 11,000 people die in road accidents a year, but still bad enough to realize I was much more likely to come a cropper in this bush taxi than from malaria or hippo damage. In a continent where disease and starvation are commonplace, traffic accidents also take a terrible toll.

Dodgy cars, buses and roads all combined with even dodgier drivers (a recent UN report revealed that 94 per cent of traffic accidents in Africa were alcohol related) were a sobering mix. Over the past three years traffic fatalities across the continent had risen by a massive 300 per cent. The situation in Lagos was particularly bad, with public buses now being morbidly described by locals as *danfos*, flying coffins.

For the first time on my journey I was gripped by an intense fear. Only minutes out of Kano and we were nudging 100 miles an hour, the taxi rattling so hard it felt like it might break up in the ether. Our driver, yet to have his first shave, was driving as if an immortal. If he did have an Achilles heel it was now stuck firmly to the accelerator pedal. He was hurtling along, thumb lazily shifting the steering wheel like a Gameboy joystick. He overtook every other vehicle on the road, *every* one of them, even the purring Mercs and Toyotas. I surveyed my fellow passengers, expecting them to be similarly aghast, but no, they looked blissfully unconcerned. Either they were Prozac fiends or had seen this all before.

Try as I might I could not stop ogling at the obscene speed we were clocking. When we shot past a vehicle with the logo NIGERIA TRAFFIC CRIME PREVENTION UNIT on its boot, I could not help but let out a nervous laugh. Part of me wanted to lean out of the window and tell them we had been kidnapped, Mrs Suleyman was about to give birth, Dennis Hopper had planted a bomb in our boot. Do whatever you have to, just please, please, slow us down.

When we pulled over for our first pit stop, Cool Thumb Luke jerked the steering wheel too fast and we screeched to a halt with a clumsy skid. By this stage Mrs Suleyman had clearly had enough too, and she launched off in a tirade of infuriated Hausa. Several of the other passengers joined in. The boy looked suitably humbled and I was glad. Perhaps he would drive a little more slowly on the next stretch.

He didn't. We thundered off along the asphalt, Mrs Suleyman tut-tutting, while I simply shut my eyes and tried to cat nap. But soon we were on a smaller road and little Achilles had no choice but to ease his heel off the accelerator to contend with the potholes. Now we were firing along on slightly fewer cylinders I was able to strike up a shrill conversation with Mrs Suleyman.

She was heading south for the funeral of her uncle, she told me. She was from a small village in the north but had studied in Kano, where she met Mr Suleyman, a doctor. She now worked as a nurse in the same hospital as him, in a ward specializing in patients with weak bones. She said Nigerians had weak bones because they did not drink enough milk, never took enough calcium in their diets, especially in the desert-like north of the country. The lusher south with its grassland and big ports had more access to good milk.

I asked her whether she was a Muslim.

'Yes, I am Muslim, a Hausa, like many people in the north,' she said, chewing on a bar of nut brittle. 'But Jebba, where you are going, is full of Yoruba people. A Christian place, like much of the south-west. Then there are the Ibo people in the south-east. Nigeria is very complicated. There are so many different people and languages mixed up.' She stopped and laughed. 'It must be one of the most complicated places in the world.'

I mentioned to Mrs Suleyman about the 2002 Miss World contest which had been due to be held in Nigeria, but after some savage riots in the town of Kaduna – near to where we had taken our first pit stop – had been subsequently staged in London. The Miss World furore had caused particular unrest in the northern regions of Nigeria where Sharia, a strict interpretation of Islamic law, had been resurgent and where the contest was viewed as decadent and immoral. Miss World was further jeopardized when several of the contending girls pulled out in protest over the fate of a young Nigerian woman who had been sentenced to death by stoning after giving birth out of wedlock.*

'Yes, there are some problems with Muslims and Christians in the north,' said Mrs Suleyman, finishing off her nut brittle.

---

*The woman in question, 30-year-old Amina Lawal from Sokoto, a town in the far north-west of Nigeria, has since been acquitted.

The car was picking up pace again and I was struggling to hear her. 'There are good Muslims and good Christians.' She raised her voice above the roar of the engine. 'Sometimes they are okay together, sometimes they fight. This is Nigeria. This is the real Africa. Some of the places you have been so far are not the real Africa. You have been in places where few people live. Nigeria is the most crazy, crowded, dirty place. But it is wonderful too. I am glad you have taken time to see it.' She was shouting now. 'Nigeria is the real Africa.'

Defeated by the engine, angry not to be able to converse more, Mrs Suleyman shrugged her shoulders. I tried to ask her more questions but it was hopeless, our driver was once again testing his machismo and mortality in equal measures. I stared grimly ahead, but I was more road savvy now and, oblivious to all the cavalier overtaking, fell into a head-bobbing slumber.

* * *

A couple of hours later I was decanted into the heart of Mrs Suleyman's real Africa: the little town of Jebba. Mrs Suleyman, ever the nurse, gave me a bag of limes and some nut brittle to keep my energy up. 'You look pale,' she told me as we parted. 'Very sick.' She was right. I had been decidedly peeky throughout the journey but put it down to the roller-coasting high jinks of our driver. I'd be fine once I'd decompressed and had something to eat.

On Jebba's main street I wolfed an omelette butty, then flagged down a bike, a sturdy 250cc Jincheng, ridden by a balding, heavy-jowled man, who reminded me of a plump Ray Charles. He spoke little English but his eyes lit up when I mentioned Mungo Park. He patted his saddle, indicating for me to ride pillion. He clearly knew where Park's monument was situated.

273

Rather than heading over the Niger, he sheered off down a series of narrow side streets, lined by shacks with corrugated iron roofs. Chickens scuttled for cover and wood smoke hung in the fetid, motionless air.

'White man! White man!' shouted a group of youths at a mechanics' workshop, one waving a tyre lever in salute.

The road had now tapered into a track of hard mud. It was clear Jebba was nothing more than a large village, but an attractive one, surrounded by little hills and hemmed in by a wide, purling stretch of the Niger.

My driver decelerated and kicked down his bike's foot stand. A handsome, colonial-style building stood opposite. Oh bugger it! He'd misunderstood and taken me to the railway station. I jumped off the saddle and tried to explain via a series of a frenzied charades that we were in the wrong place. The driver smiled, grabbed my arm and led me onto the deserted platform. He pointed at a stack of scrap metal next to the station master's hut.

'Mungo Park,' he said.

I walked up to the rusting heap and noticed a sign jutting up beside it:

HISTORIC MONUMENT OF MUNGO PARK: RELIC OF THE SS DAYS SPRING, WRECKED AT JEBBA ON OCTOBER 7th, 1857.

I stared at Park's legacy in amazement. 'Mungo Park, Mungo Park!' repeated my driver happily, pointing at a huge metal propeller amongst the other debris. I shot off a couple of photos and surveyed the remains of the boat in wonder.

Whatever the SS *Days Spring* was, however remarkable its history, it had absolutely nothing to do with Mungo Park. Park's canoe, donated by King Mansong of Ségou, had been made of wood, half-rotten wood at that. It may have had paddles and bullock hides for fending off spears, but that was about it. The propeller of this ship (yes, ship!) at Jebba railway station, looked like it might have powered a small frigate, not a barely watertight canoe.

Then there was the date the *Days Spring* had sunk, 7 October 1857. An exceptional year, no question. The Indian Mutiny sparked off, Hollywood was founded and Joseph Conrad born, but as for Mungo Park, his canoe had capsized with all on board a good half-century before. Still, I had to admit, finding this bizarre tribute to the explorer was an unexpected bonus, however historically off kilter.

'Mungo Park,' my driver insisted once again, pointing towards his bike. This time, he must mean the monument, I prayed. We remounted and weaved back through the cluttered streets onto the main drag and over the Niger. Seeing the river again was a boon to my morale after my Kano hiatus, and my spine tingled with happy recognition. The Niger had been my journey's compass, both physical and emotional. At times in Mali the great river had looked tired, thin and seedy but now, some 300 miles from its mouth, it was once again wide and vigorous, flanked by nature: trees, grass and wild, fecund blossoms.

The motorbike peeled off the main highway, down some potholed switchbacks and over a railway track. I could see where we were heading now. A stone obelisk high on a hummock beside the river bridge prodded the overcast sky. The driver turned off the bike's engine and we walked up a path fringed with scrub and cracked boulders.

And there it was. Nothing special, rather bland in fact, much as Park's obelisk on the Gambia River had been. But the river view, a view I had longed to see for weeks, was commanding. There were crows wheeling on the thermals, spinneys of conifer and, of course, pretty, industrious Jebba far below. I sensed the size, look and character of Jebba would have appealed to Park. It was much like a Nigerian Selkirk. He would have enjoyed looking down on this proud little community.

I turned back to the monument. Dwarfed by the titanic masonry was a small metal plaque. It glowed against the stone, occasionally winking in the sun. My driver shucked up a cigarette from his top pocket and offered me one. I smiled but turned it down. I was high enough already as I reverentially ran my fingers over the plaque's burnished epitaph:

To Mungo Park 1795 and Richard Lander 1830 who traced the course of the Niger from near its source to the sea both died in Africa for Africa

* * *

It was only right that Richard Lander's name should be engraved beside Mungo Park's. Both their fates were inextricably linked to the Niger, the pair of them equally blessed with unflagging derring-do.

We last left the remarkable Richard Lander returning home from Nigeria in triumph in 1828, after surviving extreme thirst, a near fatal brew of poison and the death of his friend and master, Hugh Clapperton.

The young Cornishman soon settled back into Truro life, married a local girl, fathered a daughter and secured a humdrum job as a porter at a customs house. But, like Park, it was not long before his Niger Sirens got the better of him. Small-town life failed to stimulate Lander and, despite still suffering the odd malarial attack, he quickly volunteered for another African mission. This time not as a servant, but as a leader.

Lander was prepared to set off with very little money (always a plus with the Colonial Office). His one proviso was that he should be joined by his bookish younger brother, John, a printer on the *Royal Cornwall Gazette*. By December 1829 the two brothers had received their instructions: to solve the mystery of the Niger's termination by whatever means possible. Having been furnished with trading items (mirrors, combs, needles, pipes), some basic foodstuffs and medicines, the Landers sailed from Portsmouth on 9 January 1830.

Six weeks later they arrived at Badagri. Ironically they weren't to know they were only 200 miles west of their goal, the Niger's mouth. They could have simply sailed down the coast. Instead they made plans to travel north until they reached the Niger and then follow it downstream.

The King of Badagri was no more sanguine than during Richard Lander's last visit. The blood-thirsty monarch barely gave the two brothers – both pale, long-nosed and curly-haired – a second glance: he was too absorbed with the imminent execution of 300 prisoners. He did, however, after a substantial gift of gold dust, grant the two white men permission to travel north.

This was a good start and Richard Lander, already an old Africa hand at the tender age of 26, cleverly paved the way forward by pretending his party merely wished to track down Mungo Park's papers. It was an innocent excuse that stirred up no suspicion from the local rulers.

But it wasn't all plain sailing on the first leg. Despite Richard's practical verve, his brother, John, was not proving much of an explorer. Not only was he prim, revolted by the blacks' 'jetty countenances' but constantly falling sick, so much so the brothers at times only managed four miles a day. John's condition was so bad that at one stage Richard admitted: 'I expected every moment to be his last.'

But the younger Lander soldiered on and the pair of them reached Bussa in mid-June. Here Richard was re-united with the corpulent widow, Zuma, whose amorous overtures he and Clapperton had spurned on his last journey. Once again Lander resisted, noting that Zuma's girth had expanded yet further, to the extent she could now hardly squeeze herself through the doorway of her hut.

The brothers also visited the rapids on the Niger where Park and his crew had died and noted: 'Black, rugged rocks rose abruptly from the centre of the stream. The Niger here, in its widest part, is not more than a stone's throw across . . .'

They asked the King of Bussa, who had been a young child when Park died, if he had any of the explorer's belongings. The only item that came to light was a book of logarithms that belonged to Park. Not being interested in this, the Landers returned the book to its owner, who prized it as a fetish.*

The King of Bussa gave the two Cornishmen a clapped out canoe to continue upstream. Much of the route was tough going, with shallow water and dense vegetation impeding progress. In late June they reached the town of Yauri where they were shown a double-barrelled gun that had belonged to Park. They exchanged it for one of their own fowling pieces.

In early August they began paddling downstream in a variety of vessels before securing, in the town of Rabba, a 15-foot canoe, similar to an English punt. Bought from a chief with the gloriously apt name, the King of Dark Water, it cost them 10,000 cowries.

---

* The book was later purchased by Lieutenant John Glover RN in 1858. It is now in possession of the Royal Geographical Society in London.

Their new boat proved up to the job and, despite storms, hippos, crocodiles and the natives 'gazing at us with visible emotions of amazement and terror', by October they were near the Niger's end. They knew for sure when to their delight a seagull flew overhead. The ocean could not be far away now.

Days later the Landers became the first European explorers to reach the Niger's main tributary, the Benue, which intersects the great river some 200 miles from the sea. Here they narrowly avoided being sucked into a whirlpool before defusing an even more testing situation. While resting on the bank, a group of armed, near-naked natives converged on them. Showing extraordinary *sang-froid* the brothers threw down their arms and approached their attackers with friendly waves. It was a wise tactic and the tribesmen softened, believing them to be 'Children of Heaven' who had dropped from the skies.

The next stretch was straightforward, their canoe plashing its way serenely along a belt of forest where European traders were already a familiar sight. So quiet was it that the Landers observed: 'the banks seemed to be entirely deserted, and the magnificent Niger to be slumbering in its own grandeur.'

Less than 150 miles from the sea the brothers entered the realm of the Ibo river pirates. It did not take the pirates long to strike. Near the settlement of Damuggoo 50 large war canoes straddled the river, blocking the Landers' way. Richard spotted a Union Jack among the many flags displayed, giving him a brief spark of hope. This was soon dashed when he realized dozens of muskets were trained on him. His brother, John, paddling in a separate, recently donated canoe, capsized, losing his journal and Mungo Park's gun.

The brothers, now captured and at the pirates' mercy, sat withering in the sun, naked and destitute. Only some local woman showed sympathy, bringing them coconuts and plantains. Over the following week – it was now mid-November – the two brothers were held captive by various Niger delta dignitaries. Slowly the sorry-looking pair were shuttled down river until reaching the stinky, mangrove-infested region of Brass, where King Boy, their main captor, was chief.

During this time the brothers vented their frustration in their journal, noting that in most African towns and villages they had been treated with 'universal kindness' but on this stretch were 'classed with the most degraded and despicable of mankind . . .' Soon, however, their future looked more certain. Now they were near the coast, the egotistical King Boy wanted to sell the brothers to the captain of an English brig currently docked in Brass.

This did not prove an easy transaction. On King Boy's orders Richard Lander approached the brig captain, an irascible man called Lake, to pay for him and his brother to be released. Lake refused to cough up any money at all. Lander was horrified; he had been treated by one of his own countrymen in a manner even more vainglorious than that of King Boy. In despair Lander was forced to plead with the brutish Lake one more time and finally managed to strike a deal.

But even then Lake never intended to pay a bean. Once he had the Landers on board, he shouted at King Boy: 'I won't give you a bloody flint.' He then sailed directly into the open sea. Richard Lander was uncomfortable with the double cross but was nevertheless glad to be free. The Landers parted company with Lake at Fernando Po, caught a connecting ship to Rio and another bound for Portsmouth, where they anchored on 9 June 1831.

The Landers returned as heroes – the mouth of the great river no longer a geographical mystery. Even John Barrow, who for years had trenchantly insisted the Niger joined the

Nile, was forced to eat humble pie. The brothers' journal was published for a thousand guineas and translated into several languages. Richard was the first recipient of the Royal Geographical Society's gold medal and had a statue put up in his native Truro. For all this, neither brother received barely any money from the Colonial Office for their efforts.

John, the home bird of the two, found work at a Truro customs house while tireless Richard still could not clip his wings. Within two years he set off to the Niger for the third time as part of a trade-seeking mission. In the spring of 1834 he was ambushed by some natives roughly 100 miles from the Niger's mouth. He later died of his wounds, not long after his thirtieth birthday.

'Poor Lander,' observed Dr Oldfield, a surgeon based on the Niger at the time, 'he fell a victim to his too great confidence in the natives. Had his generous heart allowed him to be more suspicious and better prepared against their treachery, he would have escaped their murderous design.'

Both Park and Lander, two courageous men obsessed with the Niger, boasted many similar qualities and suffered near identical deaths. But whereas Park had been a victim of his own fears and suspicions on his second expedition, it seems Lander had retained a trustful heart to the end.

CHAPTER 20

A LITTLE MIRACLE

ANOTHER blistering April morning: my journey almost over. I had trailed the explorer for over 2,000 miles now: tramping, paddling, Peugeot 504ing, doing all I could to keep up with his illustrious shadow. Of course, my journey had been a breeze compared to his; a gallivant, a splendid privilege. But the relentless movement was still taking its toll and as my bus pulled into New Bussa, a scruffy town some 50 miles north of Jebba, my head swam with thoughts of home.

Now only one piece was left in my Park jigsaw – the site of his death. This would be hard to pinpoint. The rapids where his canoe capsized had, for over forty years, been submerged by Kainji Lake, a vast, artificial stretch of water just north of New Bussa dominated by Kainji dam, one of the largest in Africa, its roaring cascade of water generating electricity for most of Nigeria.

Having tracked down a New Bussa guest house and dumped my kit, I forged a plan. First up, I decided, I needed a boat. With this I could sail across to the approximate spot Park had drowned. My task was made all the easier when I bumped into

Clement, a schools' inspector from Lagos, who was staying in the room opposite, the only other guest. He told me he wasn't working today and would be happy to help me out.

Before departing Clement kissed a silver crucifix hanging from his neck and combed his tight frizz of hair. He then fired up his scooter which had a sign 'NO FOOD FOR THE LAZY MAN' above its number plate. Judging from Clement's ample girth, indolence was not his thing.

We sped off to a sprawling concrete building west of town, the HQ of the surrounding Kainji Lake National Park. Clement marched me down a series of stygian corridors. On one wall hung a photo of several dead men lined up like battle casualties. They were surrounded by camouflaged soldiers with rifles. 'The dead men are poachers,' whispered Clement, seeing me gawp. 'Wildlife is very rare here. Killing poachers is the only way to stop them.'

Clement weaved on through to a cubby-hole at the rear of the building. It belonged to Mr Alba, a dapper, bespectacled fellow with a coop of chickens squawking under his desk.

Once Clement explained what I needed there was a lengthy pause. Mr Alba eyed me up with a sort of forensic zeal, his stare as unselfconscious as a child.

'So you want to find Mungo Park?' Mr Alba asked.

'Yes, the place where he died,' I explained, adding a bit about my journey and the reasons for embarking on it. There was another long pause and another long stare. Even the chickens fell silent.

'Very well,' said Mr Alba, sudden, decisive. 'You can have a boat for four hours. It will cost you 50 American dollars. You will be accompanied by a guide called Joseph.' He bellowed out Joseph's name, and a tall, regal man with thinning tufts of white hair appeared behind us. He seemed to materialize Jeeves-like from out of nowhere, a huge orange gourd under his arm.

'Can't I go with some other people?' I asked. 'I thought groups toured the lake. Fifty dollars seems a lot.'

'We have very few groups,' mused Mr Alba. 'You and Mr Clement are the only tourists now. Joseph is a very good guide. He can take you to the village of Old Bussa near to where Mungo Park died. This is good value.' He stopped and glowered at me like a benign cat. I don't think I had seen him blink yet.

'All right then,' I said, throwing caution to the wind, 'let's do it.' This was, after all, my journey's swansong.

'Good! Joseph take this.' Mr Alba handed Joseph a rusty flintlock rifle leaning against his desk. It looked like the sort of gun that would be far more dangerous to actually fire than to be targeted in its cross hairs. 'Good luck to you all,' said Mr Alba, remaining rooted to his desk. He seemed happy to have clinched a deal.

As Clement and I followed Joseph to his truck I asked him why we needed a gun.

'Bandits,' said Joseph, grinning. His smile was generous, gap-toothed and full of silver caps. I only hoped the bandits were amateurs. I feared a Napoleonic rifle and my slender grasp of the art of t'ai chi would prove dubious deterrents.

'And what do we need this for? asked Clement, pointing at the large gourd Joseph held under his other arm. 'Is it another weapon?'

'This?' Joseph seemed surprised by the question. 'This is our life-jacket. It floats very well. If we sink, we can all hang on to it.'

* * *

It soon became clear we would not need a life-jacket. Kainji Lake was as placid as a canal and our motorized launch skimmed swiftly over its glassy surface. Just before hitting the open water a clutch of black ducks sprang up from a reed bed. They flew so fast it was as if they had been catapulted. The only other evidence of life during the two-hour trip to Old Bussa was the odd fishermen's dugout.

We anchored some 20 yards out and splashed our way, waist-high in water, over to the shore. Joseph held the rifle above his head, Clement did the same with the gourd. The village of Old Bussa was still a half mile walk through tall dry grass. Midway we passed a couple of derelict buildings.

'They were holiday places,' explained Joseph, pointing at the collapsed masonry, 'built after the lake was made in the 1960s. But not enough tourists came and now, pah. Such a waste! Many villagers whose homes were submerged by the lake were angry. They had to move to New Bussa instead, village people forced into the town. They were given new homes but their lives were turned, how do you say, upside down.'

'So who lives in Old Bussa now?' asked Clement, struggling to keep up with Joseph's quick, rangy legs.

'Fishermen from out of the area. They came after the original town of Bussa was flooded and they built a new village. It's called Old Bussa because it is near to the original site.'

'Would they know about Mungo Park?' I asked, dodging a termite mound.

'I don't know. I've never asked them. The old residents of Bussa certainly knew of Park, he was part of their history too.'

We were now nearing the village and some children sur-rounded us, whispering excitedly, two of them grabbing my hands. The village was fringed by a raffia-like fence and contained huts of both thatch and mud. We walked into a central area where a huddle of old men sat under a palm tree.

Joseph pointed out the chief and I put my hand on my heart and thanked him for allowing me to visit the village. He looked at me, unsmiling. His jazzy waistcoat, its material as coarse as a sweetcorn husk, belied a serious demeanour. He answered Joseph's questions with a series of brisk nods. Another rough-hewn old man sitting astride a bicycle occasionally butted in and whooped with laughter.

'What is this man laughing about?' I asked.

'He says he wants to go to England with you. He wants to meet a white wife.'

'Hasn't he a wife here?'

'Oh, yes, and 14 children!'

'Fourteen!' The children laughed at my wide-eyed reaction. I joked that I only had one. I took out my wallet and showed the man on the bicycle a photo of Eliza. She had been on my mind a lot recently and the photo was frayed from repeated viewings. His face lit up with a smile and then he turned on me, suddenly severe.

'He wants to know why you are here,' said Joseph, translating. 'Not at home with your daughter.' It was a question I had been asked so many times, especially in the villages. How could I have a young daughter and yet be out here gallivanting around after some long dead explorer? I remembered Robert's furious reaction at the beginning of my journey in Banjul. 'What are you doing here, all alone? You must be a good Christian, my friend!'

'I miss her very much,' I said feebly. 'I'll spend lots of time with her when I'm back.'

One of the children, a tall, giggly girl with kohl-blackened eyes, grabbed Eliza's photo and pretended to run away. The old man on the bicycle caught her by the arm and took it back from her. He handed my daughter's picture back to me with a silent reverence, as if it was the most precious thing in the world.

And then, sitting there beneath the palms, sweating away in the midday shade, breathing in the thick, fetid air, I underwent a quiet epiphany. I decided I'd had enough of haggling for donkeys and coughing up bribes, enough of sledgehammer sun and iodined water, enough of nerve-shredding bush taxis and never knowing where I would next lay my head. It had been quite a journey, a terrific blend of fist-shaking despair and soul-popping wonder, but I was tired now.

Taking one last look around at this timeless place, at the goats, the lone straggly cow, the fledgling maize crop, the proud old women pumping water, the fishermen stitching their nets, the serene, inscrutable chief sitting on his haunches and the sea of smiling, curious children looking up at Eliza's photo, this child from another world, but one of them all the same, my quest to find Mungo Park seemed almost obscenely trivial. That was it, I decided, right there and then. It was time to go home.

There was only one more question.

'Has the chief heard of Mungo Park?' I asked Joseph, re-placing Eliza's photo in my money belt. Joseph translated this to the chief in his deep, musical dialect.

'No,' said Joseph, formal as an equerry. 'He has lived here for only 20 years. He has never heard of Mungo Park.'

Clement slapped my back. 'Your search is over, Thomas,' he said.

* * *

Later, blazing along in the boat, Joseph killed the engine in the middle of Kainji Lake. The weather was breaking, currents of cool, stormy air taking the edge off the heat. The water was livelier now and webbed with wrinkles. Spits of cold rain teased my sunburnt face, my first proper rain since arriving in Africa. Far ahead forks of lightning creased the sky.

287

'It is somewhere here that Mungo Park died,' said Joseph, pointing at the inky surface. 'Under here it is all rocks. This is where he drowned.'

For the final time I tried to imagine the scene: the harried Scotsman shooting the rapids, arrows zipping all around, men falling overboard, utter confusion. Park would surely have known death was imminent, but as he was sucked under what ran through his mind?

Did he curse his luck, knowing his second stab at Niger glory had proved a dismal mistake? Or did he go down with his canoe, proud in the belief that he had given the trip his best shot? Or did Mungo Park, the son of a Selkirk farmer, finally cling to the thought of Ailie and his four children, his only true lifebuoy, as the roiling river swallowed him?

* * *

That evening back at the guest house I started shaking. Nothing severe or uncontrollable, just a minor bug, I told myself, nothing to panic about. Besides, my appetite was still intact and I was well enough to trough a bowl of cassava with Clement. This was a mistake. Midway through the meal I felt all colour drain from my face. I dashed into the guest house garden and threw up violently, twice. The cassava, to be honest, had been pretty rough, but not that rough. Please, God, I prayed, don't let this be malaria.

Clement was a calming influence and I lay on a bench outside while he plied me with sweet tea and conversation. The spots of rain on the lake that afternoon had fizzled out, the storm never properly letting rip. I longed for a breeze. The night was stagnant, hotter than ever, my body febrile and slick with sweat. I was glad not to be alone.

Despite spending the best part of the day with Clement, I realized I knew next to nothing about him. This was all about to change. After bringing me a cold cloth to put over my forehead he looked me hard in the eyes.

'Have you put your trust in God, Thomas?' he asked. At first I was alarmed. Did I look that bad? So sick that he needed to save my soul right now, before I slipped away. But no, it was soon clear he was just another of Nigeria's many evangelical Christians. Being shivery and immobile I was a perfect candidate, an ailing sinner with nowhere to run.

Clement ferreted in his day pack and pulled out a video. I looked at the cover. It starred Mr T and a balding actor I vaguely recognised from *LA Law*. Clement told me it was a futuristic thriller about a group of born-again Christians fighting for their beliefs in a world of crooks and sinners. It was called something like *Judgement* or *Redemption*. He asked me if I wanted to watch it.

'I'm afraid I'm not very religious, Clement,' I replied. 'Not really my thing.'

'But Thomas, you must put your trust in Jesus,' he said, clutching my arm. 'You must save your soul. Let me tell you something, Thomas.' Clement was clearly spurred on by my silence. 'I was brought up in Lagos. My parents were good people but had no real faith. When I got my first teaching job I was posted to a little village in Cross River province, south-east of here. It was a very traditional place. One of the last areas in Nigeria where they still killed twin babies. They used to think of twins as evil, you see. Just think, if it hadn't been for the missionaries that might still be going on. Anyway, by the time I arrived it was a completely Christian village.

'If I'm honest village life bored me crazy at first.' Clement rolled his eyes for effect. 'Remember I was from Lagos, Thomas, the wildest town around. But then I got involved, I organized plays and film evenings, tried to be a part of every-thing. And, of course, I joined the church. At first the church didn't mean much but then I clicked. I began to learn what it was all about. Want to know what I learnt, Thomas?'

'Sure,' I replied, looking up at the stars as he commentated. Cicadas were churring all around. I was still shivering.

'You really want to know, Thomas?'

I nodded as encouragingly as possible.

'Sacrifice!' Clement shouted the word, grasping my arm even harder. I flinched with surprise. 'Sacrifice! Sacrifice is what Jesus taught us. To be good people we must help others, sacrifice a bit of time and energy. Be kind. Help other people turn to God.

'Recently my faith was put to the ultimate test, Thomas. I was in Jos, a beautiful town in the hills of central Nigeria. It was around the time of the 9/11 attacks in New York. There was an anti-Christian riot. Muslims took to the streets and killed over a hundred Christians. I saw two of my friends killed. I only just escaped. I have a wife and three children, Thomas. If I die what will happen to them! After this I had to decide whether to be an active Christian and continue to risk my life, or whether to simply hide my faith.'

'And are you still active?'

'Yes, I am, Thomas! Yes, I am. I know that in Europe religion is fading. Europe once was the centre of Christianity. Not now though, now it's Africa. I believe through the centuries the baton of Christ is passed from country to country. The baton is now with us in Nigeria. It is up to us to spread the word.'

'But all the killing, Clement. The Muslims killing the Christians, the Christians killing the Muslims. Religion has been so destructive here.'

'Don't always blame religion, Thomas,' Clement snapped, briefly shutting his eyes. 'Often it is tribal disputes, politics. We must have faith now, Thomas, at all costs. We need Christ more than ever.' His eyes were shining with evangelical zeal but his voice had softened. 'Nigeria has so many problems, Thomas.

Too many. I work in education, Thomas. A schools' inspector. Our literacy rates are terrible, worse than the Congo. And there is much corruption, people bribing teachers. We must stop this. Honest people should have a chance, not just the liars, the greedy, the corrupt.

'Nigeria is full of sin, Thomas, of drugs money, of thieves. But our worst problem is the leaders, so many dictators. Oh, how we suffer with these terrible men. One of our recent leaders, President Abacha, he did not rule Nigeria like a country, but like his own playground. He died while sleeping with prostitutes. They say he took too much Viagra.' I couldn't help but chuckle at this and he joined in.

'But there are good men, Thomas,' Clement said, regaining his composure. 'Look at your namesake, Thomas Sankara in Burkina Faso, he preached simplicity, told his cabinet not to fly first class, encouraged people to ride bicycles. He was killed in the 1980s by rebel officers. We need more like him. Our new president, Obasanjo, isn't great. But he's not so bad either. We have a chance with him. We don't need to develop, Thomas, just to hold on to what we've got. We need a little miracle. But it is only through Christ that . . .'

At this point my shaking got the better of me. I wanted to listen, but I was ailing, the parasites in my belly running amok, like creatures spilling through a torn fence. Clement sensed my discomfort and helped me sit up. I thanked him, straightened myself and shuffled to my room.

As I lay sweating on my bed, the fan churning overhead, I mulled over Clement's impassioned words. It had been good to hear him rail so eloquently against injustice, fed up with Nigeria's elite squandering the country's future on their own instant thrills. Nigeria, indeed everywhere I'd travelled in West Africa, seemed full of these brave, decent individuals like Clement: it was really only the regimes that stank.

291

Although I didn't share Clement's faith I could understand why it was so strong. I sensed he believed that if he prayed hard enough, dreamed hard enough, fought hard enough, he could tap into something more; more than all the chaos and dire statistics that surrounded him. He could take his country one step closer to that little miracle he so longed for.

CHAPTER 21

TO THE WORLD'S END

WHEN I WOKE the following morning, it was clear it would take a little miracle to get me back to Kano. I wasn't in good shape at all. My limbs were aching, my guts turbulent and I still had the shivers. In the night I had also managed to acquire a set of wildly ejaculating sinuses. It would be foolhardy to travel. But at the same time I desperately wanted to be at the Kano Tourist Camp, a familiar place, where I would be safe if my condition worsened.

And so at lunchtime Clement rode me on his scooter to Mokwa, the local transport depot. Weaving through the food hawkers, he pinpointed a creaky looking mini-bus heading for Kano. I walked on board, fragile as something freshly hatched, and slumped near the front. On the window was a sticker of Madonna, pouting and blowing a pink bubble of gum.

'Here, Thomas,' shouted Clement, handing me up a bunch of bananas through the window. 'Take these for the journey.' I grabbed them from him and nodded my thanks. 'God bless you, Thomas.'

'Who was that person?' said a scowling hulk of a man next to me. 'Is he your slave or something? Nigeria is independent now, you know.'

'No, he's a friend,' I said, slightly taken aback, waving at Clement as he vroomed off on his scooter. I watched NO FOOD FOR THE LAZY MAN diminish, like an optician's letter board, until it blipped out of sight.

We were off minutes later, the mini-bus travelling at the usual breakneck pace. The narrow road was at times flanked by roadside wrecks, tangled truck chassis and burnt out cars and buses.

'You are sick, aren't you?' said my tough guy neighbour, looking me up and down and rubbing his neatly trimmed sideburns. 'You cannot handle Nigeria. It's too difficult for you, isn't it?'

'I like Nigeria,' I said. 'I'm just a bit tired.' I gave him a brief description of my journey, Mungo Park, the countries I had travelled through. I hoped he might give me a break.

'Oh, so the great white man comes to look at our country.' He spat out the words, playing up to the other passengers. 'He travels down the River Niger. And now he is ill! Maybe he will die here too, like his great explorer.'

'I'm absolutely fine!' I replied, feverish, rattled. This man was smart, vindictive and wanted to bait me. I tried to ignore him. Frustratingly, before long my inflamed guts could hold on no longer and I asked the driver to pull over. I hunkered miserably behind a wispy bush before pottering back to the bus. I felt humiliated and incredibly weak.

'The white man has eaten too many yams,' joked my neighbour. He had the passengers firmly onside now and they all laughed fit to bust. Normally I would have laughed too, but I was wretched today, and just felt hurt and pissed off. The bus driver drove on, a display of geegaws – beads, crosses, photos

– dancing on his windscreen. I slumped back down next to my tormentor.

What was worse, I realized this vile neighbour of mine was right. I did cut a pathetic figure. And no, I couldn't handle it. I came from a soft land, too soft to cope long out here, West Africa, a place where people needed a spark of greatness just to survive each day. Clement, little Mohammed, Karim and Fatima, the girl on the bicycle near Niamey and a thousand others I had met on the road.

'You know where I am going, white man?' my neighbour asked. I stayed silent. 'I am going to Morocco. From there I am getting into Spain, then up into France, maybe England. I need money you see. My brother is in Marseilles. He got caught without a visa, stealing. He is in prison there. I have no visa either. What do you think of that?' He nudged me. Just from this gesture I could feel the tension within him, the violence. 'I was in university, white man, a student in Lagos, but I cannot pay for it now. I must conquer your country, like you have conquered mine.'

Conquered West Africa. It almost made me laugh. I had struggled along its parched contours for three months, and, thanks to the kindness of strangers I had got away with it, come through unscathed. But if anything, it was West Africa that had conquered me.

'What are your chances?' I asked. 'Spain will be hard to reach without papers.'

'I don't know my chances,' he harrumphed, shrugging. I noticed he was wearing an American-style baseball jacket and chino trousers. He looked in his mid-twenties but might have been younger. He could have been a student anywhere in the world. 'I do not know my chances, white man. It will be difficult I'm sure, I will need a boat. But I have no idea. All I know is I would like to stay at university in Lagos, but I cannot.' As

he spoke this time his voice turned to a whisper. I noticed his
eyes smarting with tears.

All my fear and anger evaporated. Why shouldn't this fierce,
intelligent man feel bitter, I realized. Why shouldn't he have a
pop at me? It must have been a major sacrifice for him to go to
university in the first place, his family too. And now he was
forced to join the swelling ranks of rainbow-chasers and
desperados sneaking across the Mediterranean. He clearly didn't
even want to go, he wanted to stay in Lagos and study. It seemed
such a waste, a pitiful snuffing out of this dynamic young flame.

'I wish you luck,' I said.

'Yeah, sure, we'll see.' He was gentler now, less begrudging.
After a long pause he said: 'And you see a doctor soon, you
hear.' I promised I would, relaxed against my rucksack and
soon fell asleep.

When I woke later that evening he had gone.

* * *

By the time I got back to Kano the battling parasites in my gut
had called a ceasefire. My shivers had calmed down too. Even
so, after spending a night at the Kano Tourist Camp – where
the staff seemed as happy to see me as I was to see them – I
deemed it sensible to visit a clinic the next morning. I was
recommended a place just up the road.

After a short wait an elderly nurse sat me down, stuck a
needle in the tip of my thumb and squeezed out a bead of
blood. Twenty minutes later an addled young doctor brusquely
called me in. He told me I hadn't got malaria. That was the
good news. The bad news was that he still wanted to check me
out. After an extensive session of tweaks and prods I learnt I
had a mild temperature, a chest infection, a bit of sunburn and
that I badly needed some rest.

Armed with a handful of antibiotics I returned to the camp site. I stripped off and lay under a propeller fan in the dormitory. I fell asleep at about 10.30 a.m. and did not wake until dusk. I felt much better, still very weak, but without the shivers, coughs or volcanic sinuses. I drank a pint of cold yoghurt and slumped down in front of the tourist camp's communal telly. I realized I hadn't watched TV – other than brief glimpses of African football or the *Benny Hill Show* – for months.

To my great surprise the film *Jerry Maguire*, starring Tom Cruise, was showing. I remembered seeing the film several years ago at the cinema with a girlfriend who had loved it. I had found it very schmaltzy but what the hell, it was in English, had The Who on the soundtrack and Renée Zellweger at her most beguiling.

It soon became clear my second viewing of *Jerry Maguire* was under very different circumstances. I was sick, travel-beat and more than a little lonely. The film made me hoot with laughter, sing along to Elvis's 'Pocketful of Rainbows' and by the time Jerry was telling Dorothy 'you complete me' I was in a state of absurd emotional meltdown.

In fact I was so emotional I decided to call Eliza. It was 7.30 p.m. (Nigerian time being the same as Greenwich). It was also a school night. Oh hell, she might just be up. I only wanted to quickly hear her voice. Incredibly it was Eliza who answered the phone.

'Hello.'

'Eliza, is that you! It's Daddy.'

'Daddy! You sound funny. Are you coming to baby-sit?'

'I'm a long way away, sweetheart. But I'm coming home very soon. I promise. How are you?'

And then she was off. Eliza was either chatty on the phone or didn't say a word. Tonight she was Miss Chinwag. She told me she could ride her bicycle without 'staperlizers', didn't do ballet anymore (the teacher was 'silly') – she was learning French instead – oh, yes, and there was a sleepover at a friend's at the weekend. Oh God, I thought, she sounds like a teenager already. The line began breaking up.

'I can't wait to see you, Eliza-Lou. I love you.'

'I love you, Dad.'

And then she was gone, a faint hiss was all that was left of my other life: a life I would have happily morphed back to right away. I slumped down under a tree ripe with pungent yellow blossom. Through the branches I could make out the night sky, clear as ever, a canvas of luminous pinpricks.

'I love you', I thought. They have to be the most over-used, under-valued, maudlin, manipulative, vapid and insincere trio of syllables of all time. But once in a while they live up to their promise, hit the mark, burst the poison and swell the heart. Then they are pure, ineffable, a talisman to stave off all harm, to take on the world: the very best three words.

* * *

The next morning the sickness was gone. It was as if a cleansing syringe had been stuck in my navel and surfed out all the gremlins, clearing the fog in my head at the same time. I was ready for the final leg now, to make a beeline for the mouth of the Niger: to travel 'to the world's end'.

The staff at the tourist camp told me there was a train leaving for Kaduna that morning, and, once there, I could catch a night bus to Port Harcourt, the oil-rich city where the Niger meets the sea.

My guide book warned reaching Port Harcourt might be tough. It was not complimentary about Nigerian railways, admitting: 'all services liable to suspension' and that: 'Even when running . . . and not hours late, trains are painfully slow.'

So, I was pleasantly surprised when at 9.30 a.m. (on the nose) my train chugged onto the platform at Kano station. My compartment was uncrowded, airy and offered commanding views of the flat, empty landscape. There was also a constant supply of coffee, bread rolls and Evangelicals ready to save my soul. And the laughably cheap ticket (£2.50) even included accident insurance. It was without doubt the most comfortable, best value journey to date and I was deposited at Kaduna bang on time, early in the afternoon.

The connection wasn't quite as straightforward. My Port Harcourt-bound bus, a mural of Jesus distributing loaves and fishes on its flank, filled up as the sun fell. THE LORD IS ALWAYS WITH YOU, read a sticker above the dashboard. It should have perhaps added: AND ON NIGERIAN ROADS YOU'LL NEED HIM.

Before departure a preacher stood at the end of the bus's aisle and spouted excitable truisms about the apocalypse. What was this, I wondered, a bus to Port Harcourt or the road to Damascus? Perhaps it was simply a Nigerian public service to make sure you were at one with your maker before any long journey.

The preacher's fire and brimstone sermon was mercifully interrupted when all the passengers were ordered off the bus by the ticket collector. A sour-faced dominatrix, she practically pushed us out into the night. Apparently, this was commonplace on Nigerian buses. There had been a recent spate of bus hijackings and it was important the vehicle and the passengers were thoroughly frisked for weapons. Once proved to be gun-free we all jumped back in.

The next thing I remember is waking up and feeling utterly at sea. My head was leaning against the bus window, but something was wrong. I looked out on a landscape of green. Everywhere green. And what was that noise? Drizzle. Not just drizzle, proper rain, heavy rain, dripping down the window, dimpling the soft earth like gunfire. Disorientated, I stared out at this lush new world in amazement. After three months of dry skies and hard, dun-coloured landscapes, this ambient jungle was all a bit much. I drank in the view, mesmerized.

The journey continued for another couple of hours, the jungle turning to forest, then slowly into a series of inchoate suburbs, before finally hitting the seething steam pot that was Port Harcourt. By the time I disembarked the rain had softened, but the sky remained warm, bruised and overcast. I put on my cagoule for the first time in the journey, revelling in the damp air. I shouldered my rucksack and hailed a motorbike taxi. Just one more appointment, I thought, and then I could fly home.

'Where do you want to go?' asked the biker.

'To the end of the river,' I replied.

* * *

On a creaky wharf on the tip of Port Harcourt's old town, I put on a life-jacket and jumped aboard a crowded dinghy. Our skipper revved the engine and the prow of the little boat reared up, like a motorbike mid-wheely. Soon we were belting through the largest mangrove swamp in the world, and the second largest river delta. Orange gas flares danced on the skyline.

The dinghy forged down towards Bonny Island, where we would soon splash into the Atlantic. Initially we passed only dugouts but then the river widened and a rust-caulked oil tanker sat slumped in the shallows. It looked wildly out of place, rotting and half-scuttled, as if recently torpedoed. Further up there were two far more river-worthy vessels and a fledgling oil well. Occasional speedboats zoomed by.

The Niger was radically different here. This river I had followed for hundreds of miles had often seemed more like a country than simply a belt of water. There was a patriotism amongst those who lived near its shores, whether Bozo fishermen, Fulani herders or Timbuktu Tuaregs; Malians or Nigerians; Muslims, Christians or animists.

These disparate people loved the Niger, their 'river among rivers', which, although it shrank now and then, never fully dried up. Its eternal current inspired the sort of awe and devotion that Indians felt towards the Ganges or Tibetans to the Brahmaputra, something magical and holy. But here, in the choppy, oil-blessed waters of the delta, it was another world entirely.

This was hardly surprising. Since 1958 when the first shipload of crude oil was exported from Port Harcourt the whole area has undergone extraordinary change.* Indeed, over 85 per cent of the country's oil now stems from the two states fringing the Niger's broad mouth. Billions of dollars of this black gold are exported each year, while many of the local people continue to live in abject poverty.

For all the wealth it has brought Nigeria, its oil has often been stained with blood. Not only was it a major cause of the Biafran conflict (1967–70), the country's worst civil war – up to a million Nigerians perished – but it has sparked a host of more contemporary injustices. In the early 1990s resentment towards the oil companies, especially Shell, bubbled over. Hundreds died in the ensuing battles between police and angry

* Not all aspects of Port Harcourt changed over night. When the writer Sanche de Gramont visited the town in 1972 he was shocked to witness the public execution of six young thieves, a throwback to the ritual killings Richard Lander had witnessed over 150 years before.

delta villagers, coupled with clashes between rival minority groups. The issue came to a head in 1995 when Ken Saro-Wiwa , a crusading and high-profile writer, was hanged, along with several others who had criticized Shell and the Nigerian government for misuse of oil profits. Saro-Wiwa's death sparked international outrage and prompted Shell to embrace a more generous, less covert policy towards the local people.

The dinghy finally sloshed into Bonny Island's small harbour, butting between two near identical motor boats. I walked up the wharf and ordered a bowl of pepper soup from a hawker. Looking about me as I supped the fiery brew, it seemed the island, despite all that was going on around it, was still something of a palm-fringed idyll, caught up in a rustic time warp.

That afternoon I decided to inspect. Walking along Bonny's shore, I saw fishermen still trawling in dugouts (even if buffeted by passing speedboats), villagers picking maize by hand and a monument to the Nigerians who fought for the Allies in World War Two.* I also discovered the island had once been a major depot for palm oil, in high demand in the late 1800s for making soap. Ironic, then, that a very different oil should now shape its destiny.

Just as I was leaving I fell upon a sign near the harbour: WELCOME TO BONNY ISLAND, it read. SAY NO TO DRUG ABUSE, CULTISM, VIOLENCE, RECKLESS DRIVING AND UNSAFE SEX. Next to all this a huge sinister skull had been sketched in black paint. Perhaps times were changing faster than I thought.

* * *

* Despite its troops playing valuable peacekeeping roles during the recent unrest in Sierra Leone and Liberia, Nigeria's armed forces are now in a mess. Its air force is perhaps the most wretched example, with 10,000 men but fewer than 20 working aircraft.

Later in the day I hired a small pirogue to go further out to sea. My skipper, a very dark youth in a Chairman Mao-style cap, seemed confused why anyone would want to do this. I mentioned Richard Lander's name but this drew a blank, so I told him it would take less than an hour and that I would pay him well. He grinned and fired up his tiny outboard as if to say: 'Fine by me, guv, if that's what you really want.'

We inched our way up the shore, passing a spit of sand crowned with palms and cottonwoods. The river fanned out still further and salt spray stung our faces. The sun was bright now, lancing through the dark, brindled cloud. 'Waaaaaaahh-hooooeeee' I shouted, punching the air. The skipper laughed nervously.

As we ploughed on towards the Gulf of Guinea my thoughts turned back to Mungo Park. If it hadn't been for his comeuppance at Bussa he would almost certainly have made the extra 300 miles to the sea. Following in the explorer's wake had certainly brought me closer to the man, if anything making me respect his first journey all the more, while still finding his return foray a decade later just as unfathomable. It seemed such a tragedy that this exceptional traveller ended his life in a rotten canoe firing indiscriminately at the very people he had once treated so sensitively.

For all the hero worship bestowed on Park after his death, he also came in for some sharp broadsides. His most caustic critic was the artist, John Ruskin, who thought Park greedy – despite the explorer's meagre wages – egotistical and a neglectful husband and father. Then there was the harsh but plausible claim of Major Gordon Laing (the headstrong Scot killed outside Timbuktu), that Park's second journey created a deep-rooted fear and suspicion of whites on the Niger for years to come.

So what was it that changed Park so drastically on his 1805 trip? Did he see himself less as a geographical missionary and more of an imperialist? Or had his humiliation by Ali and the Moors of Ludamar cracked his confidence? Many later travellers endured horrors in Africa, but still came back for more. Richard Lander drank poison and witnessed public executions in Badagri, Dr Livingstone, while still a relative African new boy, had his left arm savaged by a lion and Richard Burton suffered a Somali tribesman's spear in his face. But despite these near misses, the explorers all returned, their humility largely intact.

And yet, for all the waste and vainglory of his follow-up trip, there is still something special about Mungo Park. He was a genuine trail-blazer, his first expedition to the Niger almost 20 years before Livingstone was even born. To me Park will always be that wide-eyed young adventurer, who, through bravery, stamina and consummate *sang-froid*, survived two and a half years in one of the toughest spots on earth. He travelled largely alone, relying on the kindness of strangers, and was able to bring this all vividly to life through his humble and inspiring diary. If only for this, he will always be a hero in my eyes.

The pirogue bobbed precariously on the swelling tide. I soaked up the ocean view, firing off photos, jubilant, not wanting to head back just yet. The skipper was anxious though. He tapped his watch and cranked up the revs. As we turned in a wide, choppy arc I noticed a lone seagull mewing on the breeze, just as Richard Lander had 175 years before.

I shouted up at the sky, euphoric, blood-pumped, half-crazed. The world's end, I thought, that's quite far enough.

EPILOGUE

ON MY FLIGHT home from Nigeria I scanned a recent copy of *The Independent*, the first newspaper I had read for weeks.

'Rape, torture,' blazed the front page, 'and one million forced to flee as Sudan's crisis unfolds.'

Another tragedy in Africa was in the making, perhaps the worst to date, thought the reporter. A week later from the comfort of my sister's kitchen in north London I read in the Sunday papers about some anti-Christian riots. They had erupted in Kano, the Nigerian city where I had felt so at home only a month before. Two hundred people were thought to have died. Then there was a small piece about Christian Velten in *The Evening Standard*. He was still missing.

With its doomed statistics and seedy regimes there's never much good news about West Africa. And, if I was honest, much of what I had seen on my journey had been pretty wretched. But somehow when I look back now on The Gambia, Senegal, Mali, Niger and Nigeria I'm filled with a quiet joy. I think of Naya's smile and Karim's dignity, of Yusuf's ox-riding spontaneity and Clement's imperishable sense of hope. I think of strangers with generous hearts.

Of course, back home, it's easy to bathe everything in a rose-tinted glow, to romanticize the lot of the Tuaregs and the

Bozo, to airbrush the despair and loneliness, the hassles, the heat and the bleak horizons. At times the canvas of my memory becomes hopelessly blurred. 'Oh, West Africa,' I say when I'm asked. 'There's nowhere like it. It's great.' And it is great, when you're a CFA-flushed white boy on a three-month jolly. But then comes an email from Little Mohammed:

> Dear Tom. Life is hard in Timbuktu. My father is dead. I must be a doctor of the desert. It is what I can do to help my people. Don't forget me. Say hello to James. He is my good friend.

As he assured everyone he would, James moved from London to rural Hampshire, secured a local job and joined a sailing club. We still talk and laugh a lot about our time in Africa and, just sometimes, after one Guinness too many, we thrash out wildly ambitious ideas for a hospital boat on the Niger.

Of course, the Niger and its people continue to splosh around my memory. The river's explorers haunt me too; their shining adventures and lonely deaths. I discovered lots more about Mungo Park, like the fact the website of the Federal Vampire Agency suggests he was eaten by flesh-eating zombies. Further discoveries were an aeroplane, a Microsoft search engine and a restaurant in the French Alps all bearing the explorer's name.

Through my erratic research I even had the chance of meeting a live and kicking Mungo Park – the great, great (times nine) grandson of the explorer – at a pub in Chiswick. Calm, straight-talking Mungo, a 24-year-old TV producer, admitted he regularly fielded inquiries about his famous ancestor.

'I'm very proud of him,' he said. 'But I don't like to make too much fuss. If I ever have a son, though, I'll call him Mungo. No question.'

Epilogue

Up in Selkirk, Park's hometown, I struck upon John Nichol, a jovial, hyperactive biology teacher, folk singer, and actor who not only had written a play about Mungo Park, but hoped to host a tribute party in the summer of 2006 to commemorate the two hundredth anniversary of his hero's death. John and his wife Helen had even christened their young daughter Ailie, in honour of the explorer's devoted and long-suffering spouse.

In the town's old courthouse (in a cabinet next to Sir Walter Scott's slippers) John showed me a motley display of Park's kit: his scarlet Africa Corps jacket, some of his medical instruments, a ring, a sword and a pocket watch. For a man who had led such a restless life, it was a suitably Spartan legacy.

I later discovered Ailie's grave amid the yew trees and tall grass of St Mary's churchyard, where over 700 years ago the warrior, William Wallace, had been proclaimed Guardian of Scotland. It was a lovely spot with commanding views of Selkirk's fringing hills. ALICE ANDERSON, WIFE OF MUNGO PARK, read the faded, lichen-caulked slab. Several other Anderson family members were listed above her. Ailie had died in 1840, struggling to make ends meet, widowed for over 30 years.

My final stop off was at Mungo Park's statue on Selkirk's High Street. It is a proud, striking work of art with some impressive bronze panels at its base depicting Park's travels: the explorer on horseback, seeing the Niger for the first time, being nursed by a clutch of tribal women.

The statue, very appropriately, faces the Anderson family home on one side, and, far less appropriately, the REJUVENATE UNISEX BEAUTY SALON (Hairdressing and Body Piercing) on the other. Not only does the statue commemorate Park but also Alexander Anderson and George Scott, two other Selkirk sons who died on that misguided second expedition to the Niger.

But it was the last name on the memorial that really caught my eye.

Epilogue

THOMAS PARK, SON OF MUNGO PARK, DIED IN AQUAMBRO, W. AFRICA IN 1827 WHILE ENDEVOURING TO OBTAIN TRACE OF HIS DISTINGUISHED FATHER.

Thomas was Mungo and Ailie's second son. Their eldest, Mungo, died of fever in India after being sent there with his regiment at the age of 23. Then came Thomas, a vigorous, sporty youth, obsessed with his father, who landed at Accra in Ghana in 1827. Thomas perished soon after setting off into the African interior. The details remain hazy. Perhaps it was fever, perhaps starvation, although one account has him falling to his death from a tree while watching a tribal festival. He was 24-years-old. The last remaining son, Archibald, became a colonel in the Indian Army and survived until 1867. It is through him the Park blood line continues.

As I admired Park's statue I caught sight of John Nichol's balding head bobbing along the High Street. He was walking briskly, holding hands with Ailie, who was skipping fast to keep pace with her father.

Watching the pair of them, so happy in each other's company, all thoughts of the Niger drained away, usurped by a stronger current. A current my African journey had taught me to value more than ever. A current that led to one place and one place only. A splendid place. An impossible place. A place called home.

BIBLIOGRAPHY

Achebe, Chinua, (with Introduction and Notes by Aigboje Higo) *Things Fall Apart* (Oxford, Heinemann Educational Books Ltd, 1958)

Boyle, T. Coraghessan, *Water Music* (London, Granta, 1993)

Caillié, René, *Travels Through Central Africa to Timbuctoo, Volumes I and II* (London, Darf, 1992)

Dugard, Martin, *Into Africa, The Dramatic Retelling of the Stanley–Livingstone Story* (London, Bantam, 2004)

Galton, Francis, *The Art of Travel (1872), Or Shifts and Contrivances Available in Wild Countries* (London, Phoenix Press, 2000)

de Gramont, Sanche, *The Strong Brown God, The Story of the Niger River* (Boston, Houghton Mifflin, 1975)

Hudson, Peter, *Two Rivers, Travels in West Africa on the Trail of Mungo Park* (London, Chapmans, 1991)

Kapuściński, Ryszard, *The Shadow of the Sun, My African Life* (London, Penguin, 2001)

Kingsley, Mary, *Travels in West Africa, The Classic Account of One Woman's Epic and Eccentric Journey in the 1890s* (London, Phoenix Press, 2000)

Lupton, Kenneth, *Mungo Park, The African Traveller* (Oxford, Oxford University Press, 1979)

Marozzi, Justin, *South from Barbary* (London, HarperCollins, 2001)

Bibliography

Maier, Karl, *This House Has Fallen, Nigeria in Crisis* (London, Penguin, 2000)

Nichol, John, *The Travels of Mungo Park* (Selkirk, John Nichol, 1997)

Pakenham, Thomas, *The Scramble for Africa* (London, Abacus, 1992)

Park, Mungo, (with afterwords by Anthony Sattin) *Travels into the Interior of Africa* (London, Eland, 2003)

Park, Mungo, (Edited with an Introduction by Kate Ferguson Marsters) *Travels in the Interior Districts of Africa* (Durham and London, Duke University Press, 2000)

Sattin, Anthony, *The Gates of Africa, Death, Discovery and the Search for Timbuktu* (London, HarperCollins, 2003)

Theroux, Paul, *Dark Star Safari, Overland from Cairo to Cape Town* (London, Hamish Hamilton, 2002)

de Villiers, Marq and Hirtle, Sheila, *Sahara, The Life of the Great Desert* (London, HarperCollins, 2004)

Also by Tom Fremantle

The Moonshine Mule   £7.99

Across the landscape of the American civil war in the footsteps of a polecat-eating colonel – a 2,700-mile walk on the hoof from Mexico to Manhattan with Browny the mule.

'Readable, informative and very engaging.'   Jan Morris, *The Times*

'Another wonderful book.'   *Condé Nast Traveller*

Other Travel Titles

The Daily Telegraph Adventurous Traveller   £9.99
N. Gifford and R. Madden

The 'one-stop' travel guide for those who don't like easy options – from the truth about narco-mules to the lowdown on camels.

The Traveller's Companion Series   £9.99 each

A unique series of city guides combining eyewitness history and culture and written by knowledgeable and entertaining authors.

'Ideal for the cultured tourist' *TLS*

A Traveller's Companion to Dublin
A Traveller's Companion to Edinburgh
A Traveller's Companion to Florence
A Traveller's Companion to Istanbul
A Traveller's Companion to London
A Traveller's Companion to Madrid
A Traveller's Companion to Moscow
A Traveller's Companion to Prague
A Traveller's Companion to St Petersburg
A Traveller's Companion to to Venice

Other titles of interest

Children of Kali   £7.99
Kevin Rushby

Through India in search of bandits, the Thug Cult and the British Raj.

'He neither eulogizes nor extenuates . . . [is] sympathetic without being condescending, humorous without a trace of sarcasm, and imaginative without getting bedazzled by the inevitable culture shock . . . A fine piece of work.'   *Literary Review*

'Engages wittily with its subject, crossing and recrossing the borderland between law-enforcers and law-breakers.'   *TLS*

'A fascinating description of parts of India where most people will never set foot . . . highly entertaining.'   *History Today*

Hunting Pirate Heaven   £7.99
Kevin Rushby

A spectacular voyage in search of the lost pirate strongholds of the Indian Ocean.

'Frequently hilarious and always entertaining . . . a serendipitous voyage teeming with the joy of travel.'   *Spectator*

'Pirates have provided material for writers for so long that one hardly thinks there could be any literary treasures left, but here is a book that proves otherwise.'   *Guardian*

Chasing the Mountain of Light   £7.99
Kevin Rushby

The story of the Koh-i-Noor diamond, the most famous jewel in the world.

'A gem of a book . . . Rushby is an amusing writer . . .'   *Sunday Times*

'A highly entertaining book.'   *Times Literary Supplement*

312

Eating the Flowers of Paradise £7.99
Kevin Rushby

An exotic journey through the drug fields of Ethiopia and Yemen with qat and assorted companions.

'Rushby's easy style flows from start to finish and his personal touch, along with his vivid descriptions, brings to life this exotic region . . . This is the best kind of travel book, one where you feel that you are beside the author, walking, riding, sitting and listening – like some magical *jinn* that shares the entire journey.' *Wanderlust*

The Great Hedge of India £7.99
Roy Moxham

'At first I thought this remarkable book must be a hoax, but it isn't. It tells the story of one of the least-known wonders of Queen Victoria's India – a customs barrier 2,300 miles long, most it of it made of hedge. It was manned by 12,000 men and would have stretched from London to Constantinople, yet few historians mention it and most of us have never heard of it. Could anything be more astonishing?' Jan Morris

'Part history, part detective story, part travel book. Above all, it is a great read.' *Mail on Sunday*

'Observant and gently suspenseful, Moxham has written a parable at once light-handed and melancholy about the crealty and folly of empire.'
Financial Times

Tea
Addiction, Exploitation and Empire £7.99
Roy Moxham

The often violent history of tea – with many entertaining diversions – is told by someone who became a tea planter at the very end of the Empire. He tells the story of the monumental enterprise of tea cultivation, and its impact on four centuries of British and world history and also explains how tea was traded, grown, manufactured and marketed to satisfy the British thirst for fine tea and large profits.

'A very well-written book and enlightening on all aspects of the desirable shrub, from its original mass cultivation in China via tea clippers and opium wars to the invention of the tea bag.' *Financial Times*

'Cuts through the sugary, picture-book PR of the industry . . . it is the human cost that Moxham's book expertly and movingly recounts.'
The Scotsman

No. of copies	Order	Title	RRP	Total
		The Moonshine Mule	£7.99	
		The Daily Telegraph Adventurous Traveller	£9.99	
		A Traveller's Companion to Dublin	£9.99	
		A Traveller's Companion to Edinburgh	£9.99	
		A Traveller's Companion to Florence	£9.99	
		A Traveller's Companion to Istanbul	£9.99	
		A Traveller's Companion to London	£9.99	
		A Traveller's Companion to Madrid	£9.99	
		A Traveller's Companion to Moscow	£9.99	
		A Traveller's Companion to Prague	£9.99	
		A Traveller's Companion to St Petersburg	£9.99	
		A Traveller's Companion to Venice	£9.99	
		Children of Kali	£7.99	
		Hunting Pirate Heaven	£7.99	
		Chasing the Mountain of Light	£7.99	
		Eating the Flowers of Paradise	£7.99	
		The Great Hedge of India	£7.99	
		Tea	£7.99	

Grand Total £ [ ]

Please feel free to order any other titles that do not appear on this order form!
Order now and get free p&p

Name: ....

Address: ....

.... Postcode: ....

Daytime Tel. No. / Email ....
(*in case of query*)

Three ways to pay:
1. For express service telephone the TBS order line on 01206 255 800 and quote 'CRBK'. Order lines are open Monday – Friday 8:30am – 5:30pm

2. I enclose a cheque made payable to **TBS Ltd** for £ ....

3. Please charge my ❑ Visa ❑ Mastercard ❑ Amex ❑ Switch

    (switch issue no. ....)

Card number: ....

Expiry date: .... Signature ....
    (*your signature is essential when paying by credit card*)

Please send to:
Freepost RLUL-SJGC-SGKJ
Cash Sales / Direct Mail Dept, The Book Service, Colchester Road, Frating, Colchester, CO7 7DW

Enquiries to readers@constablerobinson.com
www.constablerobinson.com

Constable and Robinson Ltd (directly or via its agents) may mail, email or phone you about promotions or products. ❑ Tick box if you do not want these from us ❑ or our subsidiaries.